LIBERAL SHOCK
The Conservative Comeback

Published in 2019 by Connor Court Publishing Pty Ltd
Copyright © William Dawes (as editor)

Connor Court Publishing Pty Ltd
PO Box 7257
Redland Bay QLD 4165
sales@connorcourt.com
www.connorcourtpublishing.com.au

ISBN: 9781925826616

Cover art and illustrations by Jeremy Leasor.

Printed in Australia.

Progress of Unbelief

NOW is the Autumn of the Tree of Life;
 Its leaves are shed upon the unthankful earth,
Which lets them whirl, a prey to the winds'
      strife,
 Heartless to store them for the months of
      dearth.
 Men close the door, and dress the cheerful
 hearth,
Self-trusting still; and in his comely gear
Of precept and of rite, a household Baal rear.

But I will out amid the sleet, and view
 Each shrivelling stalk and silent-falling leaf.
Truth after truth, of choicest scent and hue,
 Fades, and in fading stirs the Angels' grief,
 Unanswer'd here; for she, once pattern chief
Of faith, my Country, now gross-hearted grown,
Waits but to burn the stem before her idol's
      throne.

At Sea.
June 23, 1833.
John Henry Newman

Some things did change. Middle class girls learned to swear
men walked on the face of the moon once the Pill had
    tamed her
and we entered our thirties. No protest avails against that
the horror of Time is, people don't snap out of it.
Now student politicoes well known in our day
have grown their hair two inches and are running the
    country.
Revolution's established. There will soon be degrees
conferred, with a fistshake and speech, by the Dean of
    Eumenides.
The degree we attained was that brilliant refraction of will
That leaves one in several minds when facing evil.
It's still being offered. The Church of Jesus and Newman
did keep some of us balanced concerning the meaning of
    'human'
that greased golden term (all the rage in the new demiurgy)
though each new Jerusalem tempts the weaker clergy.

From *Sidere Mens Eadem Mutato*
a spiral of sonnets for Robert Ellis
Lunch and Counter Lunch (1974)
Les Murray

LIBERAL SHOCK
The Conservative Comeback

Edited by

WILLIAM DAWES

Assisted by

CATHERINE PRIESTLEY and

MICHAEL WARREN DAVIS

With a foreword by **PETER HITCHENS**

Connor Court Publishing

Contents

Part II. Philosophy, France & Freedom

Part III. Markets & Mistakes

Part IV. God, Beauty & Virtue

Part V. Journeys, Realities & Practicalities

Part VI. Conservative Home, Conservative World

FOREWORD
A DANGEROUS IDEA

What Australia's most memorable Q & A episode revealed about the battle of our age.

Peter Hitchens

On my two visits to Australia I have felt a strong sense of mystery and even apprehension. How is it that a civilisation so suburban and seemingly secure should have established itself at this wild limit of the world? It might look startlingly like Britain, in fact, Sydney itself reminds me slightly of the nicer parts of Portsmouth, an old-fashioned seaport city where I misspent much of my childhood. There's something about the faintly rackety streets, and the way the parks come down to the sea, and of course the ferries and the warships, which link the two in shape and atmosphere. The last time I was there I could even faintly hear a military band thumping out a patriotic song, far away.

And yet, Australia is utterly unlike my settled, habituated, and decaying nation. It hangs suspended in a sort of void. It has inherited the language, and Magna Carta, and the Bill of Rights, and even an adversarial parliament, that priceless jewel. But beyond the city limits you will not find the deep, intimate, muddy landscape that Cromwell knew and which I can still visit, full of history and monuments, reminding us that there are in fact limits to what governments – and people – may do, binding us to habit and tradition and dampening our ardours with drizzle. Instead there are gum trees, cockatoos and then naked desert, and of course, the previous population, whose dispossession must be officially regretted but will not be rescinded any time soon. How unsettling must that be? Canberra will, I think, always look as if it has been lowered into its site from a spaceship. I am reminded by all this of Robert Frost's moving poem (which he spoke from memory at John F. Kennedy's inauguration) 'The Gift Outright', in which he recalls 'the land was ours before we were the land's'. And 'we found out that it was ourselves we were withholding from our land of living'. It isn't true anymore. Americans have now come to belong to their land, as Frost concluded, but in a cruel way: 'The deed of gift was many deeds of war'.

When I think, as I often do, that I should love to live in the beautiful, clean, optimistic world of the antipodes, I wonder if I could really cope with it, or if the transplant would ever take.

Because if you fall through the floor in Australia, you keep on falling. I sense that, once Australia finally slashes through the remaining rotted, frayed cables and ropes that tie it to its British origins, almost anything could happen. There's nothing underneath. I had a very strong sense of that void when I appeared, in November 2013, on the ABC's 'Q&A' programme. I had not expected to do so until a day or two before. Someone had forgotten to tell me it was part of my obligation to the Festival of Dangerous Ideas to which (to my great surprise) I had been invited. This was fortunate, as otherwise I might have prepared for the experience, and so made it much less exciting for me and those who watched it.

I am not trying to score a point when I say that I had never heard of Dan Savage before that evening. The failing is undoubtedly mine. I shall certainly not forget him. He came storming out of nowhere into my life, unrestrained by any visible rules. I do not think, for instance, that the BBC's version of the same format, 'Question Time', would have allowed him to speak to me as he did, let alone use phrases such as 'suck dick' and 'full of s***'. If the BBC is still a bit like cricket, in which googlies are bowled and you shield your tender parts, 'Q&A' was a lot more like ice-hockey, in which you wear body-armour, and stretcher-bearers wait in the wings. Well, I say, thank heaven for that. You'll see why in a minute. I had many times met and argued with Germaine Greer, back in England. Hannah Roisin, Dan Savage's sort-of ally, was a type I was used to. We have plenty of people like Hannah in North London. But Dan Savage himself, though I knew such people existed, was so different that he compelled me to think, very fast, as I sat there, and to go to limits I would normally have avoided.

He also engaged very closely with the audience in the Opera House. They were, mostly, his. They were born of the age of the iPhone, not the age of the book. He was their voice and face, the image of the new unrestrained world for which they had been brought up and in which they hoped to live the rest of their lives. I knew, inside two seconds, that there were two things I must not do. I must not in any way pander to him or seek his favour. And I must not allow myself to appear shocked by him, even if I was. Fear, in reasonable doses, can make you extraordinarily calm. And of course I was afraid. Here I was, disliked already for being the wrong Hitchens, and so for being alive at all – you have no idea how fierce this particular rage is among certain people. I was in a country where I did not know the code, the jokes and allusions that you can only learn by living somewhere. And if I failed or made a fool of myself, the news would not stay in Australia, but follow me home. How had I let myself in for this? Had I just flipped over a page in the contract, and missed it? But there they were, the thousands in front of me, and who knew how many watching elsewhere.

So I said a couple of prayers I reserve for such occasions, ignored the flutterings in my stomach, stayed calm, and waited for the bombardment to get going. And I watched as Dan Savage stated, again and again, the maxims and beliefs of the creed I have now come to call Selfism. It was all about what he could do with what he regarded as his own body. I had heard many times before (and have heard many times since) the key to the new belief. 'Who are you to tell me what I can do with my own body?' No doubt there were people in the hall who disagreed with him, and no doubt there were people watching at home who disagreed with him. But if they did, they must have known that night that they were on the losing side – not because they were wrong but because this Cultural Revolution has happened. What remains is, more or less, a mopping up operation in which the defeated are detected, gathered together and despatched to outer darkness of some sort, where there shall be wailing and gnashing of teeth. Of course, this is already the case in Britain, too, but there is a period of twilight between crisis and catastrophe, in which we still wait for the end. In Australia, it seems to me, 'the debate is over'. The losers must ride in their metaphorical tumbrils and queue for the metaphorical guillotine, and their only remaining role is to make the best jokes, as they mount the metaphorical scaffold, that gallows humour allows.

But let us return to the 'my own body' question. It is usually asked in an angry and ferocious tone of voice. It is common in discussions on sexual morality and on drugs, two subjects which moral conservatives cannot get away from. There are answers to it, but the whole point of the question is that we are debarred from offering them. To give these answers (you will surely know them) would be, in itself, to challenge this personal autonomy. And it is so amazingly confident of its own rectitude. What genius thought of basing the new paganism on self-worship, the idol who is always right and never fails? Looking once again at a recording of that evening, I notice how Mr Savage just cannot stop interrupting me, intoxicated by the exuberance of his own certainty. Take the point at which Mr Savage tells me, after I have referred to the intolerance of the moral left, 'You're paranoid and you're projecting by saying we are intolerant. You have...'

I responded: 'See, this is the intolerance. Because I hold an opinion different from his, he has become suddenly a qualified psychoanalyst who can tell me – who can tell me that my opinions which I am entitled to hold....'

At this point, in any normally restrained or fair debate (even one dominated by the left), Mr Savage would have known that he would make my point by interrupting me, and so would have held himself back. I also happen to think that a moderator would have intervened. But this didn't happen, Mr Savage leapt in to say, 'You're entitled to your opinions. You're not entitled to your smears.'

To this day, I don't know what 'smears' he meant. But it wasn't the moment to ask. I just carried on as if he hadn't interrupted:

'... are a pathology. And this is the absolute seed bed of totalitarianism. When you start believing that the opinions of other people are a pathology, then you are in the beginning...'

Here he was again, unworried that he might appear to be trying to shut me up, and reduced to the playground tactic of copying my accusations and turning them rather feebly against me. He might as well have said, 'And you're another'. But in fact he said, 'You're the one standing there pathologising other people's choices.' I absolutely wasn't. But because he had the crowd with him, he got away with it. I ploughed on: '...in the beginning of the stage that leads to the secret police and the Gulags.'

Then came, as it had to do, the baseless accusation against me of some sort of racial prejudice or privilege. He charged, 'You are the one sitting there saying that society is sick and damaged because other people are now free as white men used to be.' As this had less than nothing at all to do with what I was saying, I kept going, 'You'll have the whole world to yourself soon. You can't imagine anybody else is entitled to hold a view different from yours without having some kind of personal defect. That's what's wrong with you.'

This was the absolute zenith or nadir of the confrontation between our two different ideas of goodness, and our two contrasting ideas of how to conduct debate. He retorted (again turning my own words on me), 'You sit there pathologising other people's choices. You sit there saying that other people being free to live their lives by their own light in some way oppresses you, when it oppresses you in no way whatsoever. You are free not to get gay married. You are free not to use drugs. You are free not to drink. You are free to stay married to one person for the rest of your life. You are free to stay home and raise your wife's children so they always have a parent by their side. You are not free to sit there and say that other people being just as free as you are to live their lives and make their own choices in some way is damaging you personally, in some way is destroying society. People are freer now, happier now. It's a less intolerant world than it used to be because people like me are now empowered to look at people like you and say you are full of s***.'

At the heart of it, of course, is the unashamed, almost unconscious declaration that, while he absolutely denies that I am oppressed by the new orthodoxy, I am, even so, not free to criticise his opinions. He, on the other hand, is free to hurl the crudest personal abuse at me.

And then came the almost hysterical applause, during which I couldn't speak, and which I eventually denounced as what it was: a rally. I can truthfully say that it wasn't at all frightening, in a physical way. But it was distressing, because here were many young, presumably educated and gently brought-up young people, who thought this was a potent and decisive argument. This is because they have entirely embraced the Selfism of which Dan Savage spoke.

I am not sure he is what he presented himself as that night. After the programme was over, he came up to me in the green room and, with some charm and manners, expressed concern that he might have gone too far. I suspect that, like many who have now thrown themselves into the Cultural Revolution, they recall enough of what they were taught when they were young to know that there are limits we should not exceed in debate with our opponents. I reassured him that, for me, it was all in a day's work. But I was convinced that his concern was genuine, and that he is nothing like as lost to reason and tolerance as he had made himself appear. I have often prayed for him, ever since, and will continue to do so because, in truth, I rather like him and think his noisy persona is a sad consequence of living in a world where the Christian case has not been very well put, and can very readily be derided.

I am not so tender about his supporters in the audience. I think it would have taken very little more to get them on their feet, stamping the floor, and chanting slogans in alarming unison. They want self-liberation now. Most of them probably are not like Dan Savage, and do not share his desires and tastes. But they understand that if they are to have that liberation, then he too must be free to act and speak in this fashion. And that people like me must be silenced in the end (if we will not have the sense to shut up), and mocked until that can be done.

This is one of many moments in my life, mostly concentrated in recent years, when I have decided that an immediate, temporal victory just isn't possible. From then on I could do two things which would serve my cause: I could stay polite and reasonable in the face of unreason and crowd frenzy; and I could think of how this might look later.

For perhaps one day we will recall this as the high tide of 'libertarianism', when the answer to self-disciplining morality is in all cases a fervent, righteous and often very angry claim that we owe nothing to anyone but ourselves. Who are you to say I should wait around in this difficult marriage to see that my children grow up securely? Who are you to say I shouldn't smoke this joint? Who are you to say I shouldn't kill this unborn baby? Who are you to say I shouldn't buy this company, strip it of its assets and walk away with the money leaving hundreds of people jobless? Who are you to say I shouldn't smuggle these migrants past legal border controls, for money? And so on. Supposed political conservatism long ago embraced the selfism of money, while the political left were embracing the selfism of the body. Neither of them opposes the other. They have ended up in a sort of heteropolitical civil partnership, formed of the ideas of Margaret Thatcher and Deng Xiaoping, whose hideous love-child is slouching towards Bethlehem to be born.

And why shouldn't the Opera House audience have behaved as they did? Why shouldn't they squeal and yell in support of Dan Savage, like 21st century Beatlemaniacs? What authority, what teacher, what media, what literature or drama has taught them anything else? What in their homes, schools, streets, conversation and entertainment has ever told them anything else? The very universe is presented to them as a cosmic car crash without purpose or meaning, in which their actions and thoughts have no significance apart from their immediate effects, and where what is done secretly (whether you do it, or whether someone else does it) can expect neither reward nor punishment. Whichever way they look, they see an endless freedom. The end of this is the world of Mad Max, of course, but it does not come immediately. If it did, they would make the connection. They grow up in an Enid Blyton world of safe suburbs and banality and think that their pursuit of liberty is a garden game. And then they find, beyond the hedges and fences, that they are in a cruel jungle full of beasts that fight and tear. It is now more than 50 years since Leonard Cohen sang his prophetic line, which made me shiver with apprehension when I heard it then as a young Bolshevik, and which now makes me intensely sad: 'Where do all these highways go, now that we are free?' It makes me sad, because then I guessed the answer, and now I have seen it, repeatedly, in the lives of people I know, with my own eyes.

Given the chance to answer this, I named the belief that Jesus Christ was the Son of God and rose from the dead as the most dangerous idea in all human history, for so it is. If it were not so dangerous, we – and in this I include my own teenage self – would not fear and dislike it so. Oddly enough, it is when you see the power of the enemy on full display, that you most readily recognise the enormous countervailing power of the God of Love, 'whose service,' in the words of the 1662 Prayer Book's collect for peace at Morning Prayer, 'is perfect freedom'. The knowledge that what we do matters somewhere else, and why it does so, and how service can be perfect freedom, is what makes us truly free.

ACKNOWLEDGEMENT

As Catherine Priestley recounts in her afterword, this book is the product of a long, fruitful conversation. For me there is no more important interlocutor than Catherine.

Michael Davis was the first conservative writer to awak- en me to the now unavoidable distinction between mar- ket-loving liberals and community-loving conservatives. He showed me that the gravest mistake of the political right in recent decades has been the attempt at 'not caring' about issues of culture, behaviour, identity, life and leisure, by hiding behind social libertarianism. As he so perfectly explained, the reality is that 'we can't help but care'.

Damien Freeman has been a patient and sober guide through this whole process. He is a sincere, productive, and yet unpresuming patron of Conservative thought in Australia.

My appreciation for reading, challenging, proofing, discussing, supporting, or inspiring the ideas in this book must also go to Mum, Dad, Grandad, Grandma, Nan, Opa, David Corbett, Andrew Berriman, David Sergeant, Ruby Dawes, Bradley MacDonald, Lauren Brodie, Bailey Broom, Mitchell Levick, Oliver O'Toole, Adam Kadmon, Nick Cater, Rebecca Weisser, and Anthony Cappello.

INTRODUCTION

I

LIBERALISM'S LONG REACH

You're probably a liberal, and that's no good.

William Dawes

The relevance of these essays extends well beyond devotees of any particular political party. The reality is, if you're a member of any of the major parties, or if you don't think about politics, even if you make a conscious effort to avoid politics, there's a strong chance you are affected by liberal ideas. These ideas inform the flawed, hidden assumption at the centre of the everyday person's dismissive approach to politics and life. This attitude is often expressed as follows: *people should just be able to do what they want, as long as they don't harm anyone else.* This formula is repeated in as many words or less by people who consider themselves left wing and right wing. It's an escape route for anyone at a dinner party engaged in a debate that has become awkward. It is heard at family barbeques as often as on national television. It is simple and seems to please everyone. However expressed, once this assumption emerges in conversation, it is almost impossible to explain that it is not inherently sensible and that it is actually informed by a particular ideological system: liberalism. So if you don't think too hard about politics, you're probably a liberal. This also means that if you're a liberal, you're not thinking hard enough.

A crude and simple ideology

> In the war of ideas, it's the crudest and most simplified ideology that wins. During our own lifetimes we have seen spectacular examples of this. We have seen great and highly civilized countries becoming infected by epidemics of ideological insanity, and whole populations being destroyed for the sake of some irrational slogan.[1]

It is rarely the case that the best idea 'wins'. To think that the free flow of argument and counterargument necessarily arrives at the truth of a particular situation, or the truth itself, is simply naïve. The reason so many people hold this mistaken belief is that they have applied their assumptions about the *market* to the realm of *philosophy, morality and politics*. Rhetoric about the 'war of ideas' has given way to adoration of the 'marketplace of ideas'. In this fictitious marketplace the best idea will supposedly prevail in much the same way as the best business does. But we all know it doesn't work like this. The *best* eatery in Sydney may be a fine but unpretentious Italian restaurant in Paddington, family ownership spanning generations, its walls decked with fine art reflecting the owner's cultivation and eclectic taste, where diners are comforted with careful service, and delicately prepared food paired with exquisite wines – but this restaurant, superior as it may be, has no hope shaping our culture to the same ex-

---

[1] Christopher Dawson, *The Movement of World Revolution* (Washington D.C.: The Catholic University of America Press, 2013), 74.

tent as McDonalds. Likewise, the intellectual patrimony of the West is a splendid thing, but it is thwarted by 'the crudest and most simplified ideology'. That ideology, the great survivor of the 20th century's total war of ideologies, is liberalism.

Liberalism did more than survive, it triumphed – not just over the other ideologies, but against all that had come before it. Like a conquering hero, it has erected a triumphal column, towering above the public square. This monument tells a story, claiming for liberalism the credit for all that we enjoy. But when the false gods celebrated on this deteriorating memorial are questioned, they are found wanting.

The disaster

Because of the surprise Coalition win at the 2019 Federal Election, it is easy to forget that the 'conservative' side of politics has been confused, divided and incapacitated on almost every major issue in recent political memory. This is, in many respects, because of conservatives' reliance on liberal assumptions. Due to this long-term ineffectiveness mixed with temporary successes, the political and social situation has deteriorated. Our trust in institutions and each other has evaporated. There is an epidemic of loneliness, drug use and suicide in communities that seem to want for nothing material. We hear regularly of unspeakable crimes against women and children by the men closest to them. Pockets of unrelenting poverty and dysfunction persist despite years of economic growth. Political chaos is matched by the public's cynicism. Our education system fails us, and we are too ignorant to know it. A sense of economic and political powerlessness prevails over hope. A family with a mother and father in the same house is an increasingly rare indulgence for children. The source and summit of our civilisation, the Christian religion, is despised and rejected. And in response to all these manifestations of our cultural death spiral, the liberal elite on either side of the political divide (for they inhabit all major parties) profess that they are highly satisfied, so long as we have been 'free to choose' this fate. Meanwhile, conservatives don't know much about what they want, how to explain their instincts, or how to achieve any vision they might have.

There are several purposes to my introduction. An immediate aim is to convince people that the concept of a 'party of Edmund Burke and John Stuart Mill' is an unhelpful contradiction which must be abandoned. More broadly, it will hopefully make it clear that conservatism and liberalism, despite the historical fact of their cooperation against socialism in the 20th century, are ultimately incompatible. In this way, the introduction is primarily a contribution to politics. There is also a deeper, philosophical point which necessarily follows and assists the political: human nature is not suited to liberalism.

II

THE BURKE AND MILL FALLACY

The concept of a 'party of Edmund Burke and John Stuart Mill' must be abandoned.

Not long ago Paul Kelly wrote of the apparent dysfunction in the Liberal Party of Australia:

> This is not just about personalities. The crisis within the Liberal Party is permanent and deep-seated. As an institution it is now incapable of unity around a common agenda. It is riven by disputes about the policies it needs to succeed and what the Liberal Party represents.[2]

The attempt to fuse conservative disposition and liberal ideology has failed. These two strands have proven practically and intellectually incompatible. The Coalition won the 2019 election in spite of this internal collapse.

Confronted by this claim, many will repeat their reliance on the now clichéd adage: 'We are the party of Burke and Mill... and the Liberal Party has always been the custodian of the liberal and conservative tradition.'

It's a handy aphorism that was first used by the great conservative Liberal Prime Minister, John Howard.[3] But what did it ever even mean? Are Mill's liberalism and Burke's conservatism complementary? With respect to Mr How-

---

2   Paul Kelly, 'Liberals will struggle for as long as they remain the issue', *The Australian*, April 11, 2018.

3   John Howard, 'Address at the launch of the Publication 'the Conservative'', (speech presented at the launch of 'the Conservative', Parliament House, Canberra, September 8, 2005).

ard, we must acknowledge that they are not. This slogan (which had its use and its day) is an example of what the conservative philosopher Roger Scruton calls the 'Aggregation Fallacy'. This fallacy, common to political theory and practice, is explained by reference to the French Revolution. The archetypal Aggregation Fallacy, politically speaking, is the famous tripartite invocation of *Liberte, egalite, fraternite*.[4]

As it turned out, in their fervour for guillotining aristocrats, the revolutionaries didn't much think about how to realise full liberty, full equality, and full fraternity. The liberty of the individual is necessarily cut down in the pursuit of full equality for all the other individuals. And this quite literal process of cutting down aristocrats didn't do much for a sense of fraternity. As Scruton points out, shouting *liberte, egalite, fraternite* is like saying lobster is good, chocolate is good and tomato sauce is good, and so lobster cooked in chocolate and tomato sauce is three times as good. This is the Aggregation Fallacy.

A lot of violence and destruction, doublethink and injustice were met on the people of France in The Terror before anyone realised they were trying to implement a contradiction. The Aggregation Fallacy is replicated whenever the desire for good things cancels any attempt to understand the connections between them. The Liberal Party of Australia has its own version of the Aggregation Fallacy. Like revolutionary France, the Liberal Party has inflicted on itself a lot of violence and destruction, and plenty of doublethink and injustice. The Party's Aggregation Fallacy, its *liberte, egalite, fraternite* mistake, can be called the Burke and Mill Fallacy.

---

4   Roger Scruton, *The Uses of Pessimism: And the Danger of False Hope* (Great Britain: Atlantic Books, 2010), 153-165.

The Burke and Mill Fallacy

To understand the origins of the Burke and Mill Fallacy, let's examine what 'good' each of the limbs seems to offer. In his famous essay *On Liberty*, Mill offers a pocket-sized justification of absolute personal liberty limited only by the Harm Principle. Essentially, do what you want, but don't hurt anyone else. On the other hand, Burke offers the insight that for progress to be positive, it must not become divorced from precedent, because all of us are bound, socially and politically, in a communion between the dead, the living and the yet to be born. This truth places on the living an obligation to govern well and facilitate human flourishing, so that they are deserving of their inheritance, and doing justice to their descendants. Of course, rather than reading Burke's *Reflections on the Revolution in France*, Australian conservatives are probably content to define themselves by reference to John Howard's formula: a conservative is someone who doesn't think he's morally superior to his grandfather.

On the face of it, these don't seem like mutually exclusive ideas, but the combative, acrimonious relationship between 'moderates' and 'conservatives' has on more than one occasion rendered the Liberal Party incapable of setting the agenda even when in government. Again, Paul Kelly was brutally honest when he said right-wingers these days 'excel at drum-beating, making a lot of noise, writing a lot of articles and losing every substantial battle. They are fragmented, intellectually confused and strategically inept.'[5] The fragmentation is obvious. Any honest observer of the Liberal Party will admit: (1) that the conservatives despise and hold in a deep suspicion the 'small l liberals', 'moderates' or simply 'the left' of the party and (2) that the liberals reserve a deep-seated contempt

---

5   Paul Kelly, 'Barnaby Joyce and the crisis of conservatism in Australia', *The Australian*, February 20, 2018.

for their 'conservative', 'reactionary' or 'hard right' colleagues. The confusion and ineptitude simply flow downstream from this fundamental clash.

Menzies' silence

Going to the words of the Liberal Party's founder Sir Robert Menzies, while always valuable, doesn't really help in this respect either. To be honest, Menzies had to be careful and indirect, as he was uniting a disparate group of political interests together to offer Australia its only chance at an alternative to socialism. You won't find 'liberalism' (classical or otherwise) or 'conservatism' by name in the *Forgotten People* broadcasts.

It would be wilful blindness to suggest that Menzies was not instinctively conservative. Nonetheless, he insists that we read between the lines. In Australia in the mid-20th Century 'conservative' was definitely a pejorative label.[6] Not much has changed. Expressing frustration at this, after he had formed the Party but before leading it to victory, Menzies lamented:

---

6   In 1930, Sir Keith Hancock wrote an authoritative history of our young nation, explaining that 'From the political philology of Australia may be quarried a good deal of political history. *Conservative* is a word which has no currency at all; in Australia it signifies *reactionary*. Similarly, if a politician declares that he is *liberal*, his audience will understand that he is by nature *conservative*.' This will disappoint a lot of liberals who see Menzies' decision to call his party 'Liberal' as an unequivocal rejection of conservatism. Sir Keith Hancock, *Australia* (London: Ernest Benn, 1930), 12. For an indispensable explanation of the formation and transformation of the anti-socialist movements in Australian politics, see Damien Freeman, *Abbott's Right: The Conservative Tradition from Menzies to Abbott* (Melbourne: Melbourne University Press, 2018), 9-52.

> There is a cynical disposition in these days to re-ject tradition as 'reactionary', though a healthy and proud sense of continuity is one of the greatest of steadying influences and a superb element of sanity in a mad world.... In our own country the pioneers, both of government and of production, were great men, and we belittle ourselves when we speak, as we so frequently do, as if all wisdom were our sole and uninherited prerogative.[7]

Menzies is dripping with Burkean sentiment. But here, as everywhere else, he avoids the word 'conservative'. As it turned out, a model relying on a self-consciously, but cleverly concealed, conservative leading a bunch of rough-ly-defined anti-socialists, was a good electoral strategy for the Liberal Party. Until, of course, that leader's time comes to an end. When people talk of the Liberal Party's 'Messiah Complex', the phenomenon they're really refer-ring to is the movement's perennial need to return to its original model, which relies completely on a more or less self-consciously *conservative* leader who does everything he can to publicly avoid the *label*. [8]

---

[7] Robert Menzies, foreword to *Edmund Barton* by John Reynolds (Sydney: Halstead Press Pty Limited, 1949), vi.

[8] I note former Prime Minister Malcolm Turnbull's Dis-raeli Prize Speech where he claims that Menzies was obviously *not* conservative: Malcolm Turnbull, 'Disrae-li Prize Speech', (speech delivered on receipt of Policy Exchange's 2017 Disraeli Prize, Institute of Mechanical Engineers, London, 10 July 2017). Mr. Turnbull's speech relies on an oft-repeated quote of Menzies – 'We took the name "Liberal" because we were determined to be a pro-gressive party, willing to make experiments, in no sense reactionary but believing in the individual, his right and his enterprise, and rejecting the socialist panacea.' – to suggest that Menzies rejected conservatism in practice as well as in name. See above n 6 for why this is a mistake.

Menzies could never be considered a pure, ideological liberal. He resisted the urge to transform solutions to particular political problems into absolute principles. In 1964, Menzies declared in a speech to the Federal Council of the Liberal Party of Australia that 'We have no doctrinaire political philosophy'. At the time Menzies added something totally sensible, but which would shock many 'liberal' party insiders now: 'Where government action or control has seemed to us to be the best answer to a practical problem, we have adopted that answer at the risk of being called Socialists'.[9] For Menzies, being anti-socialist never meant being uncritically 'pro-market' or ideologically committed to individualism: it meant being anti-doctrine.

Howard's solution

Contemporary Liberals have made the mistake Menzies would have advised against: elevating a cosmetic solution (the Burke and Mill Fallacy) to a particular problem (factional infighting) to the status of first principle. The Burke and Mill theory was first articulated by Howard, who himself had seen vicious factional struggle during a period where the Liberal Party seemed unable to get the upper hand electorally. In declaring a ceasefire of sorts, which he was able to do after winning the internal and external battle comprehensively by 2005, he said that 'history suggested the Liberal Party is at its best when it balances and blends two traditions. The two traditions of classical liberalism and conservatism.' The Party must, he believed, 'care for both traditions and never see it as our role as Australian Liberals to see the triumph of one of those traditions to the unfair detriment or obliteration of

---

9   Robert Menzies, 'Speech by the Prime Minister, the Rt. Hon. Sir Robert Menzies' (speech presented at the Federal Council, Liberal Party of Australia, Hotel Canberra, Canberra, April 6, 1964).

the other'.[10] This pronouncement has carried a lot of currency in the Party ever since it was uttered. In fact, it has been elevated to an *a priori* principle of the Party's organisation. Let us remind ourselves why it was always wrong to do this with reference to the speech itself.

The speech, containing the Burke and Mill line, was delivered in 2005. Following the famous assertion, Howard makes it clear that he conceives of Mill as a figure signaling the economic agenda of the Party. After all, Howard thought of himself as 'socially conservative and economically liberal'. In this context Howard makes another claim which, with the benefit of hindsight, no longer rings true at all. It hasn't for some time. 'From my own personal point of view I have always thought that that [socially conservative, economically liberal] mix best suits both the needs and the temper of contemporary Australian society. Contemporary Australian society understands that we do live in a world of change, they understand that globalism is with us forever, they may not like some aspects of it but they know they can't change it and they therefore want a government that delivers the benefits of globalisation and not one that foolishly pretends Canute-like it can hold back the tide'.[11]

Could anyone legitimately claim that the average constituent today is content with the ongoing disruptive and disempowering effects of globalisation, and doesn't expect their government to do something about it in their interests? Were they ever? The political upheaval across the developed world is seen by the protagonists of these rebellions, and by the commentators opposed to them, as a revolt against a global elite who refuse to protect their

---

[10] John Howard, 'Address at the launch of the Publication "The Conservative"', Above No.3.

[11] Ibid.

own citizens or improve their lives by insisting on a world with effectively no economic or political borders.[12] Donald Trump may have his limits, but he has so far been more successful than King Canute at harnessing this discontent and presenting alternatives. It may have been possible in 2005 but no conservative leader today could (or should) give a speech claiming that Australians expect to endure the effects of globalisation without any favour or concern from their own government.

We can fairly say that things have changed. We can also add that if this unquestioning position on globalisation no longer holds, why should we assume the Burke and Mill formula does?

The present situation

The Party's recent history also plainly reveals that the attempted fusion of traditional conservatism and ideological liberalism has been failing, unable to avoid any longer its own inconsistencies. The conservative Tony Abbott, who as leader tried to perpetuate this inherited fusion, suffered the first blow in the fallout from its self-destruction, and the liberal Malcolm Turnbull momentarily triumphed. But that was never to last.

---

[12] It would be unfair and simply incorrect to put Howard himself in this category of negligent leaders blindly supporting the principles of globalisation. At crucial junctures Howard rightly protected the interests of Australians from the effects of a global market. For instance, when Hurricane Larry devastated Australian banana growers in tropical Queensland, rather than allowing the 'market' to keep prices down through the importation of fresh bananas to meet consumer demand, the Howard Government banned all fresh banana imports. It kept prices up but saved Australian banana growers from permanent destruction. See AAP, 'Government confirms ban on fresh banana imports', *The Age*, September 4, 2006.

Liberalism's moment in the Liberal Party reached its zenith when Turnbull explicitly identified himself with ideological liberalism, to the exclusion of conservatism, in his 2017 Disraeli Prize address. He declared that the party which he had seized should be guided, fundamentally, by Mill's one very simple principle in *On Liberty* and the 'open society' social liberalism advocated by Karl Popper. Turnbull's vision for the Party has been roundly rejected.

More recently, at the 2019 General Election, the political ideology and rhetoric of liberalism was dropped by Scott Morrison to the notable electoral benefit of his party. Morrison won more seats in the Coalition's third term than Turnbull's low point of 76 in its second term, following Abbott's high of 90 in its first term.

There was one relatively unnoticed incident which highlighted this subtle shift away from liberalism. On the Thursday before the election Scott Morrison pointedly distanced himself from one of the great sacred cows of ideological liberalism: uncritical admiration of the free market. It was in response to an aggressive interrogation by Leigh Sales on *7.30* regarding his housing deposit policy: 'When did the Liberal Party stop believing in the free market?'

The Prime Minister replied, 'I don't see things in such terms... I see government as a practical engagement based on your beliefs... values... about helping Australians achieve their goals... Robert Menzies had a similar scheme, Leigh, and he founded our Party because he understood it was homes, not just material, [which] were central to the Australian vision.'

Morrison was alluding to Menzies' invocation of homes material, homes human and homes spiritual in the *Forgotten People* speech. In response to Sales, Morrison chose to talk about the importance of homes – the homes humans can live in, and where families can be enriched spiritually – rather than the merits of some cold ideology, the creative destruction of the 'free market', or the redemptive qualities of 'agility' and 'innovation'. This is significant.

Despite the electoral win, the familiar risks of internal division remain. Morrison's victory does not mean that things can go back to business as usual. There are still people committed to ideological liberalism confusing the traditional, conservative instincts of Australia's great anti-socialist party.

Morrison, for the time being, has rightly distanced himself from any ideological stance and instead used his instincts with respect to the character of the Australian people and what is best for them. That is the first task of a conservative; understanding his people. This is the greater Liberal shock arising from the 2019 General Election: the Party's present shift away from liberalism.

Ideology and tradition

Another error in the Burke and Mill Fallacy is to describe Mill's liberalism as a 'tradition'. Mill, classical liberals, and libertarians cannot be considered in terms of tradition because they are adherents to an ideology. An ideology founded upon an immovable axiom, valuing individual freedom more highly than any social goal.[13] Because it is an ideology, whatever its priorities, it is inconsistent with tradition – whether it is the tra-

---

[13] Damien Freeman, *Abbott's Right: The Conservative Tradition from Menzies to Abbott* (Melbourne: Melbourne University Press, 2018), 61.

ditional society beloved by Burke, or the localised traditions of mateship and the fair go in our own country.

Juggling the utilitarian liberalism of Mill with the nuance of Burke's humble admiration for society will always be to the detriment of the latter. The fact is that Mill's ideology is easier to comprehend and regurgitate than Burke's complex appreciation of the sublime and traditional order of our communities. In my experience this practically means that liberal and libertarian ideas capture a disproportionate amount of young people joining the Liberal Party. They don't know how or can't be bothered to articulate a defence of tradition, or their own instincts, and so they say: *I should be able to do what I want, as long as I don't hurt anyone else.*

Freedom and 'freedom'

Why would conservatives now disdain liberals, since they have been such willing bedfellows in the past? Yes, it's true that liberals and conservatives united in the 20th century to fight Communism. But the reasons for this are misunderstood. Liberals don't like Marxism because it is another (much more obviously oppressive) ideology competing for world domination. Whereas conservatives fight Communism for the same reason they have always resisted liberalism: they are allergic to totalising ideological abstractions. Without the shared enemy of Communism, the alliance breaks down.

Even if they have different reasons to fight Communism, can't conservatives and liberals at least converge in their love of freedom? Well, freedom can mean a number of different things. Conservatives see freedom as freedom from slavery to sin.[14] This understanding

---

[14] Menzies hints at this view in his *Forgotten People* broadcast: 'Indeed there is much more slavery in Australia

may seem antiquated to most but it is preserved in the modern world in our acute awareness of the vice-like grip of alcohol and drug addiction. Although one can freely choose to consume these substances, it is a choice leading to dependence, where 'choosing' to have another drink, or shoot up or smoke, feels like the only choice left. If we are free from these evils, however, we can do what we ought to do: we are free to speak the truth, to do good, and to make something beautiful. This is the conservative understanding of freedom. On the other hand, liberalism informs the more popular modern notion of liberty. It involves simply freedom from *constraint*. Freedom to choose any course of action at any time. There is no purpose to this freedom. The choice itself is the goal. This could not be more different to the traditional definition.

History

Historically, conservatism can only be understood as a reaction to liberalism, ever since that revolutionary ideology burst onto the world in the 18th century.

It is worth noting that the enduring 'left wing' and 'right wing' image, which originated with the French National Assembly at the time of the 1789 Revolution, denoted a divide, not between conservatives and socialists, nor between conservatives and social democrats, but between royalist conservatives and revolutionary *liberals*.

Across the Channel, Edmund Burke railed against the French Revolution for its ideological pursuit of what the

---

than people imagine. How many hundreds of thousands of us are slaves to greed, to fear...' Sir Robert Menzies, *The Forgotten People* (Redland Bay: Connor Court - Jeparit Press, 2017), 9.

revolutionaries called a *liberal* agenda.[15] He resented this mutation of the old understanding of the word 'liberal', which had meant a generosity of spirit associated with anyone who cultivated noble characteristics.[16]

But another Englishman, Thomas Paine, a supporter of the Revolution, struck at the heart of the matter when he rebuked Burke in the first part of his *Rights of Man*, saying Burke was not registering the distinction between 'persons' and 'principles'. Paine revealed a transformation in thought: 'liberal' was no longer a characteristic of an individual person – imagine a generous and learned aristocrat – it was a set of abstract principles realised in revolution. This is when *liberality* gave way to *liberalism*.

For a long time both sides in England, Whigs and Tories (Burke was a Whig), saw this *a priori* liberalism – liberalism in principle as opposed to liberality in character – as a foreign perversion. One British publication targeted its political opponents by calling them '*liberales*', alluding to a revolutionary party which had popped up in Spain, to emphasise their strangeness.[17]

Nonetheless, ideological liberalism did find a permanent home in Anglophone politics in the 19th Century, achieving its most relied-on definition in *On Liberty* by J.S. Mill.

Mill's *On Liberty* revolves around the one very simple principle with which we are now familiar: 'That principle is, that the sole end for which mankind are warranted, individually or collectively, in interfering in liberty of action

---

[15] Helena Rosenblatt, *The Lost History of Liberalism: From Ancient Rome to the Twenty-first Century* (Princeton: Princeton University Press, 2018), 44-47.

[16] Perhaps Menzies had this meaning in mind when he called his party 'Liberal'?

[17] Rosenblatt, *Op.cit.*, 71.

of any of their number, is self-protection.'

As such, the myopic priority of liberalism is the maximisation of your personal choice, so long as you don't 'harm' anyone else. As we have already seen, it is this tantalisingly simple and fundamentally confused idea which plagues us to this day. What is 'harm', for instance? Is it merely physical harm, or emotional and psychological? Does taking offence count as harm? Is it only harm to other individuals, or to society and culture that justifies coercion?

They're all liberals

Defenders of the détente between liberals and conservatives never tire of pointing out that there is a difference between liberalism as understood in America, where it is associated with the political left, and a 'classical liberalism' which is somehow right wing.

In reality, the only distinction between *classical* liberals and *progressive* liberals is where they draw the line on justifiable state intervention. Because 'harm' is such a changeable concept, this line can move depending on how broadly or restrictively you define it. Progressive liberals support more state intervention (because they see more things as harmful), and classical liberals supposedly less. But they all see the world in fundamentally the same way: a collection of atomised individuals, whose freedoms are carved out in negative terms by the state, which has ultimate authority.

The inevitable normalisation of euthanasia should expose the totalising nature of the liberal principle. Politicians on the right and left struggle to find any argument to stop what they know instinctively to be evil. *Surely, it's up to the individual? It doesn't hurt anyone else? Who are we to discourage someone from suicide?* Liberalism has succeeded in making the liberty of the individual the only test that remains in the formulation of public policy.[18]

In the countries from which Australia takes its political cues, the United Kingdom and the USA, there has been an explosion of literature exploring the fact that liberalism and conservatism are viciously opposed. This realisation is coming to Australia. Whatever way you look at it, liberalism is not conservative. In truth, it eats at the heart of conservatism.

What has liberalism really contributed?

Accepting this shouldn't be as damaging to right-wing political movements as some fear. Liberalism is given far too much credit. We tend to attribute to liberalism everything we feel vaguely positive about – democracy, the Rule of Law, women's suffrage, McDonald's, whatever.

Anyone with a passing interest in history should know that 'None of the goods claimed for liberalism emerged with, or belong to, it. Freedom, equality, toleration, individual rights, rule of law, limits on state and market power, fair trial, *habeas corpus* — all these precede liberalism'.[19] Edmund Fawcett's *Liberalism: The Life of An Idea* is a book by liberals, for liberals, and doesn't deny the pre-liberal origins of liberal ideas. Fawcett suggests the four big liberal ideas are (1) the inescapability of conflict, (2) distrust of power, (3) Faith in human progress and (4) civic respect. The first idea, he acknowledges, was drawn in the formative years of liberalism from the 'fresh memories of religious warfare' – this is not a unique observation. The second idea 'drew on old human wisdom that power grew implacable if not checked'. The fourth idea 'had roots in religious acknowledgement of people's

---

[18] Gertrude Himmelfarb, introduction to *On Liberty* by John Stuart Mill (England: Penguin Books Ltd, 1974), 7.

[19] Phillip Blond, 'Politics After Liberalism', *First Things*, December 2017.

intrinsic worth and insistence on their moral responsibility for themselves. It had roots in law, particularly laws of property and inheritance'. The third idea – the faith in inevitable human progress in this world – was perhaps genuinely novel. But it was definitely short-lived as modern science, technology and extremely efficient means of governance and political organisation were harnessed in the 19th and 20th centuries for unprecedented levels of human destruction and regression.

Is Australia a liberal experiment?

Former politician David Kemp has begun mapping out a theory that Australia itself is a grand, broadly successful 19th century liberal experiment in volume one of his promised five-volume history of liberalism in our antipodal home. [20] This has been received very well and has encouraged a view among centre-right journalists and commentators that liberalism is responsible for every shred of goodness and every ingenious idea we now take for granted in our daily lives.

But were all the emancipatory instincts which inspired the founders of the Australian colonies really thanks to liberalism? If so, perhaps we could go further and say Jesus Christ was quoting a liberal when he opened the book of Isaiah and declared in the Synagogue that he would 'bid the prisoners go free' and 'set the oppressed at liberty'.

Kemp's thesis is no doubt a breath of fresh air to those used to the relentless negativity and condemnation of academic historians and critical theorists, not to mention the airport-lounge-republican-radical fantasies of Peter FitzSimons. But I suspect another reason the centre-right journalistic establishment continue to pump up the tyres

---

[20]   David Kemp, *The Land of Dreams: How Australians Won Their Freedom, 1788-1860* (Carlton: The Miegunyah Press, 2018).

of liberalism is that, confronted with complete, rolling defeat in the culture wars, they are desperate for an 'ism' which is theirs and which they can claim (despite all evidence to the contrary) has been very successful.

Kemp is honest in his view of the relationship between liberals and conservatives. 'Liberal parties have been targets for socially conservative, economic or religious special interests, which have sometimes defined themselves in illiberal terms.'[21] He adds that Labor has a substantial liberal wing, though subject to the 'special interests' of trade unions. He concedes that liberalism has infiltrated both sides of politics. But the image constructed of noble, aloof liberalism beset by 'special interests' demanding supplication is certainly more flattering to liberals than it is to conservatives (or trade unionists or any religious person). Conservative elder statesmen should keep this liberal aloofness in mind when recapitulating their belief in the enduring alliance between liberalism and conservatism.

It would be a great mistake to lean too heavily on liberalism in defining the anti-socialist currents in Australian history and politics.

Mateship and the fair go, for instance, aren't ideas borne of *liberalism* or *socialism*. These simple, formative concepts developed organically thanks to the supportive relationships formed by Australians in adversity. Over-hyping liberalism misses the point of Australia, and the West.

Conservatism and liberalism – the Fusionist failure

William F Buckley was an infamous American conservative, notorious for popularising and building a movement through his magazine National Review, which became

---

[21]   Ibid, 7.

known as 'Fusionism' – a pragmatic combination of traditionalist conservative, classical liberal and libertarian elements in order to form a potent political machine. This proved an extremely successful model when Soviet Communism was the central existential threat to America. Fusionism has suffered the same fate as the Burke and Mill Fallacy, with its effectiveness waning and seams coming apart with the re-emergence of the historical battle between liberalism and the conservative resistance.

In October 2017, an opinion piece in the *Wall Street Journal* acknowledged the identity crisis being endured by the right-wing American political establishment following the victory of Donald Trump the previous year. The simple question put in the heading was this: *Is 'Classical Liberalism' Conservative?* [22]

The term 'classical liberal', as Yoram Hazony pointed out, came into use in 20th-century America to denote the supporters of old-school *laissez-faire* liberalism, distinguishable from the welfare-state liberalism of figures such as Franklin D. Roosevelt. The term has crept across the Pacific and many in the Liberal Party of Australia have taken to calling themselves 'classical liberals'. In March 2016, Janet Albrechtsen lauded two younger Liberal parliamentarians from Victoria, both of whom exhibit some of the most explicit self-styling as 'classical liberals' ever seen in Australian politics. Tim Wilson and James Patterson are both products of the Institute of Public Affairs. Patterson in his maiden speech said, 'I am proud to call myself a classical liberal'. Albrechtsen said that 'both are smart, passionate and proven warriors for the values of classical liberalism'. [23]

---

[22] Yoram Hazony, 'Is Classical Liberalism Conservative?', *Wall Street Journal*, October 13, 2017.
[23] Janet Albrechtsen, 'Voices of liberalism will add cachet to Canberra', *The Australian*, March 22, 2016.

But the impact of liberal ideology extends far beyond those who proactively identify as 'classical liberals'. In the influential American journal *First Things*, Phillip Blond noted that among the ideas that compete to determine the world's future:

> only one is dominant, hegemonic, and all-pervasive – liberalism. Even though its ascendancy is relatively recent, we regard its precepts as if they were Platonic archetypes, both self-evident and manifestly good. Even those who do not consider themselves liberals unthinkingly repeat liberal platitudes.[24]

The most ubiquitous of these liberal platitudes is, of course: *people should be able to do what they want, as long as they don't hurt anyone else*. Mr Hazony simply asked: is this conservative? His answer was: no. But if not, why have conservative political institutions throughout the West been vessels and incubators for liberal ideology?

As Mr Hazony said, Trump hasn't divided the right in America. Centuries-old philosophical divisions have simply re-emerged. The conservative 'unity' sought by Never Trumpers at National Review won't be coming back. Likewise, the Abbott-Turnbull saga didn't divide the Liberal Party of Australia. It is simply the case that the fusion of Burkean conservatism and classical liberalism, the Burke and Mill Fallacy, has finally come undone.

Unable to ignore the conflict anymore, why not just let liberalism win this internal fight? The problem with allowing any political movement to become defined by ideological liberalism is that it is so unappealing. People

---

[24] Phillip Blond, 'Politics After Liberalism', *First Things*, December 2017.

ultimately recoil from rampant, selfish individualism – the paradigm this ideology devolves into. Human beings are not made that way. We are relational and sympathetic.

Marxism and Liberalism – Faction Fight

The reader may have been surprised at the earlier coupling of liberalism and Marxism as simply two ideologies competing for world domination. Right-wingers may also be wondering why, for a book of conservative essays, surprisingly little is being said of the dark, familiar phantoms of 'political correctness' and 'cultural Marxism'. These overused terms actually refer to the infiltration of all spheres of life – whether politics, art, literature, family life, or any relationship – with an obsession for analysing (and forcefully *correcting*) supposed underlying power dynamics or imbalances; in other words, Critical Theory.[25]

Critical Theory has indeed been debilitating, and fault can be laid squarely at the feet of Marx and his disciples. Many will say this should be our sole target for criticism.

Why can't we just be more optimistic about the future and positive about the past achievements of liberal democracy, and capitalism, and can't we all just enjoy this great freedom and wealth we have? It's those cultural Marxists who are the grumps raining on our parade; and all that political correctness gone mad which is ruining our free speech. We need to hold onto liberalism for dear life!

---

[25] For an accessible explanation of Critical Theory and its preoccupations, see Uri Harris, 'Jordan B Peterson, Critical Theory, and the New Bourgeoise', *Quillette*, January 17, 2018.

Well, responding to Marxist criticism with liberal optimism isn't really the conservative thing to do. Because, of course, there's not as much difference between Marxism and liberalism as we would like to think. Where Marxism obsesses over power, liberalism lauds self-interest. These two preoccupations are linked.

Maurice Cowling wrote in 1978 about just this problem. He was amused at the time by a report, *The Attack on Higher Education*, prepared by a prominent academic and liberal, Professor Julius Gould. Professor Gould lambasted the spread of Marxists at English universities, forming 'illiberal groupings' and displaying 'indifference to liberal values'. This all sounds very familiar.

But Maurice Cowling offered this conservative judgement on Professor Gould's liberal attacks on his Marxist colleagues:

> *The Attack on Higher Education* is best understood as part of a faction fight, which Conservatives should avoid, in which Professor Gould reflects merely liberal jealousy at the advances made by Marxists from the very point in the late 1960s at which university expansion was expected to confirm the stranglehold of liberal thinking on higher education.[26]

It was much clearer to Maurice Cowling then, than it is to conservatives now, that the battle between liberalism and Marxism is an ideological faction fight within which conservatives don't really fit. Both of these ideologies see everything cynically in terms of power or self-interest; and this cynicism kills the belief in truth, beauty and goodness which should be at the heart of the conservative's under-

---

[26] Maurice Cowling, 'The Present Position', in *Conservative Essays*, ed. Maurice Cowling (London: Cassell, 1978), 8.

standing of the world and man's place in it.

Who else but Mill?

The Burke and Mill formula is an unsatisfactory short-hand explanation for the intellectual foundations of the Liberal Party. A love of tradition and human society can't be matched with ideological single-mindedness. Can we discern a new formula for the Australian right, which could hope to be as successful (at least, rhetorically) in the future as Howard's seemed in its time?

Can we re-imagine the Liberal Party's political settlement without perpetuating the Burke and Mill contradiction?

Let's begin by looking at a question which begs an answer. Why Mill? As in, why did Mill have to be the 'liberal' in the 'liberal and conservative' formula? Of the litany of 'liberal' figures from the uncertain, pre-industrial origins of liberalism to today, why was Mill chosen to personify that ideology? The choice of Burke to represent conservatism is obvious. Burke is recognised as the 'father' of modern conservatism, if that is possible. Mill is not the 'father' of liberalism. Couldn't we have been the party of Burke and Locke, Constant or Rawls?

We can only guess why Mill was chosen. His name is recognisable and (to employ some corporate jargon) his ideas are quickly 'digestible', at least if we limit ourselves to *On Liberty*. It's also clear that in the context of his 2005 speech, Howard was using Mill as a signal of the party's economic programme in particular.

For a lot of Australian Liberals their *raison d'être* is a sense of superiority in economic understanding and practice. As such, there is merit in looking for a historical figure to symbolise economic sophistication.

Why not, then, find someone who at the same time defies categorisation as an ideological liberal?

Why not Adam Smith?

Burke and Smith

Adam Smith's name and his ideas have been caricatured by both left and right, time and time again. Whether as the supposed great advocate of self-interest, or the 'high priest of capitalism', this ubiquitous and flawed view of Smith with which we are familiar is distorted, relying on an assumption that what really matters is economics, not *culture*. Of course, Adam Smith made no such mistake.

Now is precisely the right time for conservatives to be re-visiting their appreciation and understanding of Adam Smith well beyond the distortions of the 1970s and 80s perpetuated by the Adam Smith Institute and other co-py-cat think-tanks.

The task has already been substantially advanced by a prominent Conservative MP and philosopher in the United Kingdom, Dr Jesse Norman, in his book *Adam Smith: What he Thought and Why it Matters*.[27] Upon reading Dr Norman's analysis, we begin to appreciate that Smith's primary target for criticism was not the state or government *per se*, but the government captured by vested interests (the merchants).

Relying on Dr Norman's analysis, and our own understanding of the shortfalls of the Burke and Mill theory, let's consider why it makes much more sense to speak of a party of Burke and Smith.

   1.   Burke and Smith understood that people

---

[27] (Great Britain: Allen Lane, 2018).

are motivated by more than self-interest

In his approach to the study of political economy, Mill understood man 'solely as a being who desires to possess wealth and who is capable of judging of the comparative efficacy of means for obtaining that end'. For Mill, there were only two traits which he thought reliably characterised mankind: 'aversion to labour, and desire of the present enjoyment of costly indulgences'.[28]

We only have to read the opening line of Smith's *Theory of Moral Sentiments* to see that he had a more complicated view of human nature: 'How selfish soever man may be supposed, there are evidently some principles in his nature, which interest him in the fortune of others, and render their happiness necessary to him, though he derives nothing from it except the pleasure of seeing it'.[29] Smith understood that there was more to our motivations than selfishness, though he did not deny its existence.

What happened to our understanding of human motivations in the period between Smith and Mill? Well almost immediately after Smith (in fact a year before Smith's death) a narrower idea of economic motivation came about thanks to Mill's teacher, Jeremy Bentham. Bentham proposed that the goodness of an action should be determined, not based on morality or the satisfaction of duty or obligation, but only in terms of the maximisation of pleasure or happiness; that is, 'the principle of utility'.[30]

---

[28]   John Stuart Mill, *On The Definition of Political Economy,* quoted in Adam Smith: What He Thought and Why it Matters by Jesse Norman (Great Britain: Allen Lane, 2018), 180-181.

[29]   Adam Smith, *The Theory of Moral Sentiments,* (England: Penguin Books, 2009), 13.

[30]   Jesse Norman, *Adam Smith: What He Thought and Why it Matters,* (Great Britain: Allen Lane, 2018), 178.

This was the first step, as Dr Norman explains, on the road to the fictitious idea of man as scientifically understandable in terms of a unifying principle of self-interest. But it was not until 1836 that this purely economic vision of man debuted in Mill's *On The Definition of Political Economy.*

How people actually lived, how society, economy and morality intermingled, was forgotten in favour of a fictitious idea of man as *homo economicus,* totally and exclusively motivated by self-interest. This assumption has led to, as Amartya Sen put it, economists now being obsessed with 'the accuracy of answers to well-defined questions posed with pre-selected assumptions'.[31] What distinguishes Smith from Mill, and links him to Burke, is his appreciation of complexity. The defiant complexity of human society.

2. *Burke and Smith shared a view of the world which prized human relationships*

A number of persistent questions characterise our political debates, even today. They should be top of the mind for any political party or movement trying to define or redefine itself. What is the nature of society? What keeps it going? Why should an individual citizen be loyal to a particular society or community? Why should we help others outside our immediate families and friends? Why should we make any sacrifice for others at all? And who is it that makes up a unified community?[32]

---

[31] Amartya Sen, 'Rational Fools', *Philosophy & Public Affairs,* 6.4, Summer 1977.

[32] See Jesse Norman, 'The Moral Basis of a Commercial Society', (Second PM Glynn Religion, Law and Public Life Lecture, The Crypt of St Mary's Cathedral, Sydney, April 9, 2018).

There have been many attempts to answer these questions politically and philosophically. One prominent approach, the standard approach of ideological liberalism, is the classical utilitarian idea that a society is legitimate only in so far as it ensures individual happiness, and in particular 'the greatest good for the greatest number'. Mill is one of the most significant historical advocates of this approach. It is also now part of the house philosophy of the educated middle class. The problem with utilitarianism is its indifference to community, and the innumerable complexities and variations which characterise human societies. It is a doctrine in which the one supreme good is the satisfaction of individual whim, regardless of place or context.

Thankfully, there are alternatives. A consistent approach to the questions posed above can be gleaned from the writings of Edmund Burke and Adam Smith, who in their time were personal friends. It involves starting with Burke, and in particular his reverence for the natural order and reciprocity within each unique community or society. We can then rely on Adam Smith to add further detail, for instance his insight that processes of exchange are not merely economic, but also moral.

Smith and Burke see men and women as social animals, beings whose nature is to be in society. This rejects the idea of man as an atom, as suggested by *homo economicus*. Smith argues that moral values and standards come not from the inside out (by reference to our own ego), but from the outside in (by reference to those around us). Moral assumptions come from our relationships with others, our sympathy towards them, through expectations and judgments running both ways. As Dr Norman points out, 'such a society's sense of virtue is not simply that of the marketplace. On the contrary — and here we must turn back to Burke — it preserves a sense of the divine, in the need to respect something apart from and above one-self, something that gives a higher meaning and a moral perspective to human lives. It does this through the proper feeling of awe that any thinking person has and should have for the complexity and value of society itself as an inheritance.'[33]

How does one come to be in 'awe' of society? In some sense it's a very strange reaction to have to your social surrounds. But consider your friends. How did each of them come to be a part of your life? Where did you meet? What have you done for them and what have they done for you? What joys and miseries have you shared? Now how many of your achievements are due to the selfless gifts of your parents, grandparents, or a teacher or mentor? To what extent have you been defined by the school you attended and the relationships and lessons gained there? Maybe not at all, but what about the peculiar, recurring traditions of your annual extended family get-together, whether for Christmas or Easter or some other occasion? Take all these relationships and all their epiphenomena and just consider what this has meant for your life. Now pan out to consider all the relationships and exchanges that define the people in your town or city, your region, and, ultimately, your country. This is roughly the process by which people like Smith and Burke conclude that we can't help but be in awe of the society we inherit and inhabit. These are the links in the series by which, as Burke put it, we proceed towards a love of our country, and of mankind.

According to Norman, the goal of government in this system is to achieve and maintain 'not merely private freedoms but a free and educated public realm, filled with the

---

[33] Ibid.

conversation of civil, honest and independent minds'. For politicians of this view, 'Leadership begins in respect for the social order, and so in modesty. It pushes leaders towards a close study of their people, all the people, and their institutions. It locates the "we" of politics at the level of the nation as a whole. And it insists on the common good, and the importance of public service and public duty'.[34]

How different this is from the principle we discussed at the outset, that every individual should be able to do what he wants as long as he doesn't hurt anyone else? How much more nuanced? How much more human!

Opportunity

Some will see the attempt to eschew such grotesque individualism as flying in the face of decades of conservative efforts to counteract collectivist socialist regimes and policies. However, we are simply addressing an inversion of the socialist problem. Our natural individuality ultimately overcame the unnatural collectivist agenda of the Soviet Empire, where the collective was artificially oriented towards and defined by the state. However, our natural *relational* qualities as human beings suffer equally when an appreciation of individuality becomes the pursuit of *individualism*. Human nature demands relationships just as much as it demands individuality.

For Australian purposes, a Party of Burke and Smith presents an opportunity. There is nothing limited or narrow about this formula. It becomes a party for everyone who approaches politics modestly and with appreciation for what they have inherited. It helps the natural party of government to be a party for its people, not an ideology. It is an opportune formula for a party which, as Abbott says, has 'never been about just one big idea', but which

---

34   Ibid.

is also anxious not to lack definition altogether in the absence of a unifying leader. As the Burke and Mill Fallacy shows, the Party is constantly looking for authoritative and credible thinkers to signal its priorities and place in history. Burke and Smith make much more sense for us because they refuse to be ideologically categorised. By dumping Mill, we're not pushing anyone away. We are refusing to entertain a view of humanity that is inhuman, and instead acknowledging a view of human society which is consistent.

III

THE DISASTER OF LIBERALISM

How liberalism has infected both sides of politics, crushing mediating institutions between the two monoliths of market and state, leaving a cultural wasteland.

Cultural wasteland

Let's consider in more detail what liberalism has done to that society we just surveyed and appreciated.

Joseph Schumpeter wrote *Capitalism, Socialism and Democracy* between 1939 and 1942, amid a total war upending old orders and order itself. In explaining how that point of wholesale destruction had been reached, Schumpeter observed that Karl Marx and his ideas, so influential on events up to that point, had burst upon a world where:

> Faith in any real sense was falling away from all classes of society, and with it the only ray of light... died from the workman's world... [35]

And so, Marx (not to mention the fascists) prophesied a false heaven, offering a perverted hope for hopeless people. Why was there nothing to counter this heresy? What had made the civilised West so vulnerable to extremist ideology? Schumpeter's catty rebuke of the *bourgeois*, chattering class of the time provides an answer. In response to their darkening world, where smog and cold reason had smothered the light for a whole mass of people which had become known as the 'working class', 'intellectuals professed themselves highly satisfied with Mill's

---

[35] Joseph A. Schumpeter, *Capitalism, Socialism and Democracy 3rd Ed.*, (New York: Harper Perennial Modern Thought, 2008), 6.

Logic and the Poor Law'.[36] That is, when confronted with a cultural crisis, the leaders of the day fell back on Mill's neat ideas about 'the greatest good for the greatest number', coupled with the loveless embrace of state welfare.

This anticipates our present disaster. Today, the liberal elite on either side of the political divide are happy to continue relying on Mill's 'one very simple principle', that each individual should be able to do what he wants as long as he doesn't interfere with another individual's right to do what she wants.

The difference is that now, along with faith, something else significant has fallen away almost completely. Civil society has disappeared. By civil society I mean 'everything that ordinary citizens do that is not reducible to the imposed activities of the central state or the compulsion and determination of the marketplace'.[37]

So what happened to civil society? Well, long before we amalgamated the local councils, we lost interest in them. When we are not complaining about the major political parties we are refusing to join them and thus normalise them. The right is constantly celebrating the seriously diminished rates of trade union membership. Meanwhile, the left trumpets the decline in church life and lauds the rise of the 'Nones'. Cooperative societies and civic organisations, if they exist, are the exclusive domain of those retirees who have not already been put in a home.

All of these forms of association, and countless more, were once the means for ordinary citizens to exercise power over their own lives and that of their families and communities. The loss of them is the loss of civil society.

---

[36] Ibid.
[37] Phillip Blond, *Red Tory,* (London: Faber and Faber Limited, 2010), 3.

There has been no better explanation of this cultural dis-integration than that of the English political philosopher Phillip Blond in his 2010 book, *Red Tory*. Broadly he explains how the liberal left and the liberal right have taken turns contributing to the disruption and chaos which has overturned civil society in the West.

In the 1960s, 'the new left' (drawn from the middle class, and distinguishable from the older more paternalist and statist left which had lost power in Britain in 1951 and Australia in 1949) preached the unshackling of personal pleasure and satisfaction as a means of public salvation. Such a doctrine, Blond argues, was toxic to the middle class and lethal to the working class. This 'sexual revolution' was 'contaminated by narcissism from the outset. For the working class this narcissism meant the dissolving of social bonds which had kept the poorest together during the worst times of the 1930s... this license to express the self allowed the advocates of liberation in the late 1960s to embrace drugs and hedonism as if personal emancipation for bohemians would lead to the liberation of all'. It's obvious that the hardest hit by personal libertarianism, particularly with respect to drugs, have been the poorest of our society. Blond points out that the new left 'opened the personal sphere to modern consumer capitalism' by commodifying sexual relations, among other things. This initiative has come to full maturity with the complete normalisation of 'dating' apps such as *Tinder*. They are 'free' for the users of course, because if you are not paying for something, you are the product.

Philip Blond points out that the political right finished the job of killing civil society by endorsing economic disruption for already displaced peoples, placing life and death in the hands of a 'creative destruction' which accelerated change at a rate faster than people could come to comprehend its aims or evaluate the damage. While figures like

Margaret Thatcher instigated much-needed modernisation of Western economies, 'the clearly un-conservative idea that the market was the ultimate arbiter of value and the measure of all things ensured that civic life was ignored and that the interests of the state and the market were viewed as synonymous'.[38]

As such, any distinction between the parties of right and left over the past half century has been somewhat illusory. Blond suggests that left and right have merely been championing different aspects of liberalism, with the social liberalisation of the '60s and '70s giving way to the economic liberalisation of the '80s and '90s.

This has resulted in a 'market state' which *enforces* individualism. It is enforced in the sense that the concept of an individual free from mutual, familial or civil obligations is not natural – it is the product of liberal ideology. To realise this new vision of man, the bureaucratic liberals of the left deliberately legislated policies which broke down familial relationships. Meanwhile, economic liberals on the right, rather than achieving a popular capitalism or 'property owning democracy', pursued a kind of market fundamentalism which has lent itself to monopolisation and control by vested interests. Both developments have had the effect of isolating the individual and increasing his reliance on the last institution standing – the state.

The 'market state' theory of forced individualism explains how we have reached a point where the supposed aim of public policy is to unshackle and liberate the individual so that he has no obligations to others, and therefore no one obligated to him. Essentially, a loner, completely reliant on the state.

---

[38] Ibid, 19.

Libertarians grow the state

Let's consider one concrete example which perfectly illustrates the propensity for advocates of unrestrained individual freedom to dramatically expand the power and remit of the state.

In 2017 there was a bill introduced in the New South Wales upper house to license voluntary euthanasia.

Dr Peter Phelps, a prominent libertarian, was one of the Liberal Party members who voted in favour of the euthanasia bill. His support was expressed publicly in the following terms: 'I disagree with euthanasia, all suicide is fundamentally illogical..., but I disagree even more strongly with limiting people's right to live or die as they choose.' [39] It is staggering to see this belief that individual whim is more important than reason, even with respect to life and death, put so expressly.

The bill did not pass the Legislative Council, falling short by only one vote. But the euthanasia push succeeded in Victoria, where it was spearheaded by Labor Premier Daniel Andrews.

It may seem odd that the socialist Daniel Andrews ends up on the same page as the libertarian Dr Phelps. But it exemplifies the influence of liberal ideology on both sides of politics; they are both affected by the same anti-rational liberal axiom, prioritising the 'freedom' of the individual above any other consideration.

Andrews claims that his Victorian legislation is the safest assisted suicide legislation in the world. And, of course, the NSW version promised to be even 'safer'. But after

---

[39] Andrew Clenell, 'Supporters 'have the votes on euthanasia' in NSW', *The Australian*, November 13, 2017.

all the checks and balances, after all the inquisitions and 'safeguards', what else does this officious process amount to, other than some bureaucrat, some emanation of the state, telling some desperate soul that 'yes, the government will allow you to die in this instance'. Is this what freedom looks like for the libertarian Dr Phelps? What do we accomplish by crossing this threshold to supposedly greater freedom, other than involving the state even more deeply in the life and death of its citizens? We are increasingly exposing the great contradiction: liberals, and by extension libertarians, actually need government. The liberal or libertarian vision for society is unnatural and counter-intuitive, necessarily diminishing culture and the institutions that temper the sovereign individual. The wasteland which results requires the state to prop up artificial 'freedoms', such as the freedom to suicide with medical assistance, because no healthy society could naturally reach the conclusion that this is a freedom worth realising. Liberals, just as much as socialists, have been responsible for the growth of the state.

Liberals and the revolution

Liberalism has succeeded in framing most political debates in terms of 'progress', 'change' and the opposition to it. Ensuring that all arguments rhetorically revolve around 'change' has led to a false dichotomy between those who accept and embrace the inexorable progress of the ages towards enlightenment, and those who stubbornly oppose it.

But the march of time is not restrained by, or thanks to, any particular political movement. For anyone to think that time was within their power would be megalomaniacal. There were no 'conservatives' or 'liberals' when the Pre-Socratic philosopher Heraclitus observed that a man cannot step in the same river twice because it is no longer the same river and he is no longer the same man. But the unstoppable progress of time provides the illusion of power to those who uncritically embrace every incidental change which is consequent upon that movement. They think that by embracing it, they are somehow in control. Joseph de Maistre made a similar observation with respect to the event which, more than any other, consumes the emotional energy of conservatives:

> It has been correctly pointed out that the French Revolution leads men more than men lead it. This observation is completely justified, and although it can be applied to all great revolutions more or less, it has never been more striking than it is in the present period. The very rascals who appear to lead the Revolution are involved only as simple instruments, and as soon as they aspire to dominate it fall ignobly. Those who established the Republic did it without wanting to and without knowing what they were doing. They were led to it by events; a prior design would not have succeeded.[40]

Liberals continue to believe they lead the 'revolution'. But everyday people who lack even the illusion of control over the immense political, economic, and – dare I say – spiritual forces they are subject to, look on with horror as 'life and death seem to be solely in the hands of a scientific and technological progress that is moving faster than man's ability to establish its ultimate goals and evaluate its costs'. [41]

Consider again the debate around euthanasia. The argument is framed in terms of a progressive view of *more*

---

[40] Joseph de Maistre, *Considerations on France*, (Cambridge: Cambridge University Press, 1994), 5.

[41] Pontifical Council for Justice and Peace, *Compendium of the Social Doctrine of the Church*, (Vatican City: Libreria Editrice Vaticana, 2010), 326.

freedom and choice, versus an antiquated 'religious' view of less freedom and choice. But to see this debate in terms of *progress*, like so many other debates, misses the point. The controversy is obviously a debate about the meaning of human life, who has power over the taking of it, and the source of a life's value. Euthanasia raises awkward questions for a lazily secular society. If man and woman are no longer made in *imago Dei*, is there any empirical way to say his or her death is more significant than that of a lame animal 'put to sleep'? But who has the time to ask these questions, let alone answer them? Apparently, no one.

This is really where we need to locate the difference between a liberal and a conservative. Not in our attitude to 'change', but in our conception of what it means to be human.

IV

WHICH WAY CONSERVATISM?

Where does all this leave conservatives? Who are they? What do they really want?

Even the most committed conservative finds it difficult to explain precisely what a 'conservative' is. This is because conservatism can't be understood like an ideology; it doesn't boil down to prescribed axioms. It is more like a 'cast of mind'.[42] The mind in question is *formed* by tradition, relationships and a humble appreciation of the society around it.

What's more, it is incorrect to say that the conservative cast of mind can be summarised simply as an opposition to radical *change*. Rather, it opposes any radical reformulation of the *understanding of human nature*. Where conservatives significantly differ with liberals is in how they view the human person.

The political significance of this introduction is to reveal that, whatever he or she is, a conservative is not *part* liberal. Ideological liberalism and conservative disposition cannot inhabit the same mind for long: tradition cannot flourish when competing against ideology; the freedom understood by conservatives is not the same freedom championed by liberals; a relational understanding of human nature contradicts the individualistic; and, finally, materialistic liberalism does not allow for a conservative's commitment to non-material goods.

---

[42] See Damien Freeman, *Abbott's Right: The Conservative Tradition from Menzies to Abbott,* (Melbourne: Melbourne University Press, 2018), 58-70.

As liberal-conservative Fusionism dies, significant writers are re-founding conservatism, planting it more explicitly in the religious and philosophical traditions of the West. The explanation of the 'Christian-Platonist' tradition, in James Matthew Wilson's deeply important book *The Vision of the Soul: Truth, Goodness, and Beauty in the Western Tradition*, has been critical to the editor's understanding of what precisely it is on which conservatives intellectually depend.

For this reason, I don't want to leave the conservative reader thinking it is sufficient simply to swap out or rearrange one or two historical characters – Burke or Mill or Smith – in order to properly address the liberal disaster. It's true that the Burke and Mill Fallacy must be abandoned. It's also true that if conservatives in Australia are looking for a better rhetorical formula to signify their priorities, 'Burke and Smith' makes more sense. This is a contribution to practical political questions, but the deeper answer to the liberal disaster, and the question of human nature and human flourishing, is not really about any of them.

To address the deeper questions, the conservative must desire as many other minds as possible to be cast in the mould of Western tradition; the revelations of Jerusalem; the philosophy of Athens; the literary, artistic and musical canon. Conservatives must advocate for a society where it is understood that there is more than matter, self-interest and the power of the will. There are non-material things that make our lives meaningful: Truth, Goodness, and Beauty. The path to human flourishing is to say what is true, to do what is good and to make what is beautiful.[43]

---

[43] With thanks to my friend Michael Warren Davis, who first articulated a version of this phrase, appropriating T.S. Eliot's: 'To do the useful thing, to say the courageous thing, to contemplate the beautiful thing: that is enough for one man's life.'

Ancient wisdom, ever new

Observations regarding the superficiality of modern life are unoriginal. Anyone can see the pervasiveness of commercialisation, our obsession with new gadgets and possessions, and our addiction to all forms of instant communication and media.

The terrifying thing for modern man, though, is that when he goes in search of deeper answers, turning to the intellectual authorities of the last three centuries, he finds that, far from adding another dimension to his understanding of human nature and happiness, our 'intellectual parents' only provide a 'school of disenchantment'.[44] For Marx, there is nothing beyond human nature other than the capacity for production. For Kant, there is nothing to beauty other than satisfaction of individual taste. For Hobbes, there is nothing inward to man apart from matter; there is no soul. For Nietzsche, every supposed truth is simply the production of a will to power. University-educated people are therefore left just as impoverished as everyone else by being schooled in the insights of their 'intellectual parents'. It is merely confirmed for them that Truth, Goodness, and Beauty are nothing more than 'subjective projections, mass delusions, or ideological conveniences'.[45] Only matter is real.

We started this introduction identifying the flawed, hidden assumption at the heart of our cultural and political malaise: *people should just be able to do what they want, as long as they don't harm anyone else.* We have come to understand that this is undeniably inspired by the central axiom of liberalism as expressed by Mill: 'That principle

---

[44] James Matthew Wilson, *The Vision of the Soul: Truth, Goodness, And Beauty in the Western Tradition,* (Washington D.C., The Catholic University of America Press, 2018), 47.

[45] Wilson, *Ibid.,* 55.

is, that the sole end for which mankind are warranted, in-dividually or collectively, in interfering in liberty of action of any of their number, is self-protection.' Apparently, this approach will ensure the greatest happiness for the greatest number.

It's obvious that Mill is another one of these 'intellectual parents' who denies, rather than affirms, the existence of anything beyond the material. The one very simple prin-ciple of liberalism – that the key to human happiness is doing what we want, subject to not directly harming oth-ers - in fact relies on the denial of such things as Truth, Goodness, and Beauty.

How has this affected our understanding of human na-ture and happiness? Well it has meant that the individual now judges the merits of his actions solely by the question of whether and to what degree they satisfy him, not how they affect others. It means, for the most part, we now avoid speaking the truth in love to people who are harm-ing themselves through destructive choices as long as they seem satisfied because the Harm Principle only applies if they are harming 'others'. Of course, liberalism has blind-ed us to the obvious truth that we are defined less by our sovereign selves, than by our relationships with and be-haviour towards others.

Edmund Burke articulated this in a very helpful way, say-ing of course that society 'becomes a partnership not only between those who are living, but between those who are living, those who are dead, and those who are to be born.' This is why he has become totemic for conservatives, who still insist on this relational, intergenerational under-standing of human nature.

The great Metaphysical poet John Donne captured the sentiment even more perfectly when he said that 'No man is an island, / Entire of itself' and 'Each man's death diminishes me, / For I am involved in mankind'.

Of course, these instincts with respect to the value of our relationships precede even the 18th century Burke and 16th century Donne. They are ancient. St Augustine of Hippo, whose treatise *The City of God* defined European political thinking for a millennium, famously declared elsewhere that it is through our relationships with others that we know God himself:

> Nay, but thou dost see the Trinity if thou see'st love.[46]

St Augustine was meditating on 1 John iv 16: 'God is love'. Augustine observed that when we love someone – whether it's our children, spouse, a friend, parents, a brother or sister – we come to know that feeling of *love* even more than we know the person we love.[47] Familiarising ourselves with this type of sincere, pure love necessarily involves coming to know God. If God is love, then wherever you see love, you see the Trinity.

Augustine's declaration has the force and undeniable clarity of truth. And when we encounter it, we begin to understand why it has been so destructive for individuality to become *individualism*, and for liberality to become *liberalism*. In the words of Les Murray: 'Most rhymes in -ism and -ation / are nothing but cabals, though, out to take over the nation / compared with true persons...'[48] We can

---

[46] Augustine of Hippo, 'Doctrinal Treatises of St Augustine: On the Holy Trinity', in *A Select Library of the Nicene and Post-Nicene Fathers of the Christian Church Volume III: On the Holy Trinity; Doctrinal Treatises; Moral Treatises ed. Philip Schaff,* (USA: Hendrickson Publishers, 1995), 123-124.

[47] Ibid.

[48] Les Murray, 'Sidere Mens Eadem Mutato: A Spiral of

now comprehend the fatal error of having elevated isolation and self-trust on a throne when we are so obviously dependent on so many others for meaning and happiness.

Another great Australian, Christopher Pearson, once spoke of the 'mnemonic power of beauty' which reminds us that we are all 'in search of a reality we are taught by our nature to hope for – a deep and hospitable ordering of the world in which we are not estranged and have a place'.[49]

It won't be easy to emerge from the cultural disaster wrought by ideological liberalism; to re-integrate those relationships, human and spiritual, which have disintegrated; or to rediscover that 'deep and hospitable ordering of the world' which we long for. How can we defeat the ideology of individualism, the creed of self alone? There is no simple principle, formula or programme for revitalisation. Confounded as I am, I can only remind myself that there is a Person, of course, who assures that, even to the end of time: *I am with you.*

Sonnets for Robert Ellis', in *Collected Poems*, (Carlton: Black Inc., 2018), 111.

[49] Christopher Pearson, *A Better Class of Sunset: The Writings of Christopher Pearson*, (Ballarat: Connor Court, 2014), 362.

THE ESSAYS AND THE AUTHORS

The authors of the essays which form this collection would not all describe themselves as 'conservative', but together the essays form a book unconfused by any attempted fusion with liberalism for the library of the conservative who cares, the conservative who cares to understand the origin of his instincts, or who cares to understand where it all went wrong, how we lost, and how we might revive our civilisational inheritance. The essays address many of the sources of anguish among conservatives confused by liberal ideas: drugs, euthanasia, education, market fundamentalism, sex, commercial surrogacy, foreign policy, populism, *et cætera*. Essentially, I hope that the material in this book will remind conservatives of their intellectual foundation and provide a more sophisticated platform for all of us who are instinctively conservative, but at sea among the flotsam of the liberal disaster.

Part I. Death, Drugs & Sex

THE CHOICE THAT ENDS ALL CHOICE

The next great cultural threshold to be enthusiastically charged over is likely to be the legalisation of euthanasia. **Catherine Priestley** addresses how this is a perfect example of the all-encompassing application of the liberal principle. All desire is treated as legitimate and indeed demands realisation, even if it is as irrational as state-licensed suicide. Among other things, it is symptomatic of our culture's uneasy relationship with suffering, and our aversion to anything which might suggest we cannot exercise power and control over every aspect of our life.

Catherine Priestley has written for The Spectator Australia *and* The Daily Telegraph.

THE NEW SMOG

Competing with euthanasia to be the most transgressive, imminent act of social destruction is the legalisation of recreational cannabis use. **David Sergeant** presents a meticulously researched paper, exposing liberal arguments for legalisation before forwarding a coherent case for robust, effective prohibition.

David Sergeant is a conservative researcher in the House of Commons and a fellow at the Bow Group think tank. He writes an opinion column for The Spectator Australia.

EMPIRE OF AVARICE

It might shock some right-wing political pundits to hear that the campus rape culture is not a fiction. Something is deeply wrong in the way men and women interact today, particularly at universities. Conservatives see it, and the left sees it. Liberals and libertarians choose to ignore it. **Michael Warren Davis** explains why there is a rape culture and why conservatives are the only ones with any hope of ending it.

Michael Warren Davis is the editor of Crisis *magazine. He previously served as US editor of the* Catholic Herald *and assistant editor of* Quadrant.

BORROWED WOMBS

Bill O'Chee, by reference to the debate around commercial surrogacy, and the tragic episode of Baby Gammy, explains how left and right have cooperated in elevating every personal desire to the status of 'inalienable right'. This has not only added to every political consideration a litany of new, competing rights, but has downgraded higher order rights such as the right to life into the same bloody contest.

Bill O'Chee was a National Party member of the Australian Senate from 1990 to 1999, representing the state of Queensland. He has written regularly for Fairfax Media (now Nine) and The Spectator Australia.

Part II. Philosophy, France & Freedom

ROMANCE AND SOCIALISM IN J.S. MILL

Helen Andrews has re-examined the life of John Stuart Mill: the person who, more than any other in Anglophone politics, personifies the principles and goals of liberalism. Andrews can't help but see the connection between John Stuart Mill's anxiety about rules and customs regulating behaviour, and his own transgressive personal life. The clarity with which she exposes these connections compels us to re-examine how readily we apply the principle of Mill and why we expect this to bear positive results.

Helen Andrews will publish her first book with Sentinel in 2020. Previously she was managing editor of the Washington Examiner magazine *and a 2017–18 Robert Novak Journalism Fellow. She has written for many publications including* The New York Times, First Things, *and* American Affairs.

LIBERTY, LIBERALS, AND THE GAY WEDDING CAKE

A strange consequence of the enormous influence of Mill is that his 'one very simple principle' has come to define progressive as well as conservative politics. Salvatore Babones argues that the ubiquity of liberals and liberalism has led to a confusion of 'rights' and 'freedoms', as both 'progressives' and 'conservatives' ultimately embrace the autonomy of the individual. Comparing the historical experiences of the United States, the United Kingdom, and Australia, he argues that, as liberals have transitioned from promoting a 'freedom' agenda to a 'rights' agenda, they have, by a slight inflection of priorities, become inescapably authoritarian, and a threat to democracy."

Salvatore Babones is an associate professor at the University of Sydney whose current research focuses on comparing civilisations. His most recent book is The New Authoritarianism: Trump, Populism and the Tyranny of Experts *(Polity Press, 2018)."*

LIBERTY AND LICENCE

Liberalism has caused another kind of confusion in Australia: that between a certain type of freedom and another, between liberty and licence. What type of 'freedom' should the Liberal Party of Australia promote? The liberty familiar to Burke, or the licentiousness which issues from Mill's principle? **Damien Freeman** traces through the history of the Liberal Party, revealing just what 'freedom' has meant for anti-Labor forces in Australian politics.

Damien Freeman is a Fellow of the PM Glynn Institute, Australian Catholic University, and Editor of the Kapunda Press. His most recent book is Abbott's Right: The conservative tradition from Menzies to Abbott *(MUP, 2017).*

DE GAULLE AND THE FRENCH RIGHT

In our perennial search to understand and define the conservative side of politics in Australia, we instinctively turn to supposed analogues in Anglophone political history. Perhaps we're looking in the wrong place in our hope of explaining someone like Sir Robert Menzies? **Nathan Pinkoski** explains the 20th century history of the French right. He analyses the role of Charles De Gaulle and more than one line jumps out as reminiscent of Menzies: 'De Gaulle elevated prudence and diminished doctrine. This had the advantage of flexibility, but the disadvantage of lacking clarity about basic principles. De Gaulle was obviously a conservative, but he never attempted to form a conservative political party. Yet inevitably he created a "party."' This appears to mirror the 'non-doctrinaire' strategy of Menzies perfectly, not to mention the long-term confusion we are presently dealing with. More broadly, understanding the current and fascinating French predicament is essential for anyone hoping to comprehend the political moment we inhabit.

Nathan Pinkoski is a Postdoctoral Research Fellow at St Michael's College, University of Toronto. He has previously been a Lecturer in Politics at Princeton University.

Part III. Markets & Mistakes

'FREE MARKET' MYTHS

There is no doubt that the uncritical admiration of the 'free market' (which used to define the political right) is being ever more frequently brought into question. No one writes better on the hypocrisy and contradiction which inheres in shallow 'free market' rhetoric than **Adam Creighton**. His essay details his observations regarding the illusory distinction between the 'private' and 'public' spheres, encouraging a more honest view of the mutual reliance between commercial enterprise and government regulation; a relationship which can be responsible for corruption as well as prosperity.

Adam Creighton is Economics Editor at The Australian. *He was a Journalist in Residence at the University of Chicago's Booth School of Business in 2019. His writing has also appeared in* The Economist *and* The Wall Street Journal.

THE REAL ADAM SMITH

Much of the misplaced faith in markets, and the disavowal of 'the state' by those in conservative circles has sprung from a mischaracterisation of Adam Smith and his writings. **Paul Sagar** exposes a long-running misrepresentation of Adam Smith which has placed him unquestioningly on the side of absolutist free-marketeers: 'While Smith might be publicly lauded by those who put their faith in private capitalist enterprise, and who decry the state as the chief threat to liberty and prosperity, the real Adam Smith painted a rather different picture. According to Smith, the most pressing dangers came not from the state acting alone, but the state when captured by merchant elites.' This essay and the one preceding it are both important for those who see the market as a tool to help citizens, rather than an object of worship. A more sober view of the market among conservatives is essential in the long wake of the GFC.

Paul Sagar is lecturer of political theory in the Department of Political Economy at King's College London. His most recent book is The Opinion of Mankind: Sociability and the Theory of the State from Hobbes to Smith *(Princeton University Press, 2018).*

Part IV. God, Beauty & Virtue

BEAUTY AND THE WEST

When people try to define conservatism they usually fall back on the figure of Edmund Burke, suggesting conservatism was born in reply to revolution. The great conservative philosopher Roger Scruton has said that conservatism can only be understood as a reaction to liberalism, ever since liberalism burst onto the world in the 18th century. But what tools have conservatives been using to respond to liberalism? Are they adequate? What wisdom are we drawing on? From where do our instincts originate? There is an ancient understanding of human nature which inheres in the conservative cast of mind. **James Matthew Wilson** brings this to light, explaining that man's nature, as understood by the conservative, is oriented, by design, for and towards Beauty. This is the most important essay in this collection for the reader hoping to better understand the true intellectual and spiritual roots of conservatism.

James Matthew Wilson is Associate Professor, Religion and Literature at Villanova University. He is the author of many essays on philosophical theology and literature, with a particular focus on the relation of artistic form and metaphysics, especially as manifested in poetry. His most recent books include The Vision of the Soul: Truth, Goodness, and Beauty in the Western Tradition *(The Catholic University of America Press, 2017), and* The Hanging God *(Angelico, 2018).*

DUMB AND DUMBER

One of the main preoccupations of a conservative must be education. **Blaise Joseph** explains how the utilitarian ideas of Mill and others have come to define our uninspired education system. At the same time as students are being denied their cultural patrimony, they are being encouraged to be creative without any direction or content to inspire their 'inner' genius. For this aimlessness in education we can thank Jean-Jacques Rousseau. The true object of education should be instilling Virtue in the young.

Blaise Joseph is a research fellow in education at The Centre for Independent Studies and a former secondary school teacher. He has written research papers on school funding, evidence-based education policy, and national testing in Australia.

THE MERITS OF CAMPION COLLEGE

It is revealing of the changeable definition of the word 'liberal' that the triumph of liberalism has been to the detriment of the 'liberal arts' in higher education: that is, the traditional study of the humanities as manifested in the philosophical, literary and artistic canon. Universities have gone from places preoccupied with the passing on of inherited wisdom, to places obsessed with novelty in all fields. Former High Court judge, **Dyson Heydon**, in a recent and challenging speech, sang the praises of one small institution which is reintroducing young people to the romance of tradition in learning. In praising Campion College, he explores how the big universities have become embarrassing in their neglect, trading on inherited prestige whilst not adequately passing on inherited wisdom and effective methods of teaching. This is the first time the speech has been published in full.

Dyson Heydon AC QC is a former Justice of the High Court of Australia. He served from 2003 to 2013. He had previously served as Dean of the Sydney Law School and as a Justice of the New South Wales Court of Appeal.

THE RELIGION OF HUMANITY

Assaults on traditional modes of education have been historically linked with an expansive secularist agenda. But does the secularism which defines the modern West completely lack a religious character? Does it really displace religion with atheism, or just another religion? How many readers are aware that liberal thinkers such as Auguste Comte and Mill himself devised more or less detailed versions of a formalised Religion of Humanity, complete with rituals and hierarchies to compete with the Old Religion? These bizarre manifestations have not lasted, but the worship of man in place of God continues almost explicitly. **Daniel Mahoney** explores this phenomenon and exposes the extent of its subversive reach, even into the Church itself.

Daniel J. Mahoney holds the Augustine Chair in Distinguished Scholarship at Assumption College. He is the author, most recently, of The Idol of Our Age: How the Religion of Humanity Subverts Christianity *(Encounter Books, 2018).*

Part V. Journeys, Realities & Practicalities

DON'T MENTION THE WAR

Tony Abbott, a statesman who has done much to encourage the self-awareness of conservatives in this country, explores how the label 'conservative' has occasionally been misused by decidedly un-conservative politicians for decidedly un-conservative ends. Nonetheless, he argues that the alliance of liberals and conservatives should persist, though he is not under any illusion that liberals and conservatives are just different sides of the same coin.

Tony Abbott served as the 28th Prime Minister of Australia from 2013 to 2015, and as parliamentary Leader of the Liberal Party from 2009 to 2015. His career and writings have been definitive for conservative politics in Australia for a generation.

FAMILIES: THE LIBERTARIAN BLIND SPOT

John Anderson explains that what libertarians misunderstand in their perennial war with government is that 'the market' is not their best means of defence. No, the human family is the best social challenge to state control. A family is not an optional extra for a good life, and yet our politics continues to treat it as such.

John Anderson is a sixth-generation farmer and grazier from New South Wales, who spent 19 years from 1989 in the Australian Parliament. He served as a senior Cabinet minister in the Howard Government, including six years as Leader of the National Party and Deputy Prime Minister.

A LEGISLATOR'S JOURNEY

Nick Minchin gives an account of his journey from youthful libertarianism to mature conservatism, showing how the tension between libertarianism and conservatism revealed itself during certain crucial votes in his long public life as a legislator.

Nick Minchin served as a Liberal member of the Australian Senate representing South Australia from 1993 to 2011 and was a Cabinet minister in the Howard Government and Leader of the Government in the Senate. He later served as the Australian Consul-General in New York, USA.

Part VI. Conservative Home, Conservative World

THE REVIVALIST

Have you ever looked upon a monolithic, concrete Brutalist tower and thought 'why do cities have to be so ugly nowadays'? Have you ever allowed yourself to acknowlerhdge that the 20th century was an unmitigated disaster for architecture, and the relative attractiveness of public spaces? Maybe you've also realised that things are so dire, that the tired rhetoric of 'conservatism' doesn't really capture the urgency of the situation. In that case, you may well be one of **Oliver JJ Lane's** Revivalists. Many millennials are openly wondering whether a house in the provinces might be a better option for their new family, relative to a cardboard-box-style apartment in the outer suburbs of their decaying metropolis. This is the essay for them.

Oliver JJ Lane is the Editor in Chief of Breitbart London / Europe.

DEMOCRACY, POPULISM, AND LIBERALISM

Roger Kimball explains why the 'populist' or 'nationalist' democratic revolts in America and Europe might not be ends in themselves. What is actually meant by 'populism' or 'nationalism'? Why are these terms constantly reiterated as if they were inherently negative, implying a necessary and immanent devolution into demagoguery? It may be the case that they are the last defence against the self-destruction of the Western nation-state from within. 'Perhaps the greatest threat to the West lies not in its external enemies, no matter how hostile or numerous, but in its inner uncertainty—an uncertainty that is all-too-often celebrated as an especially enlightened form of subtlety and sophistication—about who we are.'

Roger Kimball is Editor and Publisher of The New Criterion and President and Publisher of Encounter Books. He is an art critic for National Review. Mr. Kimball's latest book is The Fortunes of Permanence: Culture and Anarchy in an Age of Amnesia (St. Augustine's Press, 2012).

A TRADITIONALIST FOREIGN POLICY

Traditionalists have a clear attitude to local communities and the nation. Less well understood is their stance towards other nations and foreign policy generally. The wars of the late 20th and early 21st century resulted in part from extreme confidence in liberalism and its applicability to other cultures. What would traditionalists have done differently? What have they done throughout history? How would they approach the rise of China? All these extremely important questions are addressed by **Daniel McCarthy**.

Daniel McCarthy is director of the Robert Novak Journalism Fellowship Program at The Fund for American Studies and editor of Modern Age: A Conservative Review. *He writes regularly for* The Spectator USA, *and comments on U.S. politics for ABC Radio National's 'Late Night Live.'*

Part I.
Death, Drugs & Sex

THE CHOICE THAT ENDS ALL CHOICE
Liberalism has made euthanasia inevitable.

Catherine Priestley

> There is an immense mystery at the heart of being human: the paradox of opposing and accepting suffering. To abandon either side of the paradox is the real problem of evil.[1]
>
> *Scott Samuelson*

When an Australian scientist travelled to Switzerland to access euthanasia, the public and media were electrified with interest. He was 104 years old. The question of how human beings ought to live and end their lives, usually considered a private matter, was debated in public. Some commentators were champing at the bit to give their two cents. Consider the following by *Sydney Morning Herald* columnist Peter FitzSimons, who wrote after Dr Goodall's death:

> So where are you now, you fierce opponents of euthanasia and the right-to-die? How many of you, honestly, can look at the triumphant – you heard me – passing of the 104-year-old Australian scien-

---

[1] Scott Samuelson, "Suffering, not just happiness, weighs in the utilitarian calculus," *Aeon*, June 6, 2018.

tist David Goodall in Switzerland on Thursday and say that he got it wrong...? I ask again, to those in this country, who oppose such a dignified way of ending one's life... How many of us, if given the choice between ending it this way, and ending it with the ghastly descent most very old people experience, would not choose Mr Goodall's way? Not you opponents of right-to-die? Fine. It's not your choice. It's our choice. And it's like your damn hide to maintain that Goodall was wrong, and the rest of us have no right to choose how we go.[2]

Behold the explosive rage of an ideologue who believed his supreme right to choose had been curtailed. This anger, which pulsates regularly from the pages of *The Herald,* creates thousands of passive liberals who feel that supporting human rights and human dignity requires supporting euthanasia. Euthanasia eliminates suffering and therefore it is compassionate and good.

Euthanasia and assisted suicide involve deliberately ending the life of a patient or assisting them as they do so. Supporters of euthanasia can be broadly divided into two categories: the 'dying with dignity' movement, which believes euthanasia can eliminate un-relievable suffering; and the 'rational suicide' movement, which believes that autonomous individuals must have supreme choice over their own lives.

Both believe terminally ill people should have the right to commit suicide safely; otherwise, they are condemned to unnecessary suffering and are potentially forced to take their own lives in a gruesome and unregulated way. Supporters are quick to say that euthanasia isn't harming anyone else except the rational individual who is making

---

[2]   Peter FitzSimons, "David Goodall leads the way with choice we should all get to have," *The Sydney Morning Herald*, May 13, 2018.

the choice, and that those who oppose it are viewing the matter selfishly, forcing their own morality onto others. Opposition to euthanasia is considered a disgusting violation of personal autonomy, as Peter FitzSimons is only too ready to point out.

The case of Dr David Goodall

In May 2018, Australian academic Dr David Goodall flew to Switzerland to access euthanasia because it was unavailable to him in his own country. Dr Goodall was not ill. He was of sound mind. He simply wanted to die. Dr Goodall's story elevated the euthanasia debate, beyond the question of suffering, to what rights we have over our own death. Could suicide be condoned, rational and justified?

Titled "On His Own Terms", the ABC documentary following Dr Goodall's journey begins with his grandson Duncan reading the last questions his grandfather had to answer before being able to inject himself with a lethal drug.[3]

"Do you agree your mental capacity is completely fine?" Duncan asks.
"Yes."
"Do you have an incurable illness?"
"No," he says, annoyed at the suggestion.
"Are you in unbearable pain?"
"No."
"Are you influenced by others?"
"No."

When citing reasons, Duncan says, "Just leave it as '[In order to] end my suffering." His grandfather pipes up with a correction: "In order to end my life."

---

[3] "On His Own Terms," Foreign Correspondent, Australian Broadcasting Corporation, July 12, 2018.

One can't help but warm to Dr Goodall. He is a man of activity and self-reliance, filmed commuting to work at 102, and acting in theatre productions at 99. His daughter-in-law says, "I don't know how we'll manage without David."

Although we're watching Dr Goodall's journey to death, the documentary seems to emphasise his capacity to participate in and enjoy life. His visit to family in the French countryside and interaction with nature are joyous and Romantic. Despite this, his utilitarian mindset shapes his view of the world, undoubtedly informed by the Enlightenment values which characterise the natural sciences. There is a moment which seems to capture the paradox; in trying to show the ABC journalist a special view of the French countryside, he must climb a series of stairs. It is difficult for his frail body to manage; hands struggle to grip; legs to lift. The filming tries to show how Dr Goodall has lost agency and quality of life. Yet, despite the struggle, he still sees and appreciates the view.

Dr Goodall's grandson Duncan has trouble rationalising the decision. Early in the documentary, he is indignant that his grandfather has had to travel so far to "do something he has every right to do." After his grandfather has passed, Duncan is conflicted. He says, "We think human life has a value and [we] should save it at all costs... but there are times when that actually isn't the case."

The philosophy that made personal choice the supreme good

Dr Goodall supported the rational suicide movement. He was a member of euthanasia advocacy group Exit International, which organised an international press conference on his behalf shortly before his lethal injection. The founder of Exit, Philip Nitschke, was interviewed in the ABC's documentary.

When Australia became the first country to legalise euthanasia in 1996 (albeit, only for eight months), Nitschke was the first doctor to legally administer a lethal injection.[4] There is no doubt that Nitschke practices a dark art. He has written a book called *The Peaceful Pill,* which details "practical advice on end of life strategies such as over-the-counter and prescription drugs, gases and poisons."[5] He runs workshops based on the book which detail how people can end their lives.[6]

Nitschke knows euthanasia is a philosophical question, not a medical one. It's about our civilisational ethic, not the practicalities of a government policy. His leading argument in favour of rational suicide is that people have a right to die in a way that is "reliable, peaceful and at a time of their choosing". He told *The Guardian* in 2015, "[Euthanasia] should be an essential human right. In other words, you don't have to be sick to qualify for voluntary euthanasia. Everybody qualifies. I see too many people now who want to die for social reasons, not medical reasons. They may not be my reasons. They may not be yours. But they are certainly the individual's."[7]

Mill's philosophy – personal choice

Philip Nitschke and Peter FitzSimons are singing from the same hymnbook. Their argument for euthanasia is

---

4 "Philip Nitschke", Exit International, accessed June 24, 2019, https://exitinternational.net.

5 "The Peaceful Pill Handbook", The Peaceful Pill Handbook, June 29, 2019, Online.

6 'Euthanasia advocate Philip Nitschke suspended by the Medical Board of Australia', *ABC News,* July 24, 2014.

7 Melissa Davey, "Philip Nitschke: I don't judge people at all if they want to die," *The Guardian,* December 27, 2015.

powered by liberalism, which declares the freely made choices of rational, autonomous individuals to be the supreme good.

Euthanasia supporters can be passionate warriors such as Nitschke and FitzSimons, or they can be more relaxed and "laissez-faire". All have embraced the philosophy of John Stuart Mill, who wrote in *On Liberty*:

> The sole end for which mankind are warranted...in interfering with the liberty of action of any of their number is self-protection... His own good, either physical or moral, is not a sufficient warrant. He cannot rightfully be compelled to do or forbear because it will be better for him to do so, because it will make him happier, because, in the opinions of others, to do so would be wise or even right... In the part [of his conduct] which merely concerns himself, his independence is, of right, absolute. Over himself, over his own body and mind, the individual is sovereign.[8]

Mill's famous axiom leaves no room for those opposing euthanasia. After all, interfering to protect a man from doing physical harm to himself – indeed, committing suicide – is not a good enough reason to deny him personal choice. The "my body, my choice" mantra that's popular with euthanasia supporters today clearly relies on Mill's principle. Dr Peter Phelps, a former member of the Legislative Council for the Liberal Party, explained his support for euthanasia as follows: "The key principle of classical liberalism is this: You own your life. I will say it again: You own your life."[9]

Mill wanted to see his idea completely govern the rela-

---

8   John Stuart Mill, *On Liberty*, (Penguin Books Ltd, 1974), 68.
9   Dr Peter Phelps, 'Euthanasia Bill 2017', *Facebook*, November 17, 2017.

tionship between individuals and society. Could he have envisaged what a popular success it would be?

The Harm Principle, personal choice, personal autonomy, liberty of the individual – however we wish to describe it – has been so successful as an organising philosophy that it has wiped out all absolutes except itself.[10] Other competitors, such as the pursuit of truth, fear of God, tradition, authority, justice, prudence, temperance and natural order have all bowed to the individual's liberty. As Gertrude Himmelfarb says in her introduction to the Penguin edition of Mill's *On Liberty*, "Liberty remains, for good and bad, the only moral principle that commands general assent in the western world."[11]

Liberty is good. But when treated with a spirit of system that makes it the sole animating principle of a civilisation, the axiom of an ideology, the outcome is chaotic.

Following Dr Goodall's death, the left-leaning US media outlet *Vox* wrote that society was moving to a paradigm where individual liberty was the ultimate moral good, but added "it's worth recognizing what we lose when we collectively change our value system to accommodate its supremacy."[12]

Utilitarianism

Reference to the supremacy of choice, subject to the Harm Principle, is ubiquitous. But how to choose?

Mill has played a role here too: he was schooled in Jeremy

---

[10] Gertrude Himmelfarb, introduction to *On Liberty* by John Stuart Mill (Penguin Books Ltd, 1974), 1.

[11] Ibid, 49.

[12] Tara Isabella Burton, 'What we lose when we gain the right to die', *Vox*, May 21, 2018.

Bentham's utilitarian philosophy. Utilitarianism offered a framework for making choices. One could simply ask: "Does this action result in the greatest happiness for the greatest number?" If yes, utility was increased and the action deemed moral.[13] Utilitarian thinking also entered economics in the 1870s, with influential economist William Stanley Jevons devising a "pleasure-pain" calculus to psychologise how much consumption would be required to induce labour.

It is obvious that human beings are more than pleasure-pain calculators. But when pushed on issues of ethics, many today reveal themselves to be soft utilitarians. In the case of Dr Goodall, observers may have commented: "Well, if he's not enjoying life, what's the point?" For all its inadequacies, utilitarianism is an ever-present decision-making method, as faintly perceptible as mist blanketing a winter frost.

Mill and the centre-right

John Stuart Mill is considered a foundational thinker for centre-right political parties; the Liberal Party in Australia holds him up as the authority on individual freedom. But few know that Mill used his utilitarian philosophy to justify his long-term affair with a married woman. As Helen Andrews articulates powerfully in this collection, the affair brought destruction to Mill's relationships with friends and family and, we can assume, misery to Taylor's husband. Yet, Mill was able to justify his affair as rational using his utilitarian framework because the pleasure outweighed the pain.

When centre-right parties embrace Mill's philosophy,

---

[13]   Paul Collier, *The Future of Capitalism,* (Allen Lane, 2018), 9.

his liberalism, they make it very difficult for themselves to mount an argument against euthanasia. When they champion freedom of the individual combined with a utilitarian approach to decision making, they are failing to offer people a vision of what it means to be human. Instead, centre-right parties hope people will vote for them out of a desire to be left alone. They vacate the field on moral and social issues.

Rousseau and the left

Liberalism manifests itself clearly when politicians of the centre-right articulate support for euthanasia, saying that choice should reign supreme. There is also strong support for euthanasia in centre-left parties. The question is, who is influencing them?

A philosopher who seems to have similarities with Mill is Jean-Jacques Rousseau, titan of leftwing progressivism, fueler of the French Revolution.

Rousseau and Mill are both able to justify extreme licentiousness. Rousseau famously said that "man is born free but everywhere lives in chains"; those chains being society, family, institutions and civilisational norms that constrain human behaviour. As Mill railed against a society that judged his affair, so Rousseau railed against those things that limited the absolute free-will of the individual to pursue his inner desires.

We can hear Mill and Rousseau in the pro-euthanasia speeches of parliamentarians; Liberal MPs will talk about personal choice as an inalienable right; Labor MPs will speak about bringing compassion to suffering people by throwing off the shackles of our religious past.

Why euthanasia will eventually be legalised

I recall discussing David Goodall's decision with a colleague, who said that Goodall "obviously felt his life had no value". I asked, "Do you think his life has value?" He responded, "Yes of course, everyone has value, but he obviously felt he didn't."

Both of these positions can't be true at the same time – either the life has value, or it doesn't. And if the life has value, can it be justified to end it? This is not a question that liberalism answers. Instead, the philosophy tells us that Goodall's freedom to choose is more relevant than whether his life retains intrinsic value or not. As Phillip Nitschke says, they may not be your reasons; they may not be mine; but they're certainly the individual's. Or as Mill says in *On Liberty*: "[A person's] own mode of laying out his existence is the best, not because it is the best in itself, but because it is his own mode."[14]

Having uncovered what Philip Nitschke called "the philosophical underpinnings"[15] of this debate, we can see clearly where the euthanasia question is heading.

Conservatives who are instinctively against euthanasia will have some initial success. The strongest argument is the risk – errors by medical professionals, errors in diagnoses, concealed coercion and others. The horror stories from abroad are compelling. The 24-year-old woman with PTSD euthanised in the Netherlands;[16] the elderly woman with dementia whose words, "Upsy-daisy

---

[14]   John Stuart Mill, *On Liberty*, (Penguin Books Ltd, 1974), 132-133.

[15]   "Philip Nitschke: Why suicide should be a human right", BBC HARDtalk, filmed April 29, 2015.

[16]   Matt Payton, "Sex abuse victim in her 20s allowed by doctors to choose euthanasia due to 'incurable' PTSD", *Independent,* May 11, 2016.

let's go," were interpreted as consent;[17] the woman with lung cancer whose insurance company would cover the cost of a euthanasia injection, but not the cost of a potentially lifesaving drug;[18] the reports of governments saving millions in healthcare due to efficiencies derived from euthanasia.[19]

However, the advocates will chip away, pointing to stories of tragic suffering prolonged because of the denial of choice. The question of euthanasia will be decided by the ultimate test – the liberty of the individual. It will be determined that the value of human life is not absolute. The only absolute is the freedom of the individual.

As a society, we will be content to accept some premature involuntary deaths; better than one person being denied their liberty. Liberalism is so ingrained in our approach to politics, that the endpoint of many debates, including that around euthanasia, can be easily predicted.

Liberalism seems unstoppable. Launched hundreds of years ago by a few philosophers, it has hurtled trajectory perfect and with tremendous power to its final, deadly destination – the full embrace of euthanasia, the choice that ends all choice.

Can euthanasia relieve our suffering?

The Economist has championed euthanasia since the 1990s, guided by the liberal absolutes of personal choice

---

17 Kees van der Staaij, "In the Netherlands, the doctor will kill you now", *Wall Street Journal*, July 21, 2017.
18 Susan Donaldson James, "Death Drugs Cause Uproar in Oregon," ABC News, August. 6, 2008.
19 Sharon Kirkey, "Doctor-assisted suicide could save Canada up to $139 million each year, Alberta study suggests", *National Post*, January 23, 2017.

and individual autonomy. In 2015, it released a documentary following the journey of a 24-year-old Belgian woman, Emily, who requested euthanasia for mental suffering.[20]

Hers was a heartbreaking story. She had received psychological treatment since she was twelve years old and remained heavily medicated throughout her life. After a series of suicide attempts, she was committed to a psychiatric ward. She described her suffering like so: "It feels like there's a monster behind my ribcage... To get up from a puddle of tears and carry on... that's the hardest, picking yourself up every time when you know five minutes later, it'll be back. And you'll have to go through it all over again. That's what makes it so unbearable."

One of the psychiatrists interviewed said that most people who ask for euthanasia based on mental suffering had a long history of it, and that Emily's condition had become unmanageable. She said, "There are endless options in psychiatry... there must be a genuine belief in recovery – for some reason we don't have that belief, just like for terminal-cancer cases. Sometimes for mental suffering there's nothing left to offer."

The day arrives for Emily's lethal injection. Surprisingly, she tells the psychiatrist she can't go through with it. Emily explains, "Because the two previous weeks were relatively bearable. They were free from crisis. I don't know why. Was it because the serenity of death was so close? And that I felt okay? Or had something changed in me? I've tried not to think about the truth, because the truth is, I'd still rather not be here. So, I'm holding my breath for the future."

---

[20] "24 and ready to die", *The Economist*, https://www.youtube.com/watch?v=SWWkUzkfJ4M

But the hope we might have had for Emily only lasts a few moments. The end of the documentary tells us that in August 2018, about three years after the first posting of the documentary, Emily received the lethal injection.

The most compelling argument for euthanasia is that it will relieve someone's unnecessary, painful suffering. The journey of every human being will at some point take them to a place where they contemplate the mystery of painful, pointless suffering. No matter how privileged we are, there will be a suffering that makes us question the point of it all. Mental or physical illness, crippling fears, imminent death, horrendous tragedy, the loss of a loved one, the loss of a child; these things make us lose hope. In their darkest hour, one may see the decades stretch out before them and think, "How can I go on?"

The question is, how much suffering is sufficient to justify ending life?

An economics student who saw the world in terms of utility maximisation once told me that he supported euthanasia in principle but didn't trust the government to regulate it. "If I were a quadriplegic, I'd want my family just to end it," he said. I asked him how he would feel meeting a quadriplegic person; would he believe their life had so little utility that it should end? Would he be open about that view? "No, no," he objected.

We are the beneficiaries of great innovations in health care and overwhelming community support (at least in principle) for those with disabilities and illnesses; more so than at any point in our history. Why then did this economics student think a disability would be so intolerable?

It's not just physical suffering we find intolerable, but also mental and emotional suffering. I posed the question to another student, "If you were sixty years old and your entire family died in a house fire, would you want access to euthanasia?" He responded, "Yes, the suffering would be so great, I wouldn't see the point of carrying on."

Liberalism shapes a suffering-averse culture because it places liberty and personal choice as the ultimate goods to which every human has an inviolable right. The problem is, suffering often can't be alleviated by personal choice, and it severely restricts our sense of liberty. Combined with a utilitarian calculation that life is grossly unhappy, the case for ending suffering via euthanasia seems quite rational. Liberalism and utilitarianism fail to help us understand or deal with pointless suffering. Consequently, we are rattled by it, and we try to eliminate the suffering in the name of compassion.

Should we support euthanasia in the name of compassion?

At their core, euthanasia advocates believe it is compassionate and moral to try to eliminate suffering. They are disgusted by those who wish to prolong the pain; lines like "we treat our dogs better than this" litter the debate.

But they have misunderstood the meaning of the word compassion. It derives from Latin words which mean "to suffer with", not "to eliminate the suffering". Compassion is to take on the suffering of someone you love. In this way, when we share in someone's suffering, it is an act of love.

The philosopher Nietzsche railed against the sharing and spreading of suffering via compassion. Nietzsche valued power and strength. He resented compassion and weakness, criticised Christ's sacrifice on the Cross, and encouraged the death of the "weak and the botched".

> What is good? Whatever augments the feeling of power, the will to power, power itself, in man. What is evil? Whatever springs from weakness. The weak and the botched shall perish: first principle of our charity. And one should help them to it. What is more harmful than any vice? Practical sympathy for the botched and the weak—Christianity... Suffering is made contagious by pity; under certain circumstances it may lead to a total sacrifice of life and living energy—a loss out of all proportion to the magnitude of the cause (—the case of the death of the Nazarene).[21]

Nietzsche's determination to eliminate suffering makes him sound positively inhumane. His philosophy may be extreme, but we must confront the fact that euthanasia is not simply a rational choice made by terminally ill individuals. It is about how our society deals with the problem of suffering and evil, which is critical to our civilisational ethic.

It is good to seek an end to suffering. But eliminating suffering with death is in fact choosing a higher act of destruction; it is bringing on one's own apocalypse. People mistakenly believe our civilisation has evolved to the point where we are capable of bringing on our own death, even though no one knows what lies beyond.

We must also consider what happens when our goal is to eliminate, rather than share in, our neighbour's suffering? Could it be that we come to value the strong, not the weak? Could it be that your life has value due to its utility, rather than its humanity?

How we can deal with pointless suffering?

---

[21]   Friedrich Nietzsche, *The Portable Nietzsche*, ed. Walter Kaufmann (Viking Penguin Inc., 1982), 570.

Scott Samuelson, author of *Seven Ways to Deal with Pointless Suffering*, writes that "subordinating our lives to utility hollows them out", and that "without goods that explode utilitarianism and open us to the mystery of suffering, even the happiest life is miserable."[22]

Suffering explodes utilitarianism. It forces us away from enjoying temporal happiness and avoiding pain, taking us to the core of our humanity. It makes us question who we are, what our purpose is, and how we can carry on. This is not to discount the enormous pain we experience during our darkest hour. But as Samuelson captures so perfectly, being human involves 'the paradox of opposing and accepting suffering.' [23]

As we saw with Nietzsche, to eliminate suffering takes us down a path that is actually inhumane. This is so because the very essence of being human opens us up to suffering. Samuelson points to three brilliant examples:

> *Think of art, which by evoking our tragedies fills us with joy. Think of humour, which by registering our humiliations makes us roar with laughter. Think of forgiveness, which allows us to judge and be judged without destroying our relationships.*[24]

What does it look like to both accept and oppose suffering?

38-year-old J.J. Hanson Jr. died of a terminal illness in December 2017. After being told he had four months, J.J. in fact lived for three and a half years following his di-

---

[22] Scott Samuelson, "Suffering, not just happiness, weighs in the utilitarian calculus," Aeon, June 6, 2018.
[23] Ibid.
[24] Ibid.

agnosis. He told his wife, "We have to share this, to help other people, they need to know that it's okay for this to happen, don't be afraid." In a documentary made three weeks before his death, J.J.'s wife Kristen said, "I would fight for him, but I would also let him go."[25]

When asked about euthanasia, she said, "You'll never know – if you make that choice, if you do that, you might've lived, like J.J. If we had listened, if we had given up, we would have missed out on so much." To others in a similar situation, she says, "Try to hold onto hope – for yourself, for those around you, for people you don't even know."

Liberalism and utilitarianism are no good to us when we suffer – personal liberty and choice are usurped. And when this happens we must find other governing principles. We must find meaning beyond our own autonomy.

Someone who has been able to do this is Michael Wenham, who was diagnosed with motor neurone disease. He says his life has become "deeper and fuller" in a way he could not have foreseen, even as he has become more and more physically restricted. He and his wife may have been expected to support euthanasia. Michael says:

> After all, what quality of life do we have ahead of us? Wouldn't it be something to hold on to — the possibility that when we'd both had enough, we could call time? But it's not all about me. Society is a network of relationships, of interdependence. Our actions are never without effects. That is why life is in fact so rich. My life, when I open my eyes to look, has not been impoverished by my disabling disease; it is deeper and fuller in a way I could not have foreseen. I'm not saying it's easier.

---

[25] Patients' Rights Action Fund, "J.J.'s Final Days", *Facebook*, July 14, 2018.

It's frustrating and painful; it can be depressing. But life is still good. How is it good? I have time to sit and stare, and see things which busyness normally blinds us to, to spend time with friends and enjoy their company, to listen to new music, and family banter.[26]

There are two things that seem to drive Michael and J.J.'s determination to hang onto life. They view themselves as being part of a network of relationships and they have a strong sense of hope for the future – hope for themselves, and for those around them.

Their personal autonomy has been stripped away. Their absolute freedom to choose has been violated. Yet, they have set their sights on greater things; things which are difficult to articulate such as finding completeness, fulfilling their purpose and connecting with the part of their humanity which is eternal. This is not something we can fully understand, but this is the immense mystery of being human.

What is heartbreaking about Emily, the young Belgian woman, is that she had a glimpse of hope, but, ultimately, she was overcome by suffering. It was telling that her psychiatrist likened her condition to terminal cancer, where they had "no hope" of recovery for Emily. But no one could have known what the future held for Emily. She herself was surprised that she felt better as she prepared for euthanasia the first time. As J.J.'s wife Kristen says, "You'll never know, if you make that choice."

---

[26] Michael Wenham, "I'm terminally ill, but I still don't want assisted dying in Britain", *The Telegraph*, September 11, 2015.

Does euthanasia take away our will to live?

While liberalism remains the dominant ideology in the Western world, it will be difficult to argue that choice should not be held up as the supreme good. Euthanasia is going to be legalised because the "right to choose to end my suffering" is an incredibly effective argument.

However, giving people this choice may be an extremely harmful offering. When euthanasia is a valid option, it takes away some of our most powerful weapons in coping with life.

Firstly, euthanasia takes control of the future. By dealing with suffering thus, we displace the possibility that something might change. Secondly, there is great power in knowing that one must go on. The most awful suffering may afflict you, the greatest loss you can imagine may be realised, and yet the sun rises. The relentlessness of life rescues us from our present suffering.

Euthanasia says to us that we don't have to go on. The sun won't rise again, if you don't want it to.

Conclusion

The euthanasia question takes us to the heart of liberal ideology. liberaism has created a paradigm where personal choice and liberty are considered the supreme goods. It has cultivated the utilitarians, who equate the value of a life with its utility. It has come up short when we encounter pointless suffering.

The ethics around euthanasia fascinates the public, perhaps because we lack, yet need, a framework for understanding death. Opponents will always be on the backfoot. The "right to choose in order to end my suffering" is easy to understand and powerfully wielded by euthanasia supporters. But death is not so simple.

We must do justice to the human condition and realise that choice is not the only thing that matters to us. We must take a nuanced view that can't be reduced to a slogan. We must dig deep and discover what we know to be true: human life has an inherent value that cannot be affected by a perceived level of utility. We must find meaning beyond our own autonomy. Part of the mystery of being human is to both accept and oppose suffering.

THE NEW SMOG

Cannabis, freedom and the working class.

David Sergeant

The toxic smog that once consumed industrial cities is now a distant memory for most Western nations, but in Colorado USA a new industrial cloud of smoke chokes the communities of the working poor. Legalised cannabis is enabling the segregation of the State – increasingly divided between poorer areas of cannabis production and wealthier areas of cannabis consumption. The booming, legal market has bought up land and local businesses, leaving many disadvantaged Coloradans unable to find careers in alternative industry. All the while, their children are targeted by relentless and tailored advertising, pushed by multi-national corporations determined to introduce the next generation to a ruthlessly profitable market.

Liberals across the left-right political spectrum are pushing plans for legalised cannabis with increasing religiosity, and support for their ideas is growing amongst mainstream politicians. Many Western jurisdictions have already decriminalised the drug – a decision impossible to reverse once taken. This considered, our essay will examine the arguments used in support of the normalisation and legalisation of cannabis.

Conservatives understand that community and legislative direction can increase people's freedom. We will therefore forward coherent proposals designed to eradicate cannabis, providing a meaningful and superior alternative to legalisation.

Liberal motives

If you were to stop a sample of random people in the street and ask them what liberalism is, a varied response would be expected. Likewise, if you asked an American to summarise what they think a liberal believes, their answer would almost certainly differ to that given by a European. For this reason, it is important to settle on a consistent definition.

We will consider liberalism in its classic, philosophical conception, as: *The primacy and freedom of the individual from external restraints*. Whilst liberals on the *'left'* of the standard, albeit outdated political spectrum are most clearly affiliated with the push for legal drugs, there is growing support among libertarians, who self-identify as *'right-wingers'*. It has become clear that libertarianism is not significantly distinguishable from classical liberalism. Thus, when referring to liberals or liberalism, we refer also to libertarians and libertarianism.

The overwhelming majority of liberals who agitate for legalisation have one of three primary motivations:

1. Some believe legalising cannabis would reduce the amount of harm caused by the drug.

2. Others are motivated by liberal, individualist philosophy. This group argues that the legalisation of all drugs

would result in the expansion of personal choice and a net increase in societal utility. This is more important than any negative consequences that may result. Guided by John Stuart Mill's Harm Principle, the action of an individual is always permissible, so long as it does not result in direct harm to anyone else. Yes, some might experience personal suffering because of a decision to use cannabis, but that is a decision they have freely made. As the Australian Liberal Democrats put it so succinctly in a recent campaign slogan: *'Your Vice. Your Choice'*.

3. The third and final group of liberal proponents are motivated purely by individual interest, often shaped by their own personal, economically privileged experience of drug consumption. For this group, a world that gets high is a world that appeals to them, and this is sufficient justification for its enactment. The psychological underpinnings of this position have been revealed in a recent research paper, which noted that those *'with a higher sense of entitlement'* are *'less concerned about what is socially acceptable or beneficial'*.[1] Whether consciously or subconsciously, this group also seek to use drugs – particularly cannabis, to reshape the values of the working class, marginalise their communities and reinforce the present economic status-quo. Often nuanced enough to realise that naked self-interest remains unappealing, their ideological agenda is cloaked in claims they know to be untrue.

We will thus address the primary arguments used by all three of these liberal factions in favour of the normalisation and legalisation of cannabis.

---

[1] Science Daily, "Entitled people don't follow instructions because they see them as 'unfair'", 2017, p.1.

'Cannabis is harmless'

For many years, quality research detailing the impact of cannabis on mental and physical health was notably absent. This allowed those with a vested interest in its normalisation to shape a narrative of 'harmlessness'. Usefully, there has been a recent explosion of interest and study, resulting in the emergence of a comprehensive and diverse medical research consensus: *Using cannabis presents real and substantial health risks.*

A detailed collection of research has concluded that: '*cannabis precipitates schizophrenia in vulnerable people*',[2] and that adolescents who use the drug daily are '*five times more likely to develop depression and anxiety later in life*'.[3] Among families with a history of psychosis, regular cannabis use doubles the chances of an individual developing the mental health condition – from one in ten to one in five.[4] A comprehensive American study, utilising the latest technology in brain-scanning equipment, revealed that users had: '*abnormally low blood flow in virtually every area of the brain*', resulting in considerably higher risk of developing diseases such as Alzheimer's.[5] Moreover, analysis of expectant mothers who used cannabis found a direct correlation between their consumption of the drug and the mental wellbeing of their children. The more they smoke, the greater the likelihood that their children will report feelings of depression and anxiety at the age of ten.[6] For men under 30, using cannabis doubles

---

[2] Wayne Hall & Louisa Degenhardt, *Cannabis and the persistence of psychosis*, 2011, p.511.

[3] Dr Philip Timms & Dr Zerin Atakan P, *Cannabis and mental health*, 2017, para. 36.

[4] Wayne Hall & Louisa Degenhardt, *Cannabis and the persistence of psychosis*, 2011, p.512.

[5] Kelly Tatera, *Marijuana Users Have Low Blood Flow to the Brain,* 2016, para.1.

[6] Lidush Goldschmidt, Gale Richardson, Marie Cornelius & Nancy Day, *Prenatal marijuana and alcohol exposure*

the risk of infertility,[7] whilst youngsters who use cannabis daily are seven times more likely to take their own life.[8]

In response to this emerging research consensus, we've seen a change in tactics from the cannabis lobby. The narrative has switched from *'general harmlessness'* to *'comparative harmlessness'*. Although most liberals now admit cannabis can trigger mental trauma, they insist it is only capable of doing so in the small section of society already predisposed to mental-health issues, and, unlike other drugs, cannot be associated with disorder, violence, overdose or death.

We do not doubt that cannabis affects people in different ways. Indeed, we acknowledge that some may be able to use the drug in small recreational dosses without ever experiencing dramatic harm. Nevertheless, the evidence that cannabis can cause devastating damage to mental and physical health, irrespective of pre-existing susceptibility, is overwhelming. Similarly, detailed and compelling research has shown that changes to brain function, triggered by repeated usage of cannabis, can and does lead to violent behavior.[9] Analysis of 1,136 patients by the University of Montreal revealed that for young people with mental health issues, the correlation between cannabis usage and an increase in violence was: *'stronger than*

---

and academic achievement at age 10, 2014, p. 526.

7   Steve Connor, *Cannabis doubles younger men's risk of infertility, study finds*, 2014, para. 1.

8   *Ludovica* Laccino, *Teens who Smoke Cannabis Daily 'Seven Times More Likely to Commit Suicide, 2014, para 1.*

9   Todd M. Moorea & Gregory L. Stuart, *A review of the literature on marijuana and interpersonal violence*, 2003 – T. Schoeler, D. Theobald, J.-B. Pingault, D. P. Farrington, W. G. Jennings, A. R. Piquero, J. W. Coid & S. Bhattacharyya, *Continuity of cannabis use and violent offending over the life course*, Cambridge University Press, 2016.

that associated with alcohol or cocaine'.[10]

'Legalised cannabis would result in fewer users of cannabis'

Liberals insist the only way to reduce such harmful impacts is to regulate the market – transforming those who take illegal drugs from criminals to patients. This is a contention applied also with respect to prostitution, abortion, euthanasia and other liberal preoccupations – that criminalisation is *'unsafe'* whereas legalisation, with regulatory oversight, is *'safe'*.

Yet this argument becomes less convincing upon examination of the evidence. In every location in which there has been meaningful analysis of usage rates before and after legalisation or decriminalisation; including Portugal, Colorado, Southern Australia and Amsterdam, there is a resulting upsurge in the number of people using the drug.[11] Even within individual nations, the difference between usage rates in jurisdictions with contrasting legislative approaches is stark. 15.6% of citizens in the Netherlands have used cannabis, compared to 36.7% of residents in Amsterdam.[12] Following the mainstream promotion of

---

[10]   Jules Dugré, Laura Dellazizzo, Charles-Édouard Giguère, Stéphane Potvin & Alexandre Dumais, *Persistency of Cannabis Use Predicts Violence following Acute Psychiatric Discharge*, 2017, p.1.

[11]   Caitlin Hughes & Alex Stevens, *'What Can We Learn from The Portuguese Decriminalization of Illicit Drugs? 2010, p. 1005;* Eric Single, Paul Christie & Robert Ali, *'The impact of cannabis decriminalisation in Australia and the United States, 2000 para. 25;* S. Keyes, 2015, *Colorado's marijuana tax revenues nearly double last year's figures, 2015;* Dirk Korf, *Dutch coffee shops and trends in cannabis use, 2002, pp. 854-856).*

[12]   Dirk Korf, *Dutch coffee shops and trends in cannabis use,* 2002, pp. 854-856).

coffee-shops in Amsterdam, the rate of regular use among 18-to-20-year-olds more than doubled.[13]

In 1987, South Australia introduced the Cannabis Expiation Notice scheme, reducing the penalties for cannabis possession in the State. Statistics were then gathered between 1985-1993 to measure the effects of this legislative change. The percentage of those who had *'ever used cannabis'* jumped from 26-38%.[14] Similarly, those who stated that they would use cannabis *'if it was offered to them by a trusted friend'*, increased from 10% to 18%.[15]

The link between legality and a perception of social legitimacy is further evidenced by findings in the 2016 Australian National Drug Strategy Household Survey. When non-users were asked if they would try the drug if it were made legal – 7.4% stated that they would.[16]

It is clear that legal cannabis would mean cheaper cannabis, as prohibition drives up the price of the drug by 'at least' 400%.[17] Such a correlation has been extensively evidenced in the tobacco market. When cigarettes are reduced in price by 10%, their consumption rises by 7-8%.[18] This prohibition-cost relationship is especially pronounced in the UK and Australia, as their geograph-

---

[13] Robert MacCoun & Peter Reuter, *Drug War Heresies*, 2001, as cited in David Mineta, *Decriminalization would increase the use and the economic and social costs of drugs, n.d, para. 8.*

[14] Neil Donnelly, Wayne Hall & Paul Christie, The effects of partial decriminalisation on cannabis use in South Australia, 1985 to 1993, 2010.

[15] *Ibid.*, p.284.

[16] Australian Institute of Health and Welfare, *National Drug Strategy Household Survey*, 2016, p.128.

[17] David Mineta, *Decriminalization would increase the use and the economic and social costs of drugs*, n.d, para 7

[18] *Ibid.*

ic locations makes smuggling drugs from overseas more expensive.

Of course, for those who profit from cannabis, legalisation is welcome news. In the US state of Colorado, the CEO of the Harvest Company dispensary rejoiced that: *'People who would never have considered pot before are now popping their heads in'.*[19] Likewise, when asked why he believed cannabis use had increased in the state since its legalisation, Henson, President of the Colorado Cannabis Chamber of Commerce, argued that more people felt at ease with the drug: *'They don't see it as something that's bad for them'.*[20]

'Legalised cannabis would result in fewer users of other drugs'

Again, the evidence is demonstrable and clear: Using cannabis *does* make it more likely that people will use other drugs. A 25-year long study revealed that in 86% of cases of those who had taken two or more illegal drugs, cannabis had been the substance they had used first.[21] What's more, those who used cannabis weekly were 59 times more likely to use other illegal drugs than those who did not use cannabis at all.[22] In the United States, research revealed that only 7% of young people who had never used cannabis had indulged in other illegal drug use. Compare this to 33% of the young people who re-

---

[19] Keyes. S, 'Colorado's marijuana tax revenues nearly double last year's figures, 2015, para. 7.

[20] Ibid. para.6.

[21] D. Fergusson. J. Boden. & J. Horwood, *Cannabis use and other illicit drug use: testing the cannabis gateway hypothesis*, 2011, p. 556.

[22] D Fergusson & J Horwood, *Does cannabis use encourage other forms of illicit drug use?* 2000, pp. 505-520.

ported using cannabis regularly and 84% of those who used it daily.[23]

Cannabis users aren't taking other drugs because their dealers are forcing them down their throats or up their noses. Rather, as Gabriel Nahas explains: *'the biochemical changes induced by marijuana in the brain result in a drug-seeking, drug-taking behaviour, which in many instances will lead the user to experiment with other pleasurable substances'.*[24] Cannabis users will likely seek to experiment with other illegal drugs regardless of the legal status of cannabis. Legalisation would result only in more cannabis users and thus a higher secondary demand for and entanglement within the remaining illegal drug market.

In addition, Cannabis cannot be considered a *'soft drug'*. Its potency has increased dramatically in recent years and this trend has been accelerated in jurisdictions that have chosen legalisation. In Colorado, a state report revealed that within legally distributed cannabis products, including edibles and oils, average levels of THC (the principle psychoactive ingredient in cannabis) were between 62% and 95%,[25] whilst the most popular strains of legal cannabis contained between 17-28% THC.[26] Compare this to the cannabis of the 1990s which contained, on average, between 2% and 4% THC.[27] As is true in any

---

[23] B. Kandel, *Marijuana users in young adulthood, 1984,* pp. 200-209.
[24] Gabriel Nahas, 1990, as cited in Wayne Hall, Rosalie Pacula, Cannabis Use and Dependence: Public Health and Public Policy, 2003, p.110.
[25] Jennifer Alsever *Is Pot Losing Its Buzz in Colorado,* 2016, pp.1-10.
[26] Elizabeth Stuyt, MD, Missouri Medicine, The Problem with the current High Potency THC from the perspective of an Addiction Psychiatrist.
[27] Ibid.

crowded economic market, suppliers must compete for business. This means providing the most potent high at the lowest cost. Any attempt by the state to cap levels of THC in legally sold products or impose heavy taxes on the highest potency strains of the drug, will result only in the perpetuation of the black market, as dealers would simply produce illicit cannabis that is stronger and cheaper than legal alternatives.

'Legalised cannabis would deliver increased tax revenue'

Most philosophically consistent liberals will tell you that paying taxes isn't a favourite pastime. It seems strange therefore that they are so excited by the prospect of further government taxation and regulation. Nonetheless, the promise that legalised cannabis will deliver millions in additional tax revenue is regularly made.

There have been numerous claims and counter-claims surrounding cannabis's ability or inability to save the taxpayer money were it to be legalised. Liberal proponents insist huge savings could be made by ending legislative efforts to prevent and prosecute. Supporters of prohibition insist these savings would be dwarfed by the rise in social and medical costs triggered by increased usage. A detailed Australian study, comparing the status quo with legalisation forecasts, concluded that: 'Neither policy delivered substantially more economic benefits'.[28]

Where we can examine the evidence, it is clear the financial results are very different to those that were promised. In many US states such as Colorado, support is growing for a return to prohibition, despite an increase in tax rev-

---

[28] Marian Shanahan & Alison Ritter, *Cost Benefit Analysis of Two Policy Options for Cannabis: Status Quo and Legalisation*, 2014, p.1.

enue. Granted, the state raised $135 million through taxation on cannabis in 2015. However, $95 million of this was reinvested in public education programmes designed to counter the resulting rise in usage.[29] Coupled with the tripling of cannabis-related hospital admissions, a 30% rise in cannabis-related emergency room cases and a 44% increase in traffic fatalities involving THC,[30] most recognise that cannabis has cost the state more than it's raised.

This failed ideological experiment also requires vast government intervention and regulation, the very thing liberals supposedly oppose. In 2015, the Colorado state legislature passed 81 bills aimed at adjusting and readjusting legal provision in response to a constantly changing market.[31]

'Liberal elites should make drug policy'

If liberals truly wanted to empower individuals, they would surely consider listening to those most affected by cannabis before formulating policy.

It is clear that the strongest support for the prohibition of cannabis comes from working-class communities. This has been demonstrated in opinion polls across Australia[32] and the United States of America[33], but it is in the United Kingdom where there has been the most detailed analysis. In 2010, 30% of intermediate non-manual workers had used cannabis, compared to only 10% of

---

[29] Alsever, 2016, pp.1-10.
[30] Ibid.
[31] Ibid.
[32] Australian Government Institute of Health and Welfare, *National Drug Strategy Household Survey, 2016, P.126.*
[33] Abigail. Geiger, *About six-in-ten Americans support marijuana legalization, 2018, p.1.*

unskilled manual workers.[34] Likewise, *'restrictive views'* on cannabis were higher among those with lower educational attainment. In 2001, just 25% of those with a degree held *'restrictive'* views, compared to 40% of those with A levels as highest qualification, and 61% with no qualifications.[35] Even an Ipsos Mori poll, which found a slight majority of the overall public in favour of decriminalisation, revealed it was supported by only 25% of Asians and 41% of blacks, compared to 55% of whites.[36]

Is this really surprising? It is working-class areas that are hit hardest by crime, its working-class young people whose struggle for access to economic opportunities is greatest, and it is disproportionately more difficult for working-class users who have become dependent on cannabis to access treatment or fall back on affluent family networks. Perhaps most striking is the detrimental impact cannabis can have on the focus, self-belief and motivation of working-class young people, as well as on their education and career opportunities. Users have lower levels of dopamine in the striatum part of their brains, meaning lower levels of aspiration – the consequences of which were illustrated in a Christchurch study observing 1265 children.[37] Even after a wide ranging and comprehensive allowance for confounding factors, the study evidenced a strong correlation between educational underachievement and the use of cannabis.[38] The numbing effect the drug has on the brain of a user and its ability

---

[34] Alison Park, John Curtice and Katarina Thomson, *British Social Attitudes*, 2007, p.127.

[35] Ibid., p.126.

[36] A. Ames & R. Worsley, *Public attitudes to drugs policy*, (2013), p.17.

[37] C. Bergland, 'Does Long-Term Cannabis Use Stifle Motivation? 2013. Para.1.

[38] David Fergusson, John Horwood & Annette Beautrais, *cannabis and educational attainment*, 2003, p. 1682.

to concentrate and remember things can continue for days after use, meaning those using cannabis regularly may never be able to operate at the best of their ability or fulfil their potential.[39] Indeed, young people who had used the drug one hundred times or more before the age of sixteen were three times more likely than those who had never used cannabis to leave education without any qualifications.[40] Overall, after adjustment for confounding factors, Fergusson & Boden conclude that cannabis usage between the ages of 14 and 18 is *'associated significantly'* with *'lower levels of life and relationship satisfaction, lower income and higher levels of unemployment and welfare dependency'*.[41]

Many strong and disciplined working-class individuals manage to avoid using cannabis, despite the social pressure and targeted advertising. But they are still forced to suffer if their political representatives capitulate to cannabis on their behalf. The experiment with legalisation currently underway in the United States has revealed areas increasingly divided. Whilst cannabis dispensaries are primarily located in gentrified areas of city centres, the wealthy suburbs and trendy residential parts of the city are able to keep the drug at arms lengths. Rich users possess the wealth required to create separate spheres – a sphere for taking drugs and a residential area in which, whilst consumed, cannabis does not define their environment. Contrastingly, poor neighbourhoods have seen the arrival of industrial scale cannabis farms – buying up precious real-estate and replacing traditional businesses and employers. These areas, already struggling with deprivation and unemployment, are now veiled in a

---

[39] National Institute on Drug Abuse, *Marijuana research report series*, 2016, p. 1.

[40] David , Horwood & Beautrais, 2003, p. 1690.

[41] David Fergusson & J. Boden, *Cannabis use and later life outcomes*, 2008, p. 974.

suffocating haze of mediocrity. The strivers become the stoners and another generation is abandoned to a life of dull drift. Legalised cannabis hasn't increased poor American's choices – it is condemned them to serfdom in a private cannabis monopoly.

This considered, why are wealthy liberal elites so utterly determined to push legalisation? As we've already discussed, some genuinely believe it to be in the best interests of ordinary people. However, for others, it is their bitter disdain for the values of working-class communities that drives them. Many liberal, white collar professionals find the discipline, traditions and social conservatism of the working class deeply distasteful. In their arrogance, they assume that those who shun hedonism and expedient individualism for meaning, community and permanence are held prisoner by their '*backwardness*' and '*prejudice*'. The only way to liberate these '*poor men and women*' is to change their minds – literally alter the chemical composition of their minds. Using cannabis to contain and marginalise those with whom you disagree, while incrementally altering the values of their community is an ingenious approach. After all, it is far harder to stay true to your morals while semi-permanently intoxicated. Harder still to challenge the prevailing cultural character or economic status-quo of a nation.

There is no conspiracy theory at work here. This is not a calculated liberal masterplan and we are of course making generalisations. Not every wealthy, white-collar professional is an expedient liberal. Likewise, many middle-class users of cannabis suffer terribly.

Nonetheless, within the liberal elite there is too often a callous, individualistic contempt for those with traditional values, and a subconscious desire to ensure one of the last resistant demographics eventually concedes to their way of thinking.

The life of the bohemian left is defined by meaningless slavery to vice. Cannabis is their latest weapon.

Liberal Problems – Conservative Solutions

Conservatives realise the status-quo in many Western nations is not sufficient. Theoretical illegality is not enough. Westerners will only see their freedoms increased when cannabis is eradicated in their nations.

Advocates of legalisation insist it is time to end the 'war on drugs'. To the contrary, it is time to begin fighting it. Too many conservatives defend the concept of prohibition but remain complicit in back-door legalisation.

Law Enforcement

The legislative framework and established penalties for the possession of cannabis are, in theory, suitable and rigorous. The maximum sentence for the possession of cannabis in Australia stands at two years imprisonment.[42] In the UK, possession can be punished by up to five years behind bars.[43] Therefore, no dramatic new laws or hard-line legislation are needed. To eradicate cannabis, we require only the practical application of existing legal provision by responsible judges and a police force uniformly committed to this endeavour.

Real deterrence in the form of strict criminal penalties must be consistently enforced to stem the demand side of the trade. Police forces should operate a zero-tolerance approach, with every case of possession leading to arrest and a formal criminal record. In addition, the criminal

---

[42] Armstrong Legal, *2017*, p.1.
[43] Gov.UK, Drugs penalties, p.1.

justice system ought to implement a *'two strikes'* policy. Upon a second arrest for cannabis possession, the individual should always be given a prison sentence of meaningful length. Community policing needs to be the focus of our law enforcement, as rigorous, visible and aggressive enforcement can drive up the price of cannabis, whilst mitigating negative secondary societal consequences. Areas synonymous with youth usage require visible policing and adequate lighting provision. New housing developments should be constructed to facilitate beauty and community.

The two-tier, inconsistent response of law enforcement must also be immediately halted, with drug-snobbery and police profiling stamped out. It is vital the legal system makes an example out of incomprehensibly selfish middle-class recreational drug users, whose behaviour fuels criminality, addiction and misery, from which they are largely insulated. This growing share of the market would be obliterated if a handful of well-to-do young people were sentenced to lengthy prison terms for repeated recreational offences. Drug taking at middle-class events must be dealt with as proactively and resolutely as at working-class gatherings, with the message that drugs are ok so long as secondary behaviour does not cause a nuisance, replaced by the message that taking drugs is wrong full-stop. Similarly, distinctions between supposed *'hard'* and *'soft'* drugs are largely unhelpful. Equally important is the insistence that our police force consistently and fairly enforces the law. Politically motivated members of the police hierarchy, who have sought to enact a backdoor decriminalisation process, must stop.

Compelling evidence demonstrating the potential effectiveness of this approach is found in both Japan and South Korea. Whilst sentencing guidelines are similar to those in the UK – with possession of cannabis carrying a maximum punishment of five years in prison[44,45] – there is one crucial difference. The law is enforced fairly, consistently and unequivocally. The results are indisputable. Both nations have a cannabis usage rate comfortably below 1%,[46] with ten times fewer drug-related deaths than the United Kingdom.[47]

For those seeking evidence-based rather than ideologically driven drug policy, Japan and South Korea provide a tried, tested and overwhelmingly successful model that could and should be replicated in the West.

Treatment and Education

It is imperative to counter the false claim that only legalisation can allow for effective and compassionate treatment for those who have become mentally dependent. Judgement-free, abstinence-based assistance for those struggling but willing to cease their habitual high should be well funded and available. This should be coupled with early intervention for those who have developed mental health problems. Likewise, there is no need to shy away from the debate on drugs – the facts and the evidence regarding the harmfulness of cannabis stand in our support. Education, countering fanciful claims that cannabis is... '*Twenty-two thousand times less dangerous than alcohol*', should be comprehensive.

---

44 Swati Deshpande, 2019, TNN 'Japan drug law among world's toughest, personal possession attracts five-year jail'.

45 Benjamin Haas 2018, *The Guardian,* 'Bong arm of the law: South Korea says it will arrest citizens who smoke weed in Canada'.

46 World Drug Report, 2016, United Nations Office of Drugs and Crime.

47 *The Spectator,* 2019, It's not just Scotland's drugs shame – it's Britain's.

Of course, there could indeed be occasional situations in which cannabis might be a force for good, and it is important to remain pragmatic. Whilst it possesses no curative potential, it is reasonable to conduct a serious and evidence-based debate on the merits of tightly-regulated, prescriptive cannabinoid medication for the relief of specific symptoms in exceptional circumstances. In certain situations, morphine is of invaluable medical assistance – using heroin recreationally is of great societal and personal cost. Nonetheless, this tiny element of cannabis usage has long been hijacked by those dogmatic in their pursuit of recreational legalisation.

Conclusion

We began by considering the motivations of those liberals in favour of legalising cannabis. Most importantly, this essay has provided overwhelming evidence that legalisation would deliver a considerable increase in harm. We hope that it has changed the minds of any liberals who sincerely believed otherwise. We also hope that conservatives are now better equipped to make the case for robust, determined and effective prohibition.

Considering the demonstrable evidence that using cannabis results in serious, negative consequences for the individual, as well as for non-users and wider society, it is clear that legalisation of cannabis is not compatible with Mill's Harm Principle. Thus, those liberals who continue to support legalisation are dogmatically defined by a rigid commitment to freedom from restraint at the primary point of action. They fail to deliver a reasonable balance between positive and negative freedoms, thus failing those for whom absence of restraint is not enough. Vulnerable individuals must be protected from the personal harms inflicted by cannabis, whilst the communitarian foundations of conservatism compel us to consider the common good.

It is difficult to disprove or reason with the remaining liberals, who are motivated purely by naked self-interest and a desire to reinforce prevailing cultural direction. However, we have faith that the overwhelming majority of people will continue to reject social-Darwinism and deliberate atomisation.

* * *

Last Christmas I was staying in a hostel at Bondi Beach. Among my roommates was a Scotsman. We got chatting and he began to tell me about his experience working on a farm in Home Hill, Queensland. For the first several months of his stay he'd been friends with a fellow backpacker from France, called Smail Ayad. The friendship had been an enjoyable and normal one. One evening he watched as Smail got out of bed, swan dived off the balcony, butchered the farm dog and stabbed Ayliffe-Chung and Tom Jackson, two of his friends and fellow British backpackers to death. *'He just looked possessed.'*

My Scottish roommate didn't know what triggered Ayad's *'unrecognisable'*[48] behaviour that evening and nobody will ever be sure. But it would be wrong not to note that Mr. Ayad was a regular user of cannabis and had used cannabis on the evening of his gruesome rampage.[49]

Having grown up smoking it, cannabis and its consequences were nothing new to my Scottish friend. He had seen the drug's ability to wreak damage, loneliness and misery in his native Glasgow. Thankfully, after realising his own consumption was linked to experiences of para-

---

[48] Charlotte Willis, 2016, p.1.
[49] Bernard Lagan, *Backpacker's 'hostel killer' had used cannabis*, 2016, p.1.

noia, he told me he was trying to stop. I wish him all the best.

I wasn't sure if I should document this encounter. As has been demonstrated, the clinical and academic research is now substantial enough that there is no need to rely on anecdotal experiences to expose cannabis for what it is and what it does.

Still, liberals talk in cold terms about utility and the absence of restraint. They argue that the individual should be able to do what they want, when they want. The real people all over the world who have suffered unimaginably because of cannabis didn't want to lose their freedom – they did. As will many more, unless we begin fighting a war on drugs that should have been waged many decades ago.

As conservatives, we believe in a more ambitious and meaningful freedom. A freedom more valuable and empowering than the mere ability to make an immediate decision. If we're serious about increasing the freedom of individuals and their communities, the aim should not be the legalisation of cannabis, rather its eradication.

THE EMPIRE OF AVARICE

The campus rape culture is very real, and conservatives are the only ones who can fix it.

Michael Warren Davis

What we today call 'conservatism' is said to have its roots in the writings of Edmund Burke. So it does, in just the way that Anglo-Saxons have their roots in Mesopotamia. The resemblance is as pronounced and illustrative as that between Winston Churchill and Saddam Hussein.

In fact, not a trace of Burke can be found anywhere in the Anglosphere. John Howard famously explained that the Liberal Party was born of the marriage between Burke and John Stuart Mill; the same might just as well be said of the Conservatives in the United Kingdom and the Republicans in the United States. If so, the union was ill-advised; divorce was inevitable, and inevitably bitter. Mill got custody of the kids and turned them against their father.

For these men who claim Burke's paternity are the very 'sophisters, economists, and calculators' he so ferociously set himself against. They're the very 'political zealots' Russell Kirk (Burke's latter-day apostle to the Colonies) warned us not to fraternise with, for they 'instruct us that "the test of the market" is the whole of political economy and of morals.'

This is self-evidently true, but if the reader has any doubts, we may play a little game. Start by opening a copy of *The Spectator Australia* or the opinion section of *The Australian* to any page. Then, close your eyes and place your finger on a random word. I'll give you $1 if the one you've located is 'liberty', 'freedom', 'free trade', or the like. If it is 'tradition', 'order', 'custom', etc., you must give me $500. Any sensible reader would gladly take those odds. It is free money.

That liberals exist is an unfortunate fact of nature. Unlike gender dysphoria (or 'transgenderism'), for instance, there's ample evidence to suggest that liberalism develops in the womb and has done for millennia. (Diogenes was probably one, though he was far more vigorous and amusing than the modern liberal, who's a humourless and sluggish alcoholic almost as a rule.) One must make peace with their being-here, if only for the sake of one's own mental health. But we might at least wish they didn't call themselves conservatives.

In fact, Kirk devoted a great deal of his writings to rejecting the synthesis – or even an electoral alliance – between conservatism and liberalism. He called the system a 'secular dogmatism'. Mill, its great prophet, he despised, and called him a 'defecated intellect.'

Kirk's principal grievance with libertarians is their refusal to accept the existence of a moral order – or, if they concede that one exists, they insist that it must have no bearing on politics whatsoever. 'Good' and 'evil' don't exist as independent categories in liberal discourse, unless it is some truly gross injustice like genocide or cigarette-smoking. The liberal only speaks of good and evil as contingent on license, which they call *liberty*. Something may be called good insofar as it frees men up to behave as they like; it is wrong only if it puts some restraint upon their passions and appetites.

Consumer-capitalism is good, for example, because it provides us with a steady supply of free pornography, and cheap smartphones on which to view it. Tariffs are evil because they would drive up the cost of smartphones, forcing men to walk to the corner-store and ask the clerk for a *Playboy*. That would be embarrassing and inconvenient, which are unthinkable violations of his right to self-indulgence.

Kirk despised the liberal (or libertarian) ethos so deeply that he recommended conservatives form an alliance with the Left before they allow the Right to be infiltrated by these pinstriped degenerates:

> So in the nature of things conservatives and libertarians can conclude no friendly pact. Conservatives have no intention of compromising with socialists; but even such an alliance, ridiculous though it would be, is more nearly conceivable than the coalition of conservatives and libertarians. The socialists at least declare the existence of some sort of moral order; the libertarians are quite bottomless.

I share Kirk's sentiment, and I'd like to tease out his thesis even more. There are several prominent columnists who trade on their reputation as what we might call 'Burkean progressives'. David Brooks, David Frum, and Andrew Sullivan are the three best-known. They're more fluent in Burke's writings than their 'Burkean liberal' counterparts, but use his insights to come to basically left-wing conclusions. Reading them, one gets the impression Burke would have been a natural running-mate for Hillary Clinton.

Their approach is indeed more coherent than the Burkean liberals' because, as Kirk says, the libertarians share none of our first principles. With the Left we can at least speak the common tongue of morality. They agree that some things are good other things are evil, and the goodness or evilness of a thing ought to matter a great deal in matters of statecraft.

There is another advantage to 'dialoguing' (that hideous word) primarily with leftists: namely, that we would hardly risk confusing our own convictions with theirs. Brooks, Frum, and Sullivan are rare birds. Those who mistake the doyens of *National Review* cocktail parties for Burkeans are as common as pigeons and equally unsanitary.

I do want to be very clear, though, that what I propose in this essay isn't some kind of compromise with the Left. No: conservatives made the mistake of allying with libertarians because, whatever else we might say of them, they're generally sensible men. In fact, they're nothing *but* sensible, which is why they're all hopeless bores. They take great pride in championing drugs and pornography against us stodgy fogeys, which might be a robot's idea of what humans do for fun. Actual human beings don't consider smoking pot and masturbating to be worthy pastimes.

The third and most compelling reason to engage the Left is this: the internal contradictions in their ideology have revealed deep flaws in their worldview. The red-tinted glasses with which they survey the political landscape have cracked. They're forced for the first time to see the world as it really is, not as the raw ingredients of utopia. Their grievances with the West today are generally correct; only conservatives can explain how we've gotten here – and, more importantly, how to find the way out.

* * *

Consider the so-called rape culture, which is said to be ubiquitous on university campuses. A much-touted 2007 study by Christopher Krebs and Christine Lindquist found that 20 percent of women at two universities reported having been the victims of sexual assault (including groping or 'unwanted kissing'). Feminist trolls quickly seized upon and twisted the study. For a while, it was accepted as gospel truth that that one in five female undergraduates had been *raped*. That would mean American universities are almost twice as dangerous as the Democratic Republic of the Congo.

Conservatives were delighted to discover that progressives had misrepresented the data – in part because rape is a horrific crime, no doubt, but also because they hate buying into any feminist narrative. They're allergic to the idea that women are victims of anything but their own indiscretion. If a few scoundrels are going around smooching girls that don't want to be smooched, maybe those girls ought to stay in on Friday night and study.

'Anyway,' these conservatives say, 'if sexual assault really is higher on campus, whose fault is that? Universities are the exclusive domain of the Left. Your lab rats keep tearing each other apart. Maybe it is time to try a new model. Consent training and safe-sex seminars won't cut the mustard, it seems.' Indeed, they won't. But that doesn't give the Right the liberty to simply ignore the problem. There is indeed a rape culture on campus. And how could there not be?

In a 2007 survey by Clemson's Todd Kendall, 51 percent of college men admitted they would rape a classmate if there was no chance of their being caught. This is hardly surprising, given the disgustingly high use of porn in

American dorms. Another by Jason Carroll of Brigham Young University, conducted in 2016, found that 20 percent of male college-age men reported watching pornography every day or every other day.[1] Meanwhile, most research indicates that about 70 percent of men ages 18 to 24 use porn monthly. And this isn't tender, passionate stuff they're viewing: a 2010 study by a team of American academics suggest 83 percent of porn depicts violence against women.

Now imagine what inevitably transpires on our campuses. On any given day, one in five men are using porn. He sits in his room with the blinds drawn, his laptop open on the bed. Within seconds he has access to endless hours of films depicting men brutalising women. He might spend hours alone with his gruesome fantasies. Then he wipes his hands on his jeans, sprays on some Axe, and heads to a party. There he meets a pretty blond Freshman from a little farm town in Nebraska who's never gotten drunk before. She starts leading him on, but she's had too many tequila shots; her speech starts to slur, and her legs weaken. He half-carries her back to his virtual sex dungeon – blinds still drawn, the sheets reeking of his fetid sweat – and... well, what do we expect will happen next?

Moreover, how do we stop it from happening? As we said, consent training is useless. It is impossible to accidentally rape someone. These men know full well that what they're doing is wrong. For many, it is the *lack* of consent they find arousing. The same is true of safe-sex seminars. They don't want it to be safe: they want it to be dangerous, angry, violent.

---

[1] That number is, if anything, too low. Porn is not a subject most young men would be keen to discuss with a Mormon academic. Most are at least well-socialised enough to be embarrassed about enjoying it. (Cf. libertarians).

Do we admit that all men are in fact deranged perverts and follow the far-Left in calling for segregation of dorms, safe spaces, and the like? Basically, yes (and we should add 'ban pornography' to the agenda). Sexual consent occurs in nature, in the form of mating rituals, but it occurs on an instinctual level. In humans, consent is largely a construct, given the many cultures throughout history that practiced forced marriage. In some countries, like Afghanistan, the vast majority of marriages still aren't consensual. Consider also the prevalence of rape in war zones, particularly the Congo and during the Bosnian War. Male sexuality at a subconscious level is evidently far more barbaric than many of us realise.

I think of the chapter in C.S. Lewis's *Mere Christianity* where he discusses natural law and human custom. 'Men have differed as to whether you should have one wife or four,' he observes, 'But they have always agreed that you must not simply have any woman you liked.' This is true; but, as usual, Lewis strikes me as charmingly naïve. Surely most men would like to have any woman who caught their eye – only things could turn nasty if the same woman caught two men's eyes at once. We suspect the regional variations of *gamía* evolved more to protect men's pride than women's dignity.

* * *

Lewis published *Mere Christianity* in 1952 – a good 1,300 years after St Augustine arrived in England. His mind was conditioned by more than a millennium of Catholic and Anglican mores, ethics, and institutions. So is mine; so is yours; so is Sarah Hanson-Young's. We're too far removed from the barbarism of pre-Christian society to understand what a truly post-Christian civilisation would look like, but we catch a glimpse in the dorm-room of the average male university student. Behold, the true savage!

Not so noble, is he?

'In a moment of riot, a drunken delirium from the hot spirit drawn out of the alembic of hell,' Burke writes, we 'uncover our nakedness by throwing off that Christian religion which has hitherto been our boast and comfort, and one great source of civilisation among us.' This is precisely what we've done under the advice of secularists, liberal and progressive alike.

The difference between liberals and progressives is that the former remain inflexibly attached to the principles of the Enlightenment. They still believe in man's basic goodness. They still believe that 'rational self-interest' is the only guarantee of a stable and prosperous society. They're frozen in the 19th century, where yet greater industrialisation and yet greater freedom can cure all of mankind's woes.

Progressives, in the meantime, have tried to bring those Enlightenment principles to their natural conclusion. Inevitably, they arrive at a point where two of those principles diverge, and they must choose one path or the other. The 'campus rape culture' epoch reveals one such fork. There's an obvious tension between the Left's commitment to feminism and sexual-liberationism that can't be reconciled. If they want to protect women, they have to place some restraint on men's sexual appetites.

Conservatives in the Burkean and Kirkian tradition know this intuitively. The Left's nightmare of the barbarian horde lurking within the male collective psyche is, in fact, orthodox Christian theology. We call it *concupiscence*: 'a desire of the lower appetite contrary to reason.' It is a tendency to choose sin over virtue, which we inherited from our first parents after their exile from the Garden of Eden.

Progressives needn't believe the Book of Genesis is literally true to recognise that man is not, in fact, basically good and sweet and reasonable. This has always been perfectly evident. It used to be that they followed Marx, who said that institutions (religion, capitalism, etc.) corrupt him; today, it is much more common to find accusations that men are *inherently* sexist, that whites are *inherently* racist, and so on. Their understanding of human nature leaves a great deal to be desired, but not their observation that it is both corrupt and immutable. They've arrived by their own strange and winding path at the first and most important truth of Christianity: that man is Fallen.

* * *

I digress. Let's return to the uncomfortable but essential topic at hand: sex. And let's begin again with a statement that ought to be self-evidently true: *feminism is a Marian heresy.*

Our friends on the Left don't realise what an extraordinary role the Virgin Mary played in history. She afforded womanhood a dignity that was unprecedented in the ancient world, which (despite all its learning) was still thoroughly barbaric.

It is true, as the Wiccans point out, that Christianity lacks a divine feminine. The Godhead is decidedly patriarchal; those interested in praying to a disembodied uterus will have to look elsewhere. But the Mother of God is in every way perfect, which affords femininity greater esteem. Hera was thought to be a higher being than Mary; she was also jealous and vengeful – not clement, loving, and sweet. The Queen of the Gods didn't redeem her sex from Pandora's morbid curiosity, but the Queen of All Saints redeems it from Eve's.

The very idea of consent is Christian. Paganism gave us Zeus raping Antiope and Hades abducting Persephone; the Faith gives us Gabriel crying *Ave Maria*, and her reply, *Fiat*.

Even the most 'Enlightened' among us only believe in women's rights because their great-grandmothers called themselves daughters of Mary. This is an historical fact, and progressives lose nothing by admitting as much. If they can't bring themselves to believe in the literal truth of Christianity, they might as well be grateful for its works. Our ancestors in the Faith built that tremendous wall around the male psyche in order to contain the Vandal horde that lurks within.

If we wish to end the rape culture, and to reverse the trend of men demeaning and objectifying women, we have no choice but to reinforce that wall. That means banning smut, cracking down on men who sexually harass and abuse women, and the like. But if young men are to once again see women as Marys, and not as Antiopes and Persephones, they must conduct themselves accordingly.

I won't pursue this line of thinking further because it is better in every sense for women to take responsibility of themselves and each other. But women (rightly) have no qualms about pointing out the harmful effects of 'toxic masculinity'. Men – Christian and atheist, conservative and progressive – shouldn't hesitate to do the same with toxic femininity.

These are terms of left-wing coinage and have obvious flaws. What we call 'toxic' about modern men is usually, in fact, *un-manly*. A wiser age than our own would have called the vanity of gym bunnies effeminate, and the licentiousness of the nightclubber boyish. The same is true of what we might call toxic about modern women. They're simply un-feminine. The traditional female virtues have no stock among the university students screeching through megaphones, demanding their right to have sex without any personal consequences.

* * *

I haven't forgotten the theme of this collection, which is the soft tyranny exercised by the liberal political order: how a politics narrowly obsessed with liberty in fact makes men less free. The rule has emerged naturally from the example, I think, but let's make it perfectly clear.

The best-known definition of pornography (or lack thereof) was given by Justice Potter Stuart. The US Supreme Court was deliberating on whether the film *Les amants* by the great Malle ought to be censored under pornography laws. 'I shall not today attempt further to define the kinds of material I understand to be embraced within that shorthand description,' Justice Stuart confessed, 'and perhaps I could never succeed in intelligibly doing so. But I know it when I see it, and the motion picture involved in this case is not that.'

Looking around at the ruins of our civilisation, we can't help but come to the same conclusion. We know freedom when we see it, and this isn't freedom. All the op-ed columns and think-tank reports in the world may argue that 21st century Westerners are the freest people who've ever set foot on this Earth. (In fact, they do.) Yet we can't resist this niggling sense that we're all, in fact, slaves.

First and foremost, we're slaves to want. I don't mean that we're in desperate poverty, which is clearly not the case. But our appetites have grown so grossly out of control that we can never satisfy them. The poorest tribesman in the hottest quadrant of the Sahara may never see a working water-faucet, but give him a glass of water and he'll feel a deeper gratitude and a greater sense of contentment than we in the First World could ever conceive of.

In other words, we're addicted to *stuff*. Corporations are our dealers, and our government are the cops on the take. 'Our whole economy – indeed, our very foreign policy – is calculated to increase this appetite for material goods,' Kirk warned. The liberal has no time for such arguments, because the drug-deals are purely voluntary. Yet only the narrowest ideologue can call an addict 'free' in any meaningful way.

Secondly, we're slaves to vice. There's something amusing, even charming, about the Dutch wrecking their own economy in pursuit of their tulip-addiction. It was a quaint, harmless hobby that simply got out of control. Our wants, on the other hand, are inherently perverse. Pornography and sex are only two examples among thousands: mind-numbing pills, fatty foods, violent films, disposable clothing, plastic houses...

We've built an empire of avarice to satisfy these wants, subjugating not only our own people but entire world. We've raped the ecologies of Third-World countries and, when their governments object, simply disposed of them and installed new ones. Having plunged them into abject poverty and civil unrest, we then invite them into our own countries, so they can cut our grass and scrub our toilets for pennies on the dollar. Other countries, like China and India, are naturally more compliant. They break the spirits of the workers and march them at gunpoint into factories, so their own elites can grow rich off trade with the First World.

The Left's solution to this sorry state of affairs may be wrong. In fact, it certainly *is* wrong. But at least they recognise how sorry the state has become. They don't confuse the Golden Arches for some *Arc de Triomphe*, glorying in the march of liberal capitalism across the globe.

BORROWED WOMBS

*Commercial surrogacy: the common ground made by social-
ists and libertarians in prioritising desire over justice and
human dignity.*

Bill O'Chee

Some years ago, an Australian couple who were experiencing troubles having a baby chose to use a commercial
surrogate to carry a child conceived by in vitro fertilisa-
tion. As commercial surrogacy is illegal in Australia, they
found a surrogate in Thailand. A number of fertilised eggs
were implanted, and in due course the woman gave birth
to twins. One child was a girl, and the other a boy but,
unlike his sister, the boy was born with Down Syndrome.

When the Australian parents returned to Australia with
the girl, leaving the boy with Down Syndrome with his
impoverished surrogate mother, there was an enormous
outcry. Most of the public quite rightly thought that their
actions were selfish, yet the parents certainly didn't see
it that way. They wanted a baby, and when they were incapable of having one through normal means, they went
offshore to not only have a child, but have a child who met
their expectations.

The case of baby Gammy, as the child became known,
epitomises the increasingly common belief that individ-

uals can make choices without suffering any of the negative effects of those choices. The destructiveness of such thinking is often underestimated. In baby Gammy's case, the innate selfishness of the Australian couple impacted not only the surrogate mother, but also the twin children who were torn apart and deprived of each other in the most heartbreaking of circumstances.

While it is tempting to view the Australian parents' behaviour in terms of failed personal morality, it is more correct to see it in terms of injustice, since their choices affected more than just themselves.

It is worth harking back to a much earlier time, when in his *Digest*, the Emperor Justinian proclaimed that justice is the constant and perpetual desire to render to each person that which is their due – *justitia est constans et perpetua voluntas jus suum cuique tribuens*. This conception of justice has been a guiding principle underlying the development of both common and civil law systems, and also much of Western philosophy for almost two thousand years.

What was actually due to the Australian parents? What was due to the surrogate mother? What was due to Baby Gammy? What is the intersection between what is due to people as part of a commercial transaction, and what's basically due to every human being by virtue of their humanity?

Justinian believed that justice entails rendering to each that which is their due. This does not provide for individuals to have the freedom to pick and choose which consequences of their actions will bind them and which will not. Seen in this light, responsibility for the consequences of one's actions is a troublesome bar to moral and materialistic narcissism.

The great loophole for avoiding consequences manifests when we transform our desires into 'inalienable' rights. Within this radical articulation of rights theory, aspirations such as free university education, the provision of welfare or subsidised medical treatment are variously treated as rights, or even human rights. As a consequence, the satisfaction of individual want in every respect becomes the supreme goal of politics.

However, there is a notable difference between asserting something to be a right, and it actually being so. This raises two questions: to what extent are *expectations* necessarily *rights*, and if they are rights, what sort of rights are they?

One definition Professor John Finnis has given is that a right is a legally enforceable entitlement to participate in some portion of the *common good* of society. The common good of society is comprised of those public goods whose enjoyment by any single individual, or group of individuals, can be had *without diminishing the similar enjoyment of those goods by others*. Examples of the common good are such things as peace, good order, the rule of law, traditional freedoms, the right to private property, and personal and collective security.

To an extent these goods are transcendent and spiritual. Peace, order, safety – they are not tangible assets.

But people desire *more* than these common goods. And so, there's another class of claim which has become familiar to us. We make demands of the *common stock* of society. What's this? Well, it is comprised of those benefits which are bought and allocated from the collective, material *product* of a society.

Claims from this common stock are made for things such as subsidised healthcare, free schooling, social security benefits, and a whole range of other subsidies or benefits distributed by the government. Unlike the common good, the common stock is *finite*, and the allocation of any one portion of it to any individual or group reduces the portion available to everyone else.

From this we can see that to claim a right to the *common good* is not the same as a demand from the *common stock*.

How else can we differentiate these claims? Rights to the common good have no positive obligations. They do not have to be earned. Rights to partake of the common stock of society are different. The common stock of society is comprised of a limited pool of resources which, by necessity, must be rationed through some objective process. This is highly conditional.

Access to a publicly funded university education is a case in point. The available pool of such places is limited, which leads to the imposition of positive obligations to meet certain standards to gain entry to a course, and to achieve academic results sufficient to justify continuing in that course. A university education is not an absolute right, but an entitlement which must be earned.

Such logic rests painfully on the left wing of politics. The problem the left cannot escape, however, is that their claims to the common stock are largely rooted in a need to relieve themselves of the consequences of their choices, transferring the burden to the public purse, and thereby to their fellow citizens. But this leads to fundamentally unjust outcomes.

The political right laments the fact that demands on the common stock of society are now treated as absolute rights. But is this the real disaster? No, we should accept that the real tragedy is the fact that rights to the common good, which should not have to be *earned*, are now so often brought low; made transactional; conditional.

To illustrate how we have confused the comparative importance of the common good with the common stock, consider the supposed *right to free healthcare*; a benefit derived from the common stock of a country. This is protected hysterically – just remember the fuss over the proposal in the 2014 Federal Budget for a modest $5 co-payment for visits to one's GP.

Now compare this with our attitude to the right to life. Tens of thousands of children are aborted in Australia alone, in a shamelessly discriminatory fashion, to the extent that over 90% of children diagnosed with Down Syndrome are aborted.

The 'right' to free healthcare is more stringently protected than the right to life, which is now conditional. Baby Gammy's right to life was conditional on him meeting the expectations of the people engaging the surrogate mother to produce a 'perfect' baby. Gammy's right to peace, order, safety, life and love as a member of the human race, has been compromised by the commercial transaction involved in his conception.

A contributing factor to this failure lies in the utilitarian philosophy of Mill and others, which has percolated into much (supposedly) conservative thinking. The utilitarian formula – pursuit of the greatest happiness of the greatest number – besides impliedly elevating all personal desires into rights, makes all rights conditional on the whims and imperatives of the majority.

The flaws in such a scheme are obvious. The will of the majority (or the 'General Will' as Jean-Jacques Rousseau would have it) can be unleashed to overcome the right to private property, to privacy, and to political freedoms when they are inconvenient to the political aspirations of an individual or group. For these reasons, it ought to be obvious to most that *the greatest happiness of the greatest number* is anathema to the perceived fundamental dignity of human life which is at the heart of conservative politics.

The very purpose of rights is to be a bulwark against those who would infringe upon the dignity which inheres in every human life. Rights are independent of popular will, transactional compromise, commerce, or the actions of the state. When considered in this light, it is clear that utilitarian thinking can never be the satisfactory basis of any form of rights theory.

The rights that really matter can only be guaranteed if rights to the *common good* are distinguished from and prioritised over claims on the *common stock*.

In fact, belief in the pre-eminence of the common good over claims to the common stock should be the defining difference between the right and the left, because it represents the difference between fundamental justice, and redistributive injustice.

At a conceptual level, it is difficult to differentiate libertarianism from post-modernism in its response to moral imperatives. Post-modernism tells us there is no truth; there is only choice. In such a world, choice becomes the only true good. Libertarianism falls into this post-modernist trap because it too sees choice, rather than something transcendent and true, as the principal good. All of this makes libertarianism a post-modernist, relativist fifth column in the heartland of conservative politics.

Moreover, in the pursuit of their particular concept of individual liberty, libertarians are apt to declare or claim a range of 'inalienable rights' which are presumably intended to sit at the pinnacle of any hierarchy of rights. However, the purported existence of these inalienable rights is more a product of political rhetoric than deductive reasoning.

In fact, the most important of rights must be inviolable rights, not inalienable rights. The difference is important. A truly significant individual right must be inviolable – that is, incapable of limitation – rather than merely inalienable. An *inalienable* right might not be taken away, but might foreseeably be subject to limitation in any manner of ways. An *inviolable* right cannot be so limited.

An example will suffice to make the point. Freedom of speech might be an inalienable right, but as we have seen it is, and sometimes must be, subject to some form of limitation to protect individual dignity; it is not an inviolable right. The right not to have one's life taken, and the right to due and fair process before the law, for instance should be inviolable rights. They are inviolable because they cannot be limited, and therefore they cannot come into conflict with other inviolable rights.

All of these issues come into sharp focus when we return to the plight of Baby Gammy.

Even before he was born, his Australian parents sought to have his life aborted, because they did not feel that he met their hopes as parents, nor the expected outcome of their commercial surrogacy agreement. When the surrogate mother refused to comply, they abandoned him in Thailand and returned to Australia with his sister only.

When the pregnancies of Gammy and his sister were commercialised, their lives were cheapened in the eyes of the very people bringing them to life, and they were at peril of being treated less like people and more like products to be bought, sold, or disposed of as others wished. This meant that the inviolable rights of both children were at risk of being subordinated to the whims and aspirations of others.

This is indeed what happened. Not only did the Australian parents seek an outcome for themselves which was not justly theirs, but it was an outcome that could only be achieved by denying justice to their own children.

How is this possible? Quite simply, because socialists and libertarians have made common ground in magnifying class or personal desires over considerations of consequence or fundamental justice. They have dressed up their desires in the stolen robes of 'inalienable' rights.

True rights are based on justice, not the imperatives of personal or popular will. We turn our backs on this truth at our peril.

Part II

Philosophy, France & Freedom

ROMANCE AND SOCIALISM IN J. S. MILL

*How Mill dressed up his lack of conscience as a philosophy
and called it liberalism.*

Helen Andrews

John Stuart Mill had the worst personal life of any libertarian philosopher, a competitive category for bad personal lives. Marriage in particular has a record of making libertarian philosophers behave discreditably—that is, in a way that brings discredit not just on their character but on their ideas.

Bertrand Russell famously divorced the first of his four wives after a bicycle trip: 'suddenly, as I was riding along a country road, [I] realized that I no longer loved Alys.' Thus reasoned the most rational man in England. Ayn Rand forced her husband to endure loud and lofty protestations that forgoing an affair with Nathaniel Branden would be a sin against objectivism. William Godwin, England's first anarcho-libertarian, wrecked two marriages on his individualism: first to Mary Wollstonecraft, whom he set up in a separate apartment and communicated with by letter, and then to a harridan of no redeeming qualities apart from her ability to keep house whom he, in his solipsism, permitted to torment Mary's children.

Even in this company, John Stuart Mill is on another plane. Under the influence of his wife, Harriet Taylor, he drove his youngest brother George to suicide. His doting sisters were banished from his life over the flimsiest imagined slights to his wife's honor. He gave up his former friends and became a recluse, retiring to a cottage in Blackheath Park where he entertained virtually no one while Mrs. Mill lived. After her death, he made himself a national laughingstock by declaring in his *Autobiography* that his wife had been more poetic than Shelley and a greater thinker than himself, and that he had 'acquired more from her teaching than from all other sources taken together'—phrases written not when Mill was a grieving widower but during Harriet's lifetime, in drafts which she read and approved for publication evidently without embarrassment.

And that's only what she did to him after they wed. Their marriage was preceded by twenty years of brazen and self-righteous infidelity. When Mill met Harriet she was married to a good-natured pharmacist of enlightened political opinions, if no great intelligence, named John Taylor. After three years of growing mutual obsession, they bullied him into giving Harriet her own household, where she lived with their three children and entertained Mill on weekends. No one, not even his family, was permitted to mention Harriet's name in Mill's presence, much less to allude to the scandal their conduct had raised. His oldest friend, John Arthur Roebuck, was the only one who ever dared; Mill never spoke to him again. The couple withdrew into their private ménage, reassuring each other that it was only society's 'baby morality' (her phrase) that cast shame on their exalted passion. A bizarre story—and until the 1950s, an unknown one.

The Morbid Curiosity of Friedrich Hayek

Strange as it seems, the first biography to treat John Stuart Mill's private life was not written for more than eighty years after his death. The reason for the delay was simple. Mill's papers, including his letters to Harriet, were stored at his house in Avignon and guarded by his stepdaughter, Helen Taylor, who considered it her life's mission to uphold Mill's legacy and her mother's. When Helen died, her niece Mary Taylor took over and was if anything more protective, having some notion of editing Mill's collected correspondence herself. Mary was institutionalized for insanity in 1918, and the Avignon papers were put up for auction at Sotheby's and dispersed to the four winds.

The task of assembling Mill's letters had to await another libertarian philosopher who, true to type, was in the middle of his own soap opera. The love of his life had married another back in Vienna in the 1920s, and he had married his secretary on the rebound. Two decades later, after World War II, his lost love was widowed and he decided to get a divorce to be with her. His colleagues at the London School of Economics, who were left to nurse his first wife through a breakdown, stopped speaking to him ('As far as I am concerned the man I know is dead and I should find it almost intolerably painful to have to meet his successor,' said one). This was Friedrich Hayek.

Hayek became obsessed with the Mill-Taylor relationship. He tracked down Mill's letters across half a dozen university libraries and countless private collections—mundane work for a scholar of his stature, especially in the flush of celebrity he enjoyed after *The Road to Serfdom*. After that surprise hit, the first book he wrote to follow it up was a Mill-Taylor dual biography, which is still the only book about their marriage. The Constitution of Liberty was first outlined during a vacation Hayek and his second wife took in Italy and France that retraced exactly a journey Mill and Taylor had taken a hundred years earlier.

It was not the resemblance to his own situation that drove Hayek's obsession. It was the suspicion that Harriet had turned Mill into a socialist.

Hayek's intellectual allegiance was to the tradition of British liberalism, which since the Scottish Enlightenment has been different from anything on the continent. He loved its pragmatism, its impatience with abstraction, its celebration of bourgeois rather than romantic-heroic virtues. But sometime around World War I, that priceless legacy had been captured by socialists. The party of Gladstone and Macaulay had become the party of Laski and Keynes.

It occurred to Hayek that the same trajectory had played out in miniature in the life of John Stuart Mill. His beginnings were solidly Benthamite; the original edition of his *Principles of Political Economy* was mostly sound; but the second edition said alarmingly nice things about the Fourierists and the third edition all but endorsed Communism. 'If the choice were to be made between Communism with all its chances, and the present state of society with all its sufferings and injustices,' Mill averred, 'all the difficulties, great or small, of Communism would be but as dust in the balance.' The manuscript Mill was working on when he died, later published under the title *Chapters on Socialism*, showed that his drift toward collectivism might have proceeded even further had he lived.

Hayek imagined that figuring out what had sent Mill down the wrong path might reveal what had gone wrong with British liberalism more broadly. And to solve the mystery of Mill—*cherchez la femme*.

Utilitarian Adultery

No one can help falling in love with another man's wife. It is what happens next that determines a man's character. John Stuart Mill did not handle it well.

One might blame his unusual upbringing—the Greek lessons at three, the apprenticeship in Benthamism at ten, the isolation from other boys until his teenage years and from the female sex until well after that. But his father was just as doctrinaire and, if possible, more robotic, and even James Mill knew not to go chasing after married women. He confronted his son with a remorselessly utilitarian argument for giving Mrs. Taylor up before matters went too far, in order to facilitate the greater happiness of all three parties in the long run. John replied that 'he had no other feelings towards her than he would have towards an equally able man.'

This pretense of platonic admiration lasted from their first meeting in 1830 until the crisis of 1833. In September of that year, Harriet persuaded her husband to grant her a six-month separation, and she departed for France with the children. Unknown to Mr. Taylor, Mill followed her there in October.

After six weeks with Mill and at his urging, Harriet wrote a letter to her husband explaining that she and Mill had run the numbers, so to speak, in their utilitarian calculation, and concluded that whatever compromise would most conduce to Mr. Taylor's happiness would be all right with them as long as the two lovers were not required to 'renounce sight' of each other (which had been Mr. Taylor's opening bid). Mr. Taylor acquiesced, and soon Harriet was able to tell Mill that she had received 'one of those letters from Mr Taylor which makes us admire & love him. He says that this plan & my letters have given him delight—that he has been selfish—but in future will think more for others & less for himself.'

The way Mill and Harriet enlisted utilitarian language to justify their adultery is unattractive. Shortly before the Paris jaunt, Harriet had—with audacity entirely in character—asked Mill to write an essay explaining his position on marriage. The unpublished manuscript, found in the Avignon papers, reads in part:

> All popular morality is, as I once said to you, a compromise among conflicting natures, each renouncing a certain portion of what its own desires call for, in order to avoid the evils of a perpetual warfare with the rest. That is the best popular morality, which attains this general pacification with the least sacrifice of the happiness of the higher natures, who are the greatest, indeed the only real sufferers by the compromise; for they are called upon to give up what would really make them happy; while others are commonly required only to restrain desires the gratification of which would bring no real happiness.

The 'general pacification' of Taylor having been obtained in the Paris negotiations, the parties muddled along in their compromise for the next fourteen years. Mill and Taylor spent two nights a week and nearly every weekend together, but did not appear in public as a couple. Eventually Taylor died, and in 1851 Mill and Harriet were finally wed.

Marriage solved nothing. Quite the opposite, it led Mill to terminate relationships that had long been preserved, however tenuously, by the omertà surrounding Mrs. Taylor. Friends who expected to find their relations with Mill eased instead discovered that Harriet was settling old scores. Anyone she suspected of having gossiped about her during her first marriage or not sufficiently approving of her new one, she declared an enemy of the household, and naturally Mill adopted her grudges as his own.

The most egregious example was George Grote Mill, John's younger brother by nineteen years. John had not bothered to inform George of his marriage. Nevertheless, when he learned of it a month late and at second hand, George sent his best wishes. The letter survives; it is utterly inoffensive. His crime was to make a jovial reference to Harriet's well-known feminist opinions. ('Believing that [she] would generally rather discourage than encourage the marriage of others, I certainly was at first surprised to find her giving so deliberate an example of marriage in her own case.') This elicited from Mill a letter beginning:

> I have long ceased to be surprised at any want of good sense or good manners in what proceeds from you—you appear to be too thoughtless or too ignorant to be capable of either—but such want of good feeling, together with such arrogant assumption, as are shown in your letters . . . I was not prepared for. The best construction that can be put upon them is that you really do not know what insolence and presumption are: or you would not write such letters & seem to expect to be as well liked as before by those to whom & of whom they are written.

Many of those who received letters like this regained Mill's affection after Harriet's death—his sister Mary, Sarah Austin, George and Harriet Grote. But it was too late for his baby brother. Two years after John cut off contact, George Mill, driven into exile in Madeira by his worsening tuberculosis, committed suicide.

'The Saint of Rationalism'

So Harriet was awful—fine, but did she affect his work? That would raise the story above mere gossip. Mill maintained that everything written after *Political Economy* was effectively a joint production. Was this true, or did he misjudge her influence as badly as her virtues?

Independent testimony would settle the question, but independent testimony is just what we do not have, since so few of Mill's friends were ever permitted to make Harriet's acquaintance. Thomas and Jane Carlyle were among the tiny handful who ever met her, and they both thought Mill was out of his mind. 'Full of unwise intellect, asking and re-asking stupid questions,' was Carlyle's opinion of her. 'A peculiarly affected and empty body,' was Jane's. (In one staggering letter, Harriet recites a long list of Mill's eminent friends, including Carlyle, the jurist John Austin, and Alexis de Tocqueville, and dismisses them as 'narrow in intellect, timid, infinitely conceited ... more or less respectable puppets.')

The other obvious place to check would be their letters to each other. Alas, these are almost entirely devoid of intellectual discussion. Even allowing for the mundanity of most correspondence between husbands and wives, one might have hoped that they would, at least occasionally, discuss something other than their respiratory ailments.

Our only source for judging Harriet's influence is Mill's writing, which thankfully includes eight full years before they met. The most glaring change is the complete disappearance of a sense of humor. Few of his fans realize that Mill did not always write in the lucid, lawyerly style of On Liberty. Consider this squib from 1828, mocking the Duke of Wellington's new cabinet:

ONE GUINEA REWARD—Lost or stolen, from a

Cabinet of Curiosities near the Treasury, a Skull. It is extremely thick, and the eyes are so fixed in it, as to be unable to see beyond the length of the nose. It is also remarkably soft to the touch, and the organ of place is very strongly developed. It is entirely empty, and of no use to any person, except the owner. The reward offered, greatly exceeds the value of the article, as the owner, having recently been appointed Chancellor of the Exchequer, cannot conveniently do without it.

Or this from an article defending grave-robbing, on the Benthamite grounds that everyone benefits from having surgeons well instructed in anatomy: 'If bodies had never been dissected, sentimentalists could not have appealed to our hearts in behalf of the sanctity of the tomb, for whether we have or have not such an organ, would probably to this day have remained a problem.'

Both of these pieces were written after Mill's notorious 'mental crisis,' the life-changing depression he fell into at the age of twenty. It was not depression that robbed him of his humor. It was Harriet. In everything written after he met her, he is indignant where before he would have been biting or sarcastic. You may read *The Subjection of Women* from cover to cover, for example, and find nothing resembling wit.

But Mill's progressive leftward tilt, Hayek eventually decided, was not Harriet's fault. Mill's own principles unfolded naturally on their own. Hayek had not yet come to this conclusion when he published his Mill-Taylor book, which contains an abundance of previously unavailable primary sources but surprisingly little analysis. It took decades to dawn on him that Mill had never been a good classical liberal. 'Many years of work on John Stuart Mill,' admitted Hayek near the end of his life, 'actually shook my admiration of someone I had thought a very great figure indeed, with the result that my present opinion of John Stuart Mill is a very critical one.' One Hayek biographer went to the trouble of totting up the citations in his major works and found that Mill went from being the most frequently cited author in *The Constitution of Liberty* to being the sixth-most in *Fatal Conceit*, where every mention of Mill is negative.

Hayek should not have been so surprised. After all, the Benthamites had always been in favor of confiscatory inheritance taxes, as a way of eliminating England's landed oligarchy. The first edition of Mill's *Political Economy* was explicitly billed as 'a refutation of socialism' by its German translator, but even there Mill proposed limits on inheritance and bequest that he later claimed 'would pull down all large fortunes in two generations.' It was a very short leap from there to the position expressed in *Chapters on Socialism*, where Mill argues that socialism is no different from the limitations on property rights that have been part of Western law since Rome. English village law limited the rights of landholders to evict their tenants; why not limit the right of factory owners to fire their employees? The only reason not to would involve trust in emergent order, which, as Hayek came to realize, Mill utterly lacked where economics was concerned.

In his correspondence with true-believing socialists, Mill usually told them that he fully expected socialism to come to England one day but that at present mankind was unprepared for it. Mill had every hope that this unpreparedness would be temporary, for he had limitless faith in the power of education to shape humanity. If a single group of children could be raised to be socialists as deliberately as James Mill had raised him to be a Benthamite, then it would only take one generation to prove to the world that cooperative socialism was no utopia but an alternative within reach. Instructing this pioneer generation was one of the things he thought Harriet could have done for humanity, if she had lived.

For a thinker whose entire philosophy depended on human perfectibility, Mill had remarkably little idea how to bring it about. Not only was he silent on the mechanics of moral education, socialist or otherwise, he betrayed a total ignorance of the most basic facts of how character is cultivated—for example, that knowing the right thing to do is a lot easier than doing it. 'He who does anything because it is the custom, makes no choice,' he sneers in *On Liberty*. 'He gains no practice either in discerning or in desiring what is best. The mental and moral, like the muscular powers, are improved only by being used.' To the countless Englishmen following the same code as their grandparents—work hard, raise upright children, don't sleep with other men's wives—he offered not merely dismissal but mockery. Long after his youthful fanaticism had waned, he still contemptuously referred to Judeo-Christian morality as 'the notions of a tribe of barbarians in a corner of Syria three thousand years ago.'

Mill's nickname, given him by Gladstone, was 'the Saint of Rationalism.' He had a reputation as England's gentle philosopher, whose school, if it erred, did so only in assuming that the rest of mankind was as decent and benevolent as himself. But the more we examine him, the less plausible it is that Mill was too good for this world. Instead it begins to appear that Mill was unable to tell his readers how to become decent, benevolent people—because he wasn't one himself.

Mill and the 'Smug Style' in Pragmatic Neoliberalism

It is sometimes said that John Stuart Mill was ahead of his time, that all the radical things he believed have become the commonplaces of today. But Mill's principles were always commonplaces. 'The greatest happiness for the greatest number'? The phrase originated in 1725, and in any case it loses its punch once you grant that society should value certain kinds of happiness over others. Mill discounted all forms of happiness that did not strike him as having been rationally chosen; eighteenth-century utilitarian William Paley felt the same way about happiness that did not come from doing God's will. Which rather leaves political philosophy back where it started. Mill's real contribution was to associate philosophical banalities—like the harm principle, which sounds comprehensive until you try to pin down 'harm'—with political liberalism.

Once he popularized this connection, everyone who disagreed with him seemed to be not just against liberalism but against happiness. Once at a party, Jane Carlyle was introduced to a woman who said, 'Oh, you're the wife of the man who believes in the least good for the greatest number.' That is not what Carlyle believed, obviously. But he disagreed with Mill on politics, so that is how he has come down to us.

In that sense, at least, today's globalist Left could hardly be more Millian. In his obituary for Mill, his disciple John Morley related this description from an American visitor who came to pay his respects to the great philosopher:

> You placed before him the facts on which you sought his opinion. He took them, gave you the different ways in which they might fairly be looked at, balanced the opposing considerations, and then

handed you a final judgment in which nothing was left out. His mind worked like a splendid piece of machinery; you supply it with raw materials, and it turns you out a perfectly finished product.

Does this not sound like *Vox*? Across the distance of a century, today's rationalists share with Mill a conviction that every problem can be solved with a single basic set of analytical tools—in our case, the pragmatic neoliberalism of modern social science. This simplicity does tend to give analysis a certain superficiality; Mill's polymathic contemporary William Whewell said that 'he appears to me to write like a man whose knowledge is new.' But utilitarian calculation will give you an intelligent-sounding answer every time, and these days a compelling infographic as well.

Utilitarianism has inclined the leading lights of the modern Left to embrace some positions that Mill (and their other liberal forebears) would find odd: *Vox* executive editor Matt Yglesias once praised Bangladeshi sweatshops.[1] But they are still recognizably Mill's descendants, sharing with him a basic preoccupation with making everything in public life account for itself rationally. Any relationship of allegiance, authority, or dependence must either be translated into the language of utilitarian advantage or else discredited as an irrational restriction on personal choice.

And yet the irrational keeps bubbling up. For all his overgrown powers of reason, Mill in his private life was roiled by passions that he never understood. So instead he rationalized them. To justify his overwhelming love for Harriet, he made up a story about her being objectively the greatest human being on earth.

---

[1]   Matt Yglesias, 'Different Places Have Different Safety Rules and That's OK', *Slate*, April 24, 2013.

There is a lesson in that: in pursuing the utilitarian ideal, it is not the unformed rabble whose irrationalism betrays them, but a man's own. Today's Left spends all its time worrying about backlash from irrational populists, when it really ought to be worried about social justice warriors, masked 'antifa' thugs, and gnostic diviners of a 'privilege' that mysteriously pervades all things yet is based on studies that cannot be replicated and history that telescopes the facts.

In 1835, Harriet revealed the underlying principle of her philosophy in a letter to Mill designed to steel his resolve to persist in their relationship despite his friends' and family's disapproval.

> I have always observed where there is strong feeling the interests of feeling are always paramount & it seems to me that personal feeling has more of infinity in it than any other part of character— no ones mind is ever satisfied, nor the imagination nor the ambition—nor anything else of that class— but feeling satisfies.

Feelings were the great loophole for Mill. His fundamental metric of happiness rested on the foundation of feelings, and it turned out that his feelings were—without his fully realizing it—under his control. In order to justify his relationship with Harriet, he needed his passion for her to overwhelm anyone else's unhappiness in the utilitarian calculation, and so his feelings grew and grew until the equation balanced.

He posed as a modern Stoic who thought that with the right education and self-discipline men could channel their emotions toward higher ends. But as Harriet proved, all the incentives in Millian philosophy are to make feelings bigger, more demanding, more willful, more intense. Which may explain why the Left today is simultaneously

more utilitarian, more pragmatic-sounding, more sooth-
ingly chart-driven than ever before—and more irrational
than at any time since the 1960s.

**This article originally appeared in *American Af-
fairs* Volume I, Number 2 (Summer 2017): 199–
208.**

LIBERTY AND LICENCE

What is the Liberal Party's understanding of the true nature of personal freedom?

Damien Freeman

There is a Marxist who was at Cambridge with me. Fittingly enough, he was at King's and I at Magdalene. He must have left Australia to go up around the time that I did, and he returned to Australia around the same time. I published an article that examined Tony Abbott's discussion of liberalism and conservativism in *Battlelines* around this time. We got talking about what I understood it to mean to be conservative. He said that, on my understanding of what it meant to be conservative, virtually everyone in Australia today was conservative. I said that I thought that afforded me some degree of vindication.

What does it mean to be conservative? More to the point, in a country in which the dominant right-wing political party is the Liberal Party of Australia, what does it mean to be a conservative within the Liberal Party? I have written at some length on these questions elsewhere. I should like to return to a specific question here: what is the nature of the Australian conservative's commitment to the freedom of the individual?

An Australian conservative within the Liberal Party is

both part of a philosophical tradition and a political party. He is a successor to the conservative tradition in Australia, and also a member of the Liberal Party of Australia. This in itself need not be problematic: both the conservative tradition and the Liberal Party have a commitment to the freedom of the individual. But the commitment to the freedom of the individual within the conservative tradition is not necessarily identical to the commitment to freedom of the individual shared by all members of the Liberal Party.

In British politics, there is one member of the House of Commons who has displayed a singular interest in the philosophical foundations of modern conservatism. He is Jesse Norman MP. His thesis is unremarkable insofar as he regards Edmund Burke as the father of modern conservatism. It is, perhaps, somewhat more remarkable in that he claims that Burke is also the maker of modern politics. Norman has written the seminal study of Burke from a political perspective. He captures what Burke takes to be central to public policymaking. Norman also identifies the weaknesses in the current practice of politics, and he argues that Burke holds the key to reinvigorating public life.

Burke was an eighteenth-century Anglo-Irish parliamentarian and political theorist. His major statement of conservatism is found in his *Reflections on the Revolution in France*. The *Reflections* takes the form of a long and discursive letter—it is not a treatise. Reflecting on the French Revolution leads Burke into a discussion about the British constitution, and the difference between British and French political life before and after the Revolution. Unsurprisingly, he argues for the superiority of the British approach. But what is of enduring value is the broad approach to political change that he advocates.

Burke is not a reactionary who is opposed to change. He accepts that England has the kind of society that does change, and he does not think this is a bad thing. What he is opposed to is abrupt and radical change that is motivated by abstract ideas about what an ideal society should look like, rather than gentle and gradual change that is in conformity with tradition. Every society, he believes, has an organic structure. Change can happen, but it needs to evolve gradually in conformity with the values of the people. Politicians cannot impose change on people if that change is inconsistent with the structure of society or its tradition. Simply spouting some abstract ideas will not be any help if they are inconsistent with tradition.

Now is not the time to discuss in any detail Burke's approach to politics, but it is apposite to say something about his approach to liberty. Burke is committed to liberty, and in this sense it is tempting to label him as a liberal. But what distinguishes Burke from liberals—or libertarians—is the nature of his commitment to liberty. He does not believe that there is some abstract idea of liberty that is of fundamental importance.

Although Burke is remembered for his opposition to the French Revolution, it is less well known that he was a supporter of the American Revolution. He understood why the Thirteen Colonies declared their independence from the British Crown. He saw in their claims a commitment to *English* liberty, which they felt had been unjustly repressed in the colonies. It was central to the claims of the Americans that they had the weight of history on their side in their accusations against the British. The British were acting in a way that suppressed Magna Carta, the Americans believed. So when they stood up against the British, they were standing up for the institutions of the English tradition. This was not lost on Burke. He was emphatic that there was a peculiarly English sense of liberty;

that this is what the Americans were claiming they were entitled to, and which no enlightened Englishman would presume to deny to another Englishman, be he residing within the realm, or beyond the seas in the colonies owing allegiance to the Crown.

In 2015, I visited the British Library which staged an exhibition to commemorate the 800th anniversary of Magna Carta. One feature of the exhibition that struck me was not just the significance of Magna Carta for the American Revolution, but how much at odds the Americans were with their counterparts in France. The exhibition suggested that, whereas it was deeply important for the American revolutionaries that they could show that their cause was anchored in history, the French revolutionaries had no such interest. In France, the revolution was all about the weight of abstract ideas. The exhibits (and perhaps more so the commentary about them) suggested that whereas the French revolutionaries asserted an ideological commitment to the abstract idea of liberty that had been suppressed in France, the American revolutionaries asserted an historical commitment to the English idea of liberty that dated from Magna Carta, but which had been suppressed in the American colonies of late. Whether or not the exhibition's approach is historically accurate, it is entirely of a piece with Burke's analysis of the two revolutions.

So what would it mean to say that Burke's commitment to liberty is anchored in the concrete rather than the abstract? Burke draws a distinction between liberty and licence. Licence is the freedom to do whatever you like. It is, perhaps, the hallmark of the modern permissive society. Liberty, for Burke, is something different. It is freedom within socially sanctioned constraints. At least since 1215, English society had recognised certain domains within which (some) people were free. Gradually, over time, these domains expand, and society comes to permit its members greater and greater scope to make their own decisions about their religious, domestic and economic affairs. So Burkean liberty is more like the right to make your own decisions in affairs that your society has come to recognise are important areas in which disagreement among a society's members is legitimate, and in which its members should defer to their own conscience and judgement. That is a very different idea from Burkean licence, which is more like the right to do whatever you feel like doing in any context.

To my mind, liberals—or libertarians—have a decidedly un-Burkean approach to freedom. For them, political freedom has more to do with licence than with liberty. Even more concerningly, this freedom of the individual, on the model of Burkean licence, is seen as an end in itself. Indeed, it is seen as the ultimate end towards which all public policy should aspire. I doubt anyone in Australia would deny that freedom is—in some sense—a good thing. But there might be some dispute about whether it is the highest good, or indeed the only good, that matters in public life. Most of us have a sense that equality, security, prosperity and justice also matter. We might also disagree about whether what we mean by freedom is Burkean liberty or licence.

As soon as one admits that there is a range of political goods, one will just as soon find that these goods quickly come into conflict with each other, and that different ways of conceiving of a particular good will seem to be at odds with each other. One way around this is to develop a theory that stipulates how a particular good—such as liberty— is properly to be understood, and which then provides an argument for why this good is more important than any other good—usually, because it is thought that all other goods flow from this good. Once you have such a theory, the goal of public policy becomes one of adopting policies that promote this highest good.

So if you are a liberal or libertarian, you will have a particular way of understanding what liberty or freedom is. Such liberty will probably be something like freedom from external constraint. (Thus, I am free to the extent that no one else places constraints on what I may do.) The liberal or libertarian will then explain why such liberty is, in principle, more important than equality, security, prosperity, etc, and will explain why these are important insofar as they contribute to circumstances in which liberty can flourish, or else why maximising liberty ultimately enables these other goods. The liberal or libertarian can then afford to be blinkered when it comes to public policymaking. The government should adopt policies that maximise liberty, because liberal or libertarian ideology proves that this is what matters.

In *Abbott's Right*, I provide an account of the conservative's approach to liberty in the chapter headed 'The right cast of mind'. Liberty has a central place in the Australian tradition to which Australian conservatives are committed. But it is valued as part of a tradition, and as a value that has to be reconciled with other competing values of the tradition. So, important as conservatives might take liberty to be, they would never regard it as the fundamental end towards which public policy should be directed. Liberty is one of the central values that is manifested through the institutions of the Australian tradition, and is valued by conservatives as such. Theirs is more of a pragmatic commitment to liberty, rather than an ideological commitment, and liberty can be subordinated to other values of the tradition when it is pragmatic to do so.

This is far from a complete picture of the conservative cast of mind that I believe needs to be contrasted with the ideology of libertarianism, but it is an introduction to one of the fundamental disagreements about the nature of their respective commitments to liberty. It is also a good introduction into the difficulties that conservatives face today in articulating their distinctive cast of mind in debates about public policy. Before one can understand the situation in which conservatives find themselves today, however, there are two features of Australian history that need to be understood. The first has to do with the way political labels were understood historically in Australia. The second has to do with the circumstances in which the Liberal Party was established.

I do not have any particular commitment to the label conservative, although I do have a commitment to what it means to be conservative in the Burkean sense. Writing in 1930, in a book simply entitled, *Australia*, Sir Keith Hancock explains how political labels had come to be understood in the formative years of non-Labor politics in Australia. Conservative, he says, was understood to mean reactionary; liberal was understood to mean conservative; and nationalist could mean whatever the speaker liked. In this context, someone who had Burkean political sympathies would describe himself as a liberal rather than as a conservative. This tells us something about why Burkean conservatives still have a tendency to describe themselves as liberals rather than as conservatives in Australia today.

When Sir Robert Menzies established his party, he had to choose a name for the party. He wished to establish a party that would be neither reactionary nor socialist. Thus, he settled on the name of the Liberal Party of Australia. If Hancock is to be believed, Menzies adopted a name which would not have reactionary or socialist connotations for his colleagues. Menzies needed to attract support from all sections of non-Labor politics. This meant Burkean conservatives as much as it did liberals or what we might more precisely call libertarians.

The Burkeans and the libertarians who would join the new Liberal Party both had a commitment to liberty. For the Burkeans, the commitment was to liberty as a central value of the Australian, or, perhaps more accurately in their day, the British tradition to which they were committed. For the libertarians, it was an ideological commitment to liberty. The Burkeans and the libertarians also had something else in common: they were all fundamentally anti-socialist. In the Cold War era, the threat of communism was such that a shared opposition to socialism was enough to galvanise the Burkean and libertarian flanks of the Liberal Party. In such circumstances, the nature of one's commitment to liberty would seem less significant than the fact of it.

As the threat of communism recedes and the Cold War ends, the differences between the Burkean and libertarian flanks of the Liberal Party become more pronounced. Although there is still a shared commitment to liberty, the different nature of the commitments comes to the fore. This is the party that John Howard leads, and which he conceives of as a broad church. It is, he says, the political custodian in Australia of both Burke and Mill. The Burkeans and the Millians each have a commitment to liberty, for the Burkeans this is a commitment to liberty as it is understood within the tradition, whereas for the Millians—or libertarians—it is an ideological commitment to freedom as the fundamental political value.

Although John Howard liked to describe himself as economically liberal and socially conservative, Tony Abbott was the first national leader in Australia to brand himself as being explicitly conservative. Despite the strength of the conservative tradition, the label has been shunned in contemporary Australia in a way that it has not in the United Kingdom or the United States. This is partly because of the names of the major parties: the Conservative

Party, the Republican Party and the Liberal Party broadly cover the same ground in those countries, and are pitted against the Labour Party, the Democratic Party and the Australian Labor Party. One can see how, in these circumstances, liberal might come to be used to describe members of the Democratic Party or the Labour Party, whereas in Australia it would naturally come to be identified with people who are not aligned with the ALP, and members of the Conservative Party and Republican Party would more readily adopt the label of conservative than liberal, whereas their equivalent in Australia would feel more comfortable with the label of liberal.

None of that, however, goes to the core of the problem: what we mean by being conservative, as opposed to how the label happens to be used in political discourse. I can identify three reasons why public figures of a conservative cast of mind tend not to proclaim their conservative credentials as proudly as they might.

First, conservative is taken to mean reactionary. In his essay, 'Why I am not a conservative', F. A. Hayek builds up a case against conservatism. The conservatism that he has in mind is a form of European conservatism. Such conservatives are closer to what I would call reactionaries: they are opposed to change *in principle*. It is notable that Hayek does not regard Burke as a conservative in this European sense. Indeed, Hayek admits that it is difficult to label Burke in terms of Hayek's conception of liberal and conservative. The Burkean is not a reactionary. Hancock points out in 1930 that Australians understand conservative to mean reactionary, and liberal to mean conservative, so perhaps Hancock would have said that Australians would use the label of liberal to describe Burkeans. I feel comfortable using the label conservative as a shorthand for Burkean, but if this suggests that Burkeans are reactionary, as it might in Hayek's America or Hancock's Australia, then I would prefer to label them as Burkeans.

Secondly, conservative has been used as a label for an extremist position in Australia. Australian politics is all about claiming the centre ground. Serious politicians on the left or the right of the political spectrum in Australia want to claim that they are centre-left or centre-right. A centre-left politician needs to distinguish himself from the far-left as much as he has to distinguish himself from the right. It has become conventional to use the label of liberal for centre-right in Australia, and conservative for the far-right. I do not accept that Burkeans are necessarily on the far-right of Australian politics, let alone that they are extremists. To be a Burkean is not to be more or less extreme. It is to believe that public policy should be understood in terms of tradition, institutions and enduring values that emanate from the lived experience of a society, rather than in terms of abstract ideas or ideologies that must be imposed on societies. The Burkean is not squeamish in the face of change, but he does insist that change must be consistent with the values that are manifested through the institutions of our tradition. This ought to result in a fairly moderate approach to change. In a political discourse that uses the label conservative to mean the far-right rather than the centre-right in contemporary political debate, it is difficult for anyone to use conservative as a label for a Burkean approach.

Finally, I think it has become unfashionable to identify as conservative because the zeitgeist is antithetical to the core commitments of conservatism. There is no way around the fact that tradition, institutions and values have been unfashionable for some decades. It is the new and the ephemeral that are fashionable. This hardly leaves room for public figures courting popularity to assert their commitment to tradition, however important they might take it to be. Likewise, membership and belonging are not fashionable forms of life at the moment. This makes it hard to articulate a commitment to institutions, which by their nature are about their members' sense of belonging, and which tend to be anchored in tradition. The idea that people live their lives according to values that transcend their appetites or preferences has all but disappeared. Once, it was well understood that a statement of my values was a statement of the conduct to which I aspire. I might be better or worse at living up to my values, but my values give me a sense of what it would mean for me to live well. Now, values seem to be understood as a statement of how I actually live, rather than how I aspire to live. Transcendent values have given way to personal preferences. So again there is little room in public life for a public figure to articulate a commitment to transcendent values that seem to threaten people's transient preferences. The current zeitgeist might well prove unsatisfactory in the longer term. Should this happen, it would hardly be surprising to find a resurgence of conservatism in public discourse.

The conservative's commitment to freedom is genuine, reasonable and pragmatic. The conservative cast of mind ought to seem attractive to mainstream Australians. I do not say that the Liberal Party of Australia should be more conservative. I think it is in keeping with the party of Menzies that it provides a home for all-comers who do not see the Australian Labor Party as embodying their approach to public policy. I do say, however, that conservatives should speak up more vocally as Burkeans rather than as 'the right wing' of the party. They should not present as being more to the right of the party than other members of the party. They should present as having a Burkean commitment to liberty, rather than an ideological commitment to liberty. If only they had the confidence to do so, I believe they would find that many people across Australia would find that this is a sensible and pragmatic approach to policy making in Australia, and more people in Australia would feel comfortable describing themselves as conservative.

LIBERTY, LIBERALS, AND THE GAY WEDDING CAKE

How liberalism came to infect both sides of politics in the Anglophone West.

Salvatore Babones

In 2018, the gay wedding cake became the unlikely emblem of rights, freedom, and the struggle for the soul of liberalism. First the United States Supreme Court found in favor of the freedom of a Colorado baker to turn down a commission for a gay wedding cake. Then a few months later the United Kingdom's Supreme Court affirmed the freedom of a Belfast bakery not to decorate a cake with the motto 'Support Gay Marriage' – when they didn't. Score 2 for freedom of speech, 0 for gay wedding cake rights.

Many people think of freedoms and rights as the same thing. And in fact the same 'thing' can be a freedom in one place but a right in another. Consider the ability to say what you want in public. In the United States, freedom of speech is considered one of the age-old common law freedoms inherited from England. The United States Constitution makes this clear when it says that 'Congress shall make no law ... abridging the freedom of speech.'

The freedom comes down from time immemorial, and Congress has no right to alter it. Europeans, by contrast, enjoy an oxymoronic 'right to free speech.' Their governments have granted them the freedom to speak, sometimes, and European governments reserve the right to revoke that freedom whenever it serves the governments' interests.

A right is something that someone has granted; freedom is primordial. Freedoms can be limited, restricted, even taken away entirely, but they can't be created. You can give me a right, but you can't give me my freedom. You can, however, take away my freedom by giving someone else a right. Slavery used to work just that way. Yes, slavery is a right: the right of one person to control another. The abolition of slavery infringed the rights of millions of slave owners, but restored freedom to millions more. No slave has ever been 'given' his or her freedom; to free people means to take something away, viz.: their chains.

Marriage is an institution that grants certain (increasingly limited) rights under the law. Both the United States (since a 2015 Supreme Court decision) and the United Kingdom (since a 2013 Act of Parliament, effective in 2014) allow same-sex marriage, as does Australia (since 2017). Gays have always had the right to marry in these countries, albeit only the right to marry people of the opposite sex, which many of them have done all through history. Now they also have the right to marry people of their own sex, or of no sex at all. As a result, homosexuals now face the same level of risk to their freedom that heterosexuals have faced for millennia.

Freedoms and rights are often intermingled, and even more often confused. But broadly speaking, freedoms are free, while rights come at a price. The classic 'four freedoms' reserved in the first amendment to the Constitution of the United States – freedom of religion, speech, publication, and assembly – are all primordial freedoms that impose no obligations on anyone. When, in 1941, Franklin Roosevelt rhetorically replaced the second two 'freedoms of' with two new 'freedoms from,' he smuggled in a rights agenda under cover of freedom. His freedom from want and freedom from fear were really rights in disguise.

In Australia, freedom from want is provided by Centrelink, freedom from fear by Medicare, the police, and (for some people) the Human Rights Commission. The freedom from want that they provide is really an expensive right that someone has to pay for, and some Australians' freedom from fear of offensive speech can be enforced only by terrorizing others. We can all enjoy the 'freedoms of' religion, speech, publication, and assembly without limiting each others' freedoms of the same, but we can't all enjoy unlimited 'freedoms from' want and fear. Some people's wants are, after all, insatiable, and some people's egos are so fragile that every social interaction is pregnant with fear.

In short, rights like the 'freedom from' want and fear – to say nothing of the more expansive rights to food, clothing, housing, medical care, social services, unemployment insurance, and social security asserted in Article 25 of the United Nations Declaration of Human Rights – are what economists call 'rival goods.' Someone's right is always someone else's obligation, often the state's obligation, which means our collective obligation. Such obligations form the bonds that tie a country together. But as a fellow member of a shared community, you have every right to limit my rights, which inevitably place obligations on you as well. You have no right to limit my freedom. When one group claims the right to limit the freedom of others, sparks fly.

Of liberties and liberals

Clear thinking about freedoms and rights requires first of all that we recognize the distinction between them, but second of all that we recognize their underlying similarity. Freedoms and rights can both fairly be described as liberties. Magna Carta, the Charter of the Forest, the Petition of Right, the English Bill of Rights, and the American Bill of Rights all blend freedoms and rights together in enumerating the ancient liberties of the Anglo-Saxon peoples.

As Edmund Burke argued so elegantly in his *Reflections on the Revolution in France*, the traditional liberties of the Anglo-Saxon peoples are founded 'not on abstract principles' but inherited 'as the rights of Englishmen, and as a patrimony derived from their forefathers.' Even today, the peoples of the United Kingdom, Australia, New Zealand, Canada, and the United States, along with those of a few curious geographical odds and ends, retain many of the ancient liberties of Englishmen. Other ancient societies had their own customary liberties, but nearly all other societies wiped their legal slates clean in the transition to modernity. Only in the Anglo-Saxon countries do people retain the ill-defined liberties of their forefathers.

In most other countries, people can enumerate their rights, and date them to specific documents. Not us. Anglo-Saxon liberties predate the governments of today's Anglo-Saxon countries, and supersede them. In the United States, the freest and in many ways the most ancient of the Anglo-Saxon countries, the government is explicitly denied the right to dilute the people's ancient liberties. These liberties, to quote Burke again, constitute 'an *entailed inheritance* derived to us from our forefathers, and to be transmitted to our posterity.' We are Burke's posterity.

Which is not to say that Anglo-Saxon liberties have stagnated. They have stood the test of time precisely because they have evolved over time. That is the third and final key to clear thinking about freedoms and rights: the recognition that liberties are particular, not universal, and have evolved to fit specific social contexts. They are functional for the societies in which they have evolved. Burke's 'spirit of liberty in action' shows whether it is useful or destructive, good or bad. Freedom of speech is usually counted a blessing, until it results in an incitement to crime. Or outside the United States, in defamation. Or in Australia, just hurting people's feelings.

Liberals have been reinterpreting the Anglo-Saxon world's liberties for more than 300 years. Liberalism is the Anglo-Saxon world's oldest articulated political philosophy. It emerged in resistance to absolute rule and through that resistance it created the first functioning political space to exist outside the royal court. Before liberalism, opposition to the monarch meant rebellion against the monarch; witness the English Civil War and the beheading of Charles I in 1649. After the restoration of Charles II in 1660, English liberals created the concept of the loyal opposition. In the early 1700s, they effectively created the political public square.

Conservatives increasingly sallied into that square to engage liberals in political debate, but the very act of having a debate was a liberal idea. The conservative party of William Pitt 'the Younger' arose as an offshoot of the liberal Whig party; Edmund Burke was himself one of those conservative 'Old Whigs' who seceded from the dominant Whig faction that, for him, was moving too quickly in a 'New' direction. A century later, the British Labour Party, too, emerged as a liberal heterodoxy, though this time composed of radicals who thought the established Liberal Party was moving forward too slowly. Thus all three historical British parties started out as varieties of liberals, and in the twenty-first century no less a labourite than Gordon Brown could make the 'golden thread that runs through British history of the individual standing firm for freedom and liberty' a standard line in his stump speech.

Back in the nineteenth century, British liberals and conservatives coalesced into formal political parties, with the Liberal Party usually dominant in the elected House of Commons and the Conservative Party always dominant in the hereditary House of Lords. As the franchise was expanded in a series of Reform Bills, the United Kingdom became an increasingly democratic (and increasingly liberal) country. But the old Liberal Party disintegrated with the coming of truly universal suffrage, first for men (1918) and then for women (1928). Universal suffrage enfranchised many poor conservatives and many more poor progressives, but few new liberals. By the 1930s the Labour Party had taken the place of the Liberals as the main opposition to the Conservative establishment.

The United States was both liberal and democratic right from the beginning. It was the conservatives who started off on the wrong foot. Many of the new country's loyalist conservatives fled during or soon after the Revolutionary War. That left the liberals (represented in the United States by the Federalist Party) in command of the intellectual commons. Had the United States remained a limited democracy like the United Kingdom, the Federalists might have dominated its politics throughout the nineteenth century, as the Liberals dominated at Westminster. But liberalism is a highly refined, thoroughly intellectual tradition, and as federal elections moved toward direct popular votes in the early nineteenth century, the liberal Federalist Party was doomed.

On both sides of the Atlantic, labourism or (in America)

progressivism was the third political tradition to emerge, since it depended on the votes of the poor, who did not always enjoy the right to vote. American progressives were first organized in the Democratic-Republican Party of Thomas Jefferson and Andrew Jackson, the direct ancestor of today's Democratic Party, which for a few decades in the early nineteenth century was the only effective political party in the country. Yet American progressivism, like British labourism, was also an outgrowth of liberalism. Even Bernie Sanders, notwithstanding his own declarations, is no socialist. Actual socialism is a non-starter in American politics, as it always has been all across the Anglo-Saxon world. Like Anglo-Saxon conservatism, Anglo-Saxon progressivism and labourism are simply shades of the dominant liberal tradition.

Left, right, and liberal

The lack of any real, effective socialist party in the Anglo-Saxon world has long puzzled political scientists, because Karl Marx predicted that socialism would appear first in the most advanced capitalist countries. In Marx's day, that meant England. In the early twentieth century, the United States overtook the United Kingdom as the most advanced capitalist country, but still no socialism. By the 1950s, Marxism had become respectable (and even fashionable) at universities in all the Anglo-Saxon countries, and still the political scientists waited for the workers to rise up and demand socialism. In the 1960s many political science students tried to stage the revolution for themselves, but all that came of it was Baby Boomer angst amid an embarrassment of polyester. The US presidential elections of 1968 and 1972 went to the notably non-socialist Richard Nixon.

The Marxist idea that politics is a class war between the deserving poor and the greedy rich is derived from the

European historical experience: the peasants versus the nobility, fraternity versus privilege, atheism versus religion, red versus white, the left versus the right. In most continental European countries, the left-right distinction worked pretty well until relatively recently. Political parties could comfortably be placed on an axis running from the communist hard left to the reactionary hard right, with the center-left social democrats and the center-right Christian democrats making the running in the middle. In this way of seeing the world, social democracy is just the 'lite' version of communism – and, in fact, that's how the German Social Democratic Party got its start, as the German affiliate of the Second International. On the other wing, many postwar Christian democratic parties were havens for reconstructed fascists.

The left and right of European politics are both alien to the Anglo-Saxon world because they both fall outside the broadly accepted liberal consensus of Anglo-Saxon political systems. No American progressive or British labour politician could get elected on a promise to abolish private property. Just as surely, no sane American or British conservative would campaign for state funding of a church. All major political parties in the Anglo-Saxon world are liberal. That doesn't mean that they're in the center between left and right. They're not on the left-right continuum at all. They literally exist in another dimension.

In the Anglo-Saxon world, there is no political center, because there are no political sides. A progressive or labourite is not the opposite of a conservative. America's greatest progressive leaders at the high point of its progressive era were the Democrat William Jennings Bryan, who famously prosecuted John Scopes for teaching evolution, and the Republican Theodore Roosevelt, proponent of naval armament and the rough life. Bryan was known as the 'Great Commoner' for his support of ordinary workers, and lest anyone question Roosevelt's labourite credentials, in 1902 he ended a coal strike by threatening to send in federal troops – to support the workers against the owners. Meanwhile in the United Kingdom, the future conservative icon Winston Churchill successfully championed minimum wages and the eight hour day. In Australia, look at the histories of B.A. Santamaria's Democratic Labor Party or Robert Menzies' appeal to the 'Forgotten People.'

Thus, although being 'more left' (in the continental sense) by definition means being 'less right,' being more conservative does not necessarily imply being less progressive or labourite. The interlacing of political positions in the Anglo-Saxon world means that hardly any one party or politician represents a pure play for a particular ideology. In fact, the whole idea of ideology is anathema; party platforms in the Anglo-Saxon world have always consisted of lists of policy positions, not well-theorized statements of political principle. Most Anglo-Saxon political parties embrace a mix of conservative and progressive or labourite policies, and nearly anyone and everyone in the Anglo-Saxon world is a liberal. Liberty is the great universal value of the Anglo-Saxon world. Groups like communists, fascists, and greens that are driven by foreign ideologies have never stood a chance.

The new liberal authoritarianism

If everyone is a liberal, where do liberals stand in the Anglo-Saxon world? The United Kingdom has always had a 'liberal' major party, but the United States gets along quite well without one. Australia has a Liberal Party that suffers from a perpetual identity crisis, since the latter-day Australian Labor Party is itself largely composed of liberals. The Liberal Party of Australia is conservative by default, if only because it is not a labour party; it is the conservative elements of its platform that distinguish it from Australian Labor. In countries where everyone is more or less a liberal, liberal parties struggle to be 'for' anything in particular. For decades the main goal of the UK Liberal Democrats was to have a referendum on proportional representation, and when in 2011 they finally got it, they lost.

Yet all of the major political parties in the Anglo-Saxon world include dyed-in-the-wool liberals among their most prominent members, from Hillary Clinton and Mitt Romney in the United States to Tony Blair and David Cameron in the United Kingdom to Kevin Rudd and Malcolm Turnbull in Australia. Seeking to differentiate themselves in a political milieu that is liberal by default, they have pushed forward from the old-fashioned 'classical' liberal freedom agenda (now marginalized under the label 'libertarian') toward a new liberal discourse of rights. Not content with mere human rights, they have promoted animal rights and even planetary rights, as if the inorganic elements of the Earth itself merited political representation.

And thus the most liberal of liberal political organizations in the United States, the American Civil Liberties Union, went to bat in the Colorado wedding cake case for gay rights at the expense of personal freedom. The organization made its name in the early twentieth century defending the freedom of speech of unsympathetic figures like anarchists, communists, pornographers, Nazis, and the Ku Klux Klan. Today, it is 'determined to fight racism in all its forms' as well as 'fighting bigotry and oppression against other marginalized groups, including women, immigrants, religious groups, LGBT individuals, Native Americans, and people with disabilities.' Those are certainly worthy causes, but the shift in emphasis is telling. The liberal conscience of America now places much more emphasis on minority rights than on universal freedom.

The strategic shift in liberal politics from the promotion of freedom to the expansion of rights would be innocuous enough, were it not for the moralistic rhetoric in which it is framed. Politicians on all sides are always advancing policies that would place unwelcome obligations on others: tax increases, welfare conditions, improved building standards, and myriad other policy changes cause inconvenience to many and even suffering to some. But a proposal to raise taxes to pay for a new highway is not ordinarily construed as a moral right that must be granted in any decent society. Those who demand greater accountability for government hand-outs do not call their opponents racists; quite the contrary: they are much more likely to be called racists by their opponents.

Unlike other politicians, who tell us what they think society should do, liberals have developed the habit of telling us what society must do. They brook no (legitimate) debate. Those who oppose the liberal agenda are construed as racist, sexist, homophobic, and all the rest by definition. After all, why would you defend the freedom of a baker to refuse a gay cake commission – unless you were a homophobe? The only respectably permissible answer to that challenge is to claim that you are defending the baker's freedom of religion, and so coverage of gay wedding cake cases necessarily focuses on the bakers' religious affiliations: Christian will do; Moslem would be better.

In a free society, people are free to hold unsavory views, and even plain wrong ones. It is not so long ago that homosexuality itself was widely proscribed, and even criminalized, as morally 'wrong.' When morality is a moving target, freedom is the backstop that prevents things from getting out of hand. Lest we forget, lest we forget.

Homosexual couples can buy wedding cakes on equal terms with heterosexual couples, just as (these days) they can marry on equal terms with heterosexual couples. But liberals want to go much further, pushing what was originally a freedom agenda into a rights agenda, and demanding that society accept the obligations that these new rights entail. It is one thing to ask for rights; we all want rights. It is quite another thing to demand rights, since the only authority on which these new rights are based is the authority of liberals themselves. We can argue all we want about taxes and spending and all the other quotidian questions of practical politics, but liberals present their expansive rights agenda as a moral imperative that is above debate.

Democracy requires respect – or at least toleration – for opposing points of view, even when it comes to human rights. Respect and toleration underpin the long-term success of democracy across the Anglo-Saxon world. The three major Anglo-Saxon political traditions have always been intermingled in the same families, and even in the same individuals. As a result, liberals, conservatives, and progressives or labourites have learned to live with each other, and with each other's points of view.

But as liberals have transitioned from promoting a freedom agenda to promoting a rights agenda, they have set themselves up as the new authoritarians of the twenty-first century. They are telling the rest of the electorate: you must, on our authority, accept new obligations associated with the new rights we have identified and defined; your ancient Anglo-Saxon liberties are no safeguard against our new agenda.

Authoritarianism is nothing else but governance legitimated by demands for deference to authority. In an authoritarian system, obedience is the highest political virtue. What liberals are demanding today is unquestioning obedience to their expansive rights agenda; just like the authoritarianisms of old, they are vilifying (if not outright criminalizing) the asking of questions. Woe be unto the author, broadcaster, or professor who questions the liberal orthodoxy in any but the most generic of terms: hell hath no fury like a liberal spurned. And thus, ironically, it is the liberals who are introducing continental traditions of right versus wrong, with us or against us politics into the Anglo-American societies. They are attempting to redefine Anglo-Saxon democracy as an existential struggle between liberals and illiberals.

Forget about Brexit and Donald Trump. The greatest threat to Anglo-Saxon democracy comes from the radical rights agenda of the new liberal authoritarianism. Ancient liberties that have stood for more than a thousand years could be lost in a few election cycles... but only if we agree to give them up. Labourites and progressives seem willing to compromise on this; conservatives are made of sterner stuff. The conservatives' one weak point is the liberal influence in their own political parties, especially in Australia (where most conservatives are embedded inside a nominally liberal party), but also in the UK and even in the United States, where the arch-conservative Republican Party includes a large liberal wing that dares not speak its name. But someone has to save Anglo-Saxon democracy, and if conservatives won't stand up for ancient liberties, who will?

DE GAULLE AND THE FRENCH RIGHT

The story of another nation's failed attempt to fuse liberalism and traditionalism.

Nathan Pinkoski

Having been swindled too often by 20th century liberalism, the Anglo-American tradition of conservatism has embarked on an audacious endeavour to rethink what conservatism means and what its relationship with liberalism should be. Yet it is less certain what sources this endeavour should draw upon, since these swindles stain so many. British conservatism has a long history of defining itself by whatever the Tory Prime Minister does while in office. Australian and Canadian conservatism have been historically successful as 'big-tent' movements, but holding the tent together has paralysed successive Tory governments. American conservatism's greatest post-war successes, the 'Reagan Revolution' and the defeat of communism, are tied up with liberalism. The best American conservatism can offer is a revisionist reading of the post-war canon: reconsidering what Buckley and Kirk, Reagan, and Nixon were really all about. Yet these considerations hold back from considering other sources. This gives the old orthodoxy the upper hand; they hold fast to the triumphalist interpretation of liberal-conservative fusionism.

Every revisionist endeavour runs up against this authority, resulting in a kind of stalemate that preserves the status quo.

This stalemate, combined with the dramatically different political circumstances of the 21st century, require us to look to very different sources—even those beyond the tradition of Anglo-American conservatism. This impels a significant variation from other writers in this volume: a study of the right in France.

The reasons for doing so come from reflection on the extraordinary circumstances surrounding the 2017 French Presidential election. Initially, it appeared that the contest would be the fairly typical showdown between the left-wing *Parti Socialiste* (PS) and the right-wing Gaulliste party, recently renamed *Les Republicains*. Then came Emmanuel Macron. With a rare combination of political cunning and good fortune, Macron's ascendency showed that both of the established parties were much weaker than their partisans thought.

This is particularly true of the right, which believed that after the historically low popularity of François Hollande, it could return to power. In a sense, it did. While the right tried to portray Macron, who briefly held a junior position in Hollande's government, as a man of the left, this argument was not very persuasive in the French context. Far more than in Anglo-American countries, an essential characteristic of the French left is its anti-capitalism and hostility to globalisation. Macron, by contrast, who embraces globalization and capitalism, represents an almost total repudiation of the 20th century French left. But Macron is not a conservative in any meaningful sense. To Anglo-American liberals dismayed by political events in Britain and the United States, he is their champion, their hope that an alternative is possible even in the European countries where liberalism appears to have never held power.

René Rémond: The Rights in France

A closer study of French history helps us understand why Macron is neither a man of the left nor a conservative, and what circumstances made his ascent to power possible. The reason lies in the history of the divisions on the French right. Since the 19th century, France has not one right but three, and liberalism is one of these. Conservatism has succeeded politically and intellectually when it has understood the persistence of these divides. It has failed most miserably when it has misunderstood these. Liberalism's rise to power in 2017 and conservatism's failure to counter it effectively was no accident. It is the culmination of a gradual process begun in the 1970s, when liberalism quietly began to dominate the French right. If conservatives are to provide an adequate response to liberalism's challenge, this history must be understood.

We owe the analysis of a tripartite division of the French right to Réné Rémond in *The Right Wing in France* (*Les Droites en France*). *The Right Wing in France* was first published in 1954, but it went through successive editions and updates until Rémond's death in 2007. It is a classic of French political science and political history that remains relevant in the present.

Rémond focused on the great contraries of the left and right, which had fought across French history since 1789, and the political and cultural factors that made their divides persistent. But the right in France is itself a question. Far more than Anglo-American conservatism, France's right is characterised by a splintered, divisive political history: of ideologies, originating in parties and personalities; of regimes, touching on monarchists, imperialists, anti-imperialists, republicans, and anti-republicans; of moral and social questions, implicating traditionalists, clericalists, anti-clericalists, and secularists; and of political policies, like those who aspire to weaken the power of the state, and those who aspire to strengthen it.

Rémond concluded that all these divisions in the right could be broadly organized into three political traditions, which emerged in the 19th century and persist into the present. Taking their names from three political factions of the 19th century, these are: légitimisme, Orléanisme, and Bonapartisme. Each offers a different vision of France's greatness.

Légitimisme represents the political tradition opposed to the principles of the French revolution. Légitimisme is reactionary in the precise sense of the word. Seeing the fall of the Bourbons following 1789 as a political and moral catastrophe, it seeks to restore the monarchy. For légitimisme, France's greatness is the *ancien régime,* the political regime of the monarchy. Like Edmund Burke, légitimisme defends organic principles of change, but if it agrees with Burke's mode of defending this, the inherited wisdom of history, it frequently goes further than Burke to offer a mode of defence rooted in theology. Speaking of providence, the will of God, and the monarch as the servant of the will of God, légitimisme thus denounces written constitutions in terms stronger than Burke: to légitimisme, 'every constitution is a regicide.' But its political vision is more subtle than a crude defence of absolutism. Local and natural liberties have never had a stronger defender than légitimisme. It stridently opposes the administrative centralisation of the state, regarding it as a product of Jacobinism. Rémond's analysis of French history sees légitimisme's purest expression in the power of the royalists who ruled France from 1815-1830. But then and afterwards, légitimisme manifests itself as a version of romanticism. Often very far from political life, it prefers to express itself in political philosophy or literature, as a yearning for a return to the natural course of history arbitrarily ruptured in 1789.

Orléanisme takes its name from the Duke of Orléans, Phillipe d'Egalité (1747-1793). Although he was of royal blood, there was a brief moment during the French Revolution when he led a faction that offered a compromise between absolute monarchy and the principles of the revolution. In the decades to come, Orléanisme stood for a moderation between the *ancien régime* and the revolution: a monarchy, now secularised, whose power was constrained by liberal articulation of rights and a legislative parliament. Its purest expression in power would be during the reign of the son of Phillipe d'Égalité, King Louis Philippe I, from 1830-1848. Orléanisme is the French expression of liberalism. 'Liberal' here means liberal individualism, treating human beings as autonomous individuals who enter their social roles, morals, and market exchanges by choice. Drawing their support principally from the bourgeois elites and consolidating their social and political positions, Orléanisme is the government of the elites, the *notables*. It is sceptical of traditional sources of authority and instinctually anti-clerical, incredulous of the religious orthodoxy found in the *ancien régime*. Thus it confronts traditions that threaten the autonomy of the individual. For Orléanisme, France's greatness is primarily commercial success, coupled with freedom from traditional authority. Later, Orléanisme aligned more closely with the programme of the Third Republic, from its support for liberal economics to its anti-clerical promulgation of *laicité*.

Following 1848, the arrival of Bonapartisme confounded the pre-existing traditions of the right. Bonapartisme accepted the heritage of 1789, notably Jacobinism's centralisation of the state. From its purest expression in power under Emperor Napoleon III and onwards, Bonapartisme seeks a strong state and powerful sovereign to rule this state. It is therefore the first tradition of the right to draw directly on the forces of an explicitly national, popular sovereignty. To strengthen popular sovereignty, it weakens the powers of the *notables*, the Orléaniste elite, and places governing power firmly in the hands of the sovereign. The Bonapartiste sovereign resembles a monarch, but obtains his legitimacy directly from the people by means of national plebiscites. These plebiscites give the sovereign the justification to pursue a politics of national greatness at home and abroad. Thus Bonapartisme is more demonstrably democratic than Orléanisme: Bonapartisme's basis is popular consent through universal suffrage. The appeal of Bonapartisme is in large part the opportunity of the people to vote against the elites and entrust rule in a strong character steeped in legend (such as a descendent of Napoleon). While all these features of Bonapartisme have their origin in the revolution of 1789, making Bonapartisme somewhat ambivalent in its membership on the right, that is not its full character. In a time of new revolutionary turmoil in the wake of 1848, with the left becoming more 'red', socialist and collectivist, the rural population and part of the bourgeois sought a clear principle of authority and strength to preserve the social order. As Bonapartisme developed, this principle of authority became more and more a principle of the right. Ultimately for Bonapartisme, France's greatness lies in a great statesman who acts as the people's representative in domestic affairs and in foreign policy.

1870-1940: Coalition, Synthesis, and Collapse

Following the end of the Third Empire from its defeat in the Franco-Prussian War, France nearly restored the monarchy – but this effort failed when the divisions between the rights reasserted themselves. This gave the republican left impetus to form the Third Republic, casting the right out of political power for decades. The hard lesson for the French right was that its divisions could not be wished away or casually ignored. For the right, gaining political power required coalitions and political alignments around a common cause.

In the early 20th century, the right slowly coalesced around the cause of nationalism, giving a Bonapartiste tilt to its thought. National grandeur became the principal preoccupation of the right. Nationalism had once been the cause of the republican left. But the desire to avenge the defeat of 1871, not helped by the republican left's increasing internationalism and desire to focus on global imperial projects, created a significant gap into which the right could gradually step. This came to a head in August 1914. During the First World War, the different political factions formed the *Union sacrée,* with the goal of setting aside their differences to defend France against the Germans. Notably, the right participated, giving their support to the republican regime they once condemned; disagreements about forms of government were less important than the need to protect the nation. Notably, factions on the far left did not give their support; moreover, the left became increasingly ambivalent about defending the nation as the war progressed.

Nationalism helped win the First World War. Without the *Union sacrée* defeat would have been certain against the much stronger Germany. The basis of the right's political unity in nationalism paralleled a similar attempt to find a basis for intellectual unity in nationalism: the project of *l'Action française.* This grand attempt at synthesis around 'integral nationalism,' exemplified in the thought of Charles Maurras, borrowed from each of the three rights. From Bonapartisme, national grandeur was its objective, and it attacked the political elites that hindered this project. Against narratives of the inevitability of modern French decline, or dependency on stronger powers, Maurrassianism made the case for national independence. It argued that it was possible for a middle power like France to exercise a strong foreign policy as a means to achieve national greatness. On the home front, légitimisme defined domestic concerns. From légitimisme, *l'Action française* found reasons to attack the Jacobin administrative state in the name of defending local and natural liberties. Moreover, its political thought was anti-democratic. It advocated for the monarchy. It sought to elevate the position of the Catholic Church, but as a means to achieve nationalist ends. This instrumentalisation of Catholicism brought the condemnation of Rome. But *l'Action française* could draw from the Orléaniste playbook of anti-clericalism, to assert a national independence from Roman dogma and moral rules.

The intellectual synthesis of *l'Action française* was ambitious, but it could not hold together. Besides the inherent intellectual tensions in Maurras's project, the project translated into a vulgar scorn for the republican regime. This scorn produced a different kind of determinism than the one the project had initially sought to avoid. The right's political representatives came to believe that the republic was already doomed. When war with Germany came, then, the political representatives had already decided the outcome. The political class's ghoulish analysis of the catastrophe of the 1940 defeat was that it was inevitable. Even Maurras abandoned 'Maurrasianism' and its insistence on national independence to throw in his lot with a regime that could barely sustain the illusion, let alone the reality, of national independence. *l'Action française* ended in discord: some adherents withdrew to neutrality, others opted for resistance, and others supported Vichy.

Every reflection on the history of the French right must reckon with the stain of Vichy. Yet it must do so without any simplistic conclusions. Nowadays the simplistic conclusion is that the Vichy regime is a fascist regime; a narrative in which the French right of the early 20th century becomes proto-fascist, and nationalism becomes the essence of fascism. Yet Raymond Aron, Stanley Hoffman, and René Rémond remind us that fascism was never a major political tradition in France. It has no basis in the three rights. Orléanisme was too protective of individual liberty to have any time for fascism's predilections for collectivism. Second, fascism's key features are anti-légitimiste. Fascism is revolutionary in intention and practice, and bases this revolution on the postulates of mass democracy. It is thus much more friendly to 1789 than légitimisme. Finally, although both share a disposition in favour of nationalism, fascism is very different from Bonapartisme. Fascism and nationalism are certainly not the same—otherwise those of the French resistance, who in the name of nationalism fought the Nazi occupation, would themselves be fascists. Fascism relies on a particular political party to advance its project, and lacks Bonapartisme's focus on preserving the social order.

Consonant of Vichy's complexities, a better analysis is that Vichy tried to implement a conservative programme of protecting the established social order of French society and restoring national greatness. But its hostility to republicanism translated into a hostility to democracy, so that it pursued this programme without seeking popular approval. While it could ride the coattails of Pétain's personal popularity and an initial sympathy to its programme, without a genuinely popular basis, its descent into dictatorship was inevitable. Moreover, Vichy's domestic programme always had a tragico-comic character about it, since it required completely ignoring the German occupation. Disregarding foreign policy doomed the Vichy regime from the start, for its whole domestic programme was ultimately enslaved to a foreign power.

Vichy's failure discredited much of the French right. But it did not destroy it. Charles de Gaulle's political practice confirms that Orléanisme, Bonapartisme, and légitimisme were still operative following the war. Having read his Maurras but performed the role of Cassandra in the 1930s, de Gaulle understood that the roots of the catastrophe of May 1940 were not just on the battlefield, but lay in the decade's intellectual and political mistakes. France needed a new foundation, and this new foundation required a new, better realignment of the traditions of the French right.

De Gaulle's Coalition

For Charles de Gaulle, the Third Republic failed because its parliamentary system institutionalised the divisive conflict between France's fractious political parties. This compromised national unity in three ways. First, it gave rise to highly ideological confrontations. No ideology commanded enough strength to secure widespread support, but it perpetuated a widespread trend that became more and more aggressively critical of republicanism itself. This strengthened the hands of the anti-republicans of the left, the communists, and those of the right (who expressed themselves in Vichy). Second, the Third Republic entrenched the position and power of the political elites and notables, who governed to satisfy the interests of their own factions rather than address the broader concerns of the French people. This eroded its legitimacy. Third, the parliamentary version of republicanism translated into a weak executive. Limited by fragile coalitions and power-sharing agreements, the executive could not act efficiently enough to realise the national interest, especially in times of crisis. As the geopolitical situation of the 1930s worsened, the French state was left too weak to maintain order internally and protect itself from external threats.

De Gaulle's political solution to France's problems was

that the nation needed a constitutional regime more in keeping with the tradition of Bonapartisme. Thus he proposed a constitutional version of Bonapartisme. Having observed the disastrous effects of a weak state on France, de Gaulle conceded an important principle to the Jacobin side of the Revolution. To preserve order and muster resources in times of crisis, a strong, centralised state was necessary. Following the end of the German occupation, therefore, de Gaulle's first task was to re-establish the state. De Gaulle's next objective was to consolidate national unity by an appeal to national greatness, to grandeur. Drawing from 'Maurrassianism', he held that grandeur could be achieved by prioritising foreign policy from the basis of national independence. During the war, the pursuit of grandeur required above all else insisting on France's independence vis-à-vis the British and the Americans, in spite of the far weaker strategic position of the Free French. After the war, when domestic concerns arose, the task became more complicated. As Will Morrisey observes in his *Reflections on de Gaulle*, grandeur requires that the elevation of foreign policy to take place without subordinating domestic policy to foreign policy. De Gaulle readily acknowledged that the effort to balance both was a delicate, tricky task, requiring the virtue of moderation or *mesure* consonant with the greatest statesmen of France's past.

The final objective of de Gaulle's Bonapartisme was to re-found French republicanism on a popular and non-parliamentary basis. While de Gaulle admired the Anglo-Saxon parliamentary traditions, he did not think they were right for France. In France, what was required was a strong executive chosen not through the political parties and the elites, but by the people directly. For that reason, De Gaulle avoided any attachment to a political party, and his political thought always had an anti-notables, anti-elitist trajectory. Instead, the project of grandeur requires as its precondition the popular consent. During the war, de Gaulle appealed directly to public opinion: not just French public opinion but British and American public opinion. This appeal strengthened de Gaulle's weak hand. After the war, the basis of de Gaulle's politics was maintaining popular approval expressed by the nation as a whole. Hence on the most important political questions, he submitted himself to the plebiscite.

De Gaulle's first attempt in 1945 did not succeed. Initially, the Liberation achieved de Gaulle's aim of national unity. This enabled him to draw all of France's major parties into his post-war government. However, the parties quickly awarded themselves their old powers. As the left coalesced in opposition to de Gaulle, and his popular support faltered in the face of food shortages and economic problems, de Gaulle had two options.

First was to make himself a dictator. However, de Gaulle thought this solution was impossible after Vichy: legitimacy required democracy. His refusal to entertain dictatorship showed the limits of his Bonapartisme. While he was often accused of aspiring to be another Napoleon, of having 'the shadow of Bonaparte', he condemned Napoleon's hubris. De Gaulle's Bonapartisme was not about creating a personal cult but an attraction to combining a certain political tradition with a republican constitution.

To that end, the second option de Gaulle could have exercised would have been to rally to right-wing parties, drawing close to the Christian democrats. This step would have permitted him to consolidate his power from within the old party system and push for a new regime. However, it would have forced him to play by the rules of the very party system that had brought about the crisis of the 1930s. By this means, fundamental reform of the regime would not have been possible. Instead, de Gaulle took the extraordinary step of resigning. Ultimately, in 1946, the popular consent that was a requirement of de Gaulle's project was not available. For the sake of material comfort, the French 'rejected grandeur and returned to confusion.'

De Gaulle received another chance in 1958, as the Fourth Republic followed the path of the Third into weak, ineffectual government, exacerbated by party conflict. As the crisis in French Algeria deepened, France drifted closer to civil war. Unlike in 1946, public opinion shifted decisively in favour of de Gaulle, enabling him to return to power and found the Fifth French Republic along the constitutional lines he favoured.

The basic strategy behind De Gaulle's re-founding and subsequent government was to ally his Bonapartisme with Orléanisme. This alliance was tactically important, because de Gaulle judged that the contemporary expression of légitimisme was too attached to *l'Algérie française;* moreover, many of the strongest personalities of 1950s légitimisme were romantics about Vichy. While de Gaulle had kept ties to some of these personalities, he judged they were fundamentally mistaken about the changed political situation of 1958.

De Gaulle thought France's national greatness was no longer best served by maintaining an expensive overseas empire. He agreed with Orléanisme that in modernity, national greatness was best served by a greater emphasis on successful commerce. The circumstances demanded this shift. In 1958, the French state was in a precarious economic position, on the verge of bankruptcy. De Gaulle appointed the economist Antoine Pinay, who had the support of the businesses, to undertake a series of measures designed to liberalise the domestic economy and trade with other countries. De Gaulle pulled France out of Algeria, pursued de-colonisation, and based his domestic policy around a moderate economic liberalism. He thereby distanced himself from légitimisme and reached out to Orléanisme. Through Orléanisme, he championed technological and economic modernisation, holding off communism and socialism from the left, and légitimisme from the right. The fiscal situation dramatically improved, and he presided over one of the greatest periods of economic growth in France's history.

Yet while de Gaulle appreciated Orléanisme's economic insights, and drew the brightest of the young Orléanistes into his entourage (including Valery Giscard d'Estaing), he never permitted it to become his political philosophy. He maintained the view that the political rules the economic; Orléanisme is only worthwhile as long as is furthers national greatness and aligns with an ordered life. De Gaulle said:

> "France is like a household. The housewife wants a fridge, a washing machine, and even, if possible, a car. That is change. But at the same time, she does not want her husband out on the town, her boys putting their feet on the table and her daughters coming home at all hours. That is order... [France] wants progress but not chaos."

Economic development is 'the route that leads us toward the summits,' de Gaulle said. But it is not to be mistaken for the summit. It contributes to grandeur but is not identical to grandeur. De Gaulle had no hesitation challenging the *notables*, the elites, on behalf of the people. In 1962 he audaciously reformed the constitution so that the President was appointed directly by the people. This move lost him considerable support amongst the Orléanistes and the political elite (though Giscard d'Estaing stayed supportive). Several times, de Gaulle bypassed the political elites to seek support for his most controversial measures through plebiscites. De Gaulle's distance from Orléanisme was especially clear in his wariness of European federalisation. His goal of sustaining national independence made him sceptical of European federalisation, whatever its purported economic advantages were. De Gaulle held that supranational organisations would lack popular legitimacy and challenge national independence. Thus de Gaulle kept Orléanisme in a junior position in his coalition.

Although de Gaulle broke with the more légitimiste right – who returned the favour and despised him – this rupture was primarily a political rupture. De Gaulle himself appropriated légitimisme as a kind of personal ethic of noblesse oblige, and embodied that ethic in his role as President of the Republic. Like a monarch of the *ancien régime*, it was his solemn duty to watch over and take care of France and her people. He was careful to keep himself distant from the ordinary administrative operations of political life; like a monarch, he left administrative affairs to the Cabinet (or at least he gave this impression to the public). This served both Bonapartiste purposes, detaching him from the political elites, and légitimiste purposes, increasing the regal *mystique* of the President as the one who discerned the idea of France. Using television, he spoke directly to the people, and to these people, he spoke 'much less of themselves than of France.'

In sum, De Gaulle ruled for a decade by constitutionalising the tradition of Bonapartisme, seeking support for his most controversial measures through plebiscites. He appropriated Orléanisme's prioritisation of commercial greatness into his project of national greatness. He rejected the contemporary manifestations of political légitimisme, but took up légitimisme as a personal, Presidential ethic, holding himself to its exacting aristocratic standard.

The basis of de Gaulle's republicanism was always popular approval, and so every referendum he ever held was a drama in which he and France could ascend to new summits, or fall back into mediocrity. This raised the stakes of his referenda, but it meant he was always on the ballot. Thus when he lost a referendum over constitutional reform in

1969, he sadly but gracefully retired into private life.

Orléanisme Ascendant and the Fracture of Gaullisme

De Gaulle's greatest success was creating a lasting constitutional framework that could endure in the absence of his personality. But even the greatest statesmen cannot solve every political problem. The heights of their achievements expose their limitations. Ronald Reagan succeeded in creating a lasting political coalition with an articulate political programme that defined American conservatism. Perhaps he succeeded too well, so that American conservatism's political programme became fixed to the point of inflexibility. De Gaulle represents the problem's mirror image.

Gaullisme was not about a fixed political programme. Having sought centralisation since 1945, it pushed decentralisation in its twilight years. A defender of the French empire after the war, it became the champion of decolonisation. Its economic ideas fluctuated from dirigisme to free-market reforms. Reflecting on grand strategy, De Gaulle consistently taught that a priori doctrines had no place in politics, because they dangerously distorted political judgement. Before 1914, the grand strategy of the French political establishment held to a military doctrine of military offensive, relying on the élan of its soldiers. This a priori doctrine nearly destroyed the French army in 1914. Pétain grasped that in light of the changing technological conditions of warfare, the superior strategy was to rely on defensive firepower rather than offensive manpower. Successfully applying this strategy in 1916 and saving countless lives he became renowned as the hero of Verdun. But by the 1930s, Pétain's innovation had become an a priori doctrine. France became reliant on fixed defensive positions—the infamous Maginot Line—right at the time when she needed to invest in mobile tank corps. De Gaulle came into power in 1958 in large part to solve the Algerian crisis, and many of his supporters expected him to keep Algeria French. But again, De Gaulle refused to hold as an a priori doctrine that France required an Empire. Grasping that circumstances placed new demands on France, he folded up the flags.

De Gaulle elevated prudence and diminished doctrine. This had the advantage of flexibility, but the disadvantage of lacking clarity about basic principles. De Gaulle was obviously a conservative, but he never attempted to form a conservative political party. Yet inevitably he created a 'party.' His successors to that 'Gaulliste' party could justify their departures from de Gaulle's policies on the grounds of flexibility. But what they in fact did was weaken the position of Bonapartisme and its nationally focused objectives, and concede more and more of their basic principles to Orléanisme. Once the Orléaniste Giscard D'Estaing won the Presidency in 1974, liberalism began to dominate and define the right. He initiated a new era of European liberalism. This version of liberalism merged with a moralised philosophy of history that took its bearings from two historical forces.

First, it argued that the Second World War demanded deeper economic and political integration in Europe; this moral demand for liberalism merged with an historicist argument about the necessity of economic interdependence. This vision of European integration was not de Gaulle's, and in the 1960s, this project appeared to have lost the debate. But after de Gaulle died federalisation too slowly revived, to create the illusion that there was a political consensus around a single ideal of European federalisation since 1945 (to foster that illusion, the 1992 Maastricht Treaty took the 1957 Treaty of Rome, the 'Treaty on the European Economic Community,' and retroactively renamed it the 'Treaty on the European Community'; then in 2007 the Lisbon Treaty again retroactively renamed it the 'Treaty on the Functioning of the European Union.')

To stand against the tide of integration, liberalism argued, was to be on the wrong side of history, and to flirt with the ideologies that had reputedly brought about the First and Second World War. The catchphrase became '*nationalisme, c'est la guerre*', and the political class would nod sagely, pushing European federalisation more and more aggressively.

Second, liberalism elevated May 1968 as an event impelling the start of a new epoch, with more and more social liberalisation. Giscard d'Estaing observed that going back to the situation before May 1968 would only reproduce the circumstances that gave rise to May 1968. In some sense he was correct; one could not turn back the clock. But this became the kind of argument that justified attacking all social practices that offered restraints on individual actions. It became a reason for deepening liberalism within France.

Giscard d'Estaing began the trend that supported deeper European integration, permitting Brussels to make laws and regulations promoting individual autonomy, particularly freedom of mobility. It was Giscard d'Estaing who changed immigration laws so that family members of immigrants could also immigrate into France. Second, he and his successors were pour 68, defending a permissive social culture. Giscard d'Estaing legalised abortion and lowered the age of consent.

Third, he and his successors were anti-légitimiste. Whenever political ideas had a whiff of the old national unity conservatism, the political class gestured frantically toward Jean-Marie Le Pen and associated conservatism with the simplified conclusion about Vichy: racism, fascism, and Nazism. It became steadily clear from the 1980s that Orléanisme ruled France. As Pierre Manent has argued in 'Populist Demagoguery and the Fanaticism of the Centre,' these positions steadily became constitutive of the French right--and the French left--in the 1970s and 80s.

When the Gaulliste party returned to power under Jacques Chirac, opportunism replaced conservatism. Chirac intensified support for federalisation and backed the Maastricht Treaty. When his 2005 effort to win a referendum on a constitution for the European Union was met with a decisive defeat, he defied de Gaulle's precedent and stayed in power. While Chirac maintained the Bonapartiste rhetoric, his Orléaniste practice increasingly dismayed the Gaulliste party's base, and provoked the steady drift of conservative voters toward the Front National (FN).

Nicolas Sarkozy tried to save the right by running against Chirac's legacy. Deploying the *ligne Buisson* strategy of appealing to conservative voters of both the Gaulliste party and the FN, Sarkozy achieved an impressive first-round performance of 30% support, not seen since the 1980s. However, his eccentric Presidential style, combined with his support for the repackaging of the EU constitution as the 'Lisbon Treaty' and for EU-imposed austerity, doomed him to defeat against François Hollande. In 2017, François Fillon made moves to imitate Sarkozy's strategy, but he preferred to talk about economics and his political position was much weaker. He never outpaced support for Marine Le Pen, and well before the 'Penelopegate' scandal struck, it was easy for voters to be cynical of his intentions – Fillon had served in both Chirac's and Sarkozy's governments.

Macron grasped that since the 1990s, the right's only real political agenda was Orléaniste. Thus he could dispense with the right's conservatism, ignore both political parties and their baggage, and run as a straightforward Orléaniste—just as Giscard d'Estaing did in the 1970s. At the same time, Macron understood that the eccentric Presidential style of Sarkozy – compounded under Hollande – ran against the Bonapartiste constitution of the Fifth Republic, and was partially responsible for their unpopularity. So he, the new 'Jupiter,' restored the Bonapartiste rhetoric. But this was a rhetoric displaced from Bonapartisme itself. Macron's agenda is Orléaniste, and he makes no effort to conceal it—which provoked the massive *Gilets Jaunes* protests of 2018.

Macron's brazen Orléanisme, however, has put the right in a difficult position. Since Macron became a frontrunner and President, the Gaulliste party has had great difficulty criticising the economic programme that is the core of his agenda, since it is unclear how their programme would have been different from his. Instead it falls to the far left and Marine Le Pen to articulate a challenge to Macron's economic platform. With Macron's victory, the old Gaulliste coalition between Bonapartisme and Orléanisme is finished. The voters who once supported this coalition are splitting, fairly evenly, into two different camps. As Philippe Raynauld has observed, a characteristic example of the division of the French right lies in the little surveys *Le Figaro* asks its readers. 50% are for Macron, and 50% are against.

This split further fractures the French right. But as history teaches, these fractures are nothing new. In fact it makes clear what the fundamental divisions are on the French right. As in the past, this kind of clarity makes it possible for new alignments and coalitions to emerge—and perhaps most importantly, it teaches the right to beware of false friends. Macron's victory has helped provoke discussions about fundamental questions that were so long set aside because *'Paris vaut bien une messe'*—because gaining power was more important. That epoch is finished. The post-war right, so long fixated on the spectre of légitimisme, has gained an understanding of what its real foe is. In response it can go in search of those principles that de Gaulle practiced but did not define. From the ruins of its demise and defeat, there is hope for renewal and salvation.

Part III
Markets &
Mistakes

'FREE MARKET' MYTHS

Wrongheaded assumptions about the market and the state have captured the political right and cost citizens.

Adam Creighton

Back in that halcyon period before the global financial crisis, when labour and capital were both doing well, the terms 'left' and 'right' more or less meant something.

To be 'on the right' of politics meant supporting the conventional wisdom: lowering taxes on the wealthy, cutting welfare to encourage workforce participation, celebrating the financial services sector, and privatising government assets to boost competition.

To be 'on the left' signalled an affection for identity politics. So convincing had the supposed ideas of the right been that major social democratic parties in the US, UK and Australia all pretty much adopted its program. The economic debate had shrunk to one of degree not kind.

It was a simpler world, abruptly ended by the financial crisis in 2008.

The left is still besotted with identity politics (its elites now do quite well out of the status quo), but confusion reigns for the right. State support for the financial sector made a mockery of its free market stance. The reality turned out to be unforgiving competition for the many, and institutionalised socialism for the elites.

A new economic era seems to have emerged since 2008: wage stagnation, anger at banks, and declining respect for major political parties and the institutions of democracy and business.

Perhaps some of this isn't justified. Living standards and incomes have continued to improve for most people, as the Productivity Commission recently noted. Statistical agencies increasingly struggle to incorporate the burgeoning array of goods and services, and their rapid improvement in quality, into quality of life indices.

But perceptions matter more ultimately for politics. Credit Suisse's annual wealth report shows the share of the world's wealth owned by the top 1 per cent of households increased from 44 per cent in 2008 to over 50 per cent in 2017. The number of millionaires (in US dollars) in Australia is poised to jump from 1.2 million this year to 1.7 million by 2022, the biggest percentage jump among 23 countries in the report. Much of that arises from increases in asset prices, rather than individual effort or innovation.

Meanwhile, the bottom third of households — about five million families — had less wealth in 2018 than in 2009, according to the ABS biennial survey of income and wealth, even if the average had risen 20 per cent At the same time, particularly for men, the economy is generating fewer of the stable, reasonably paid jobs in the mining, manufacturing and agricultural sectors that perhaps bestowed more dignity than, for instance, delivering meals on a bicycle to rich people.

The dramatic shift away from repetitive, simple jobs to those entailing more human interaction has sapped men's satisfaction with their lives, according to a recent study by economists Greg Kaplan and Sam Schulhofer-Wohl from the University of Chicago and the US Federal Reserve.

It is also failing to generate enough jobs full stop. Surveys from June 2019 showed more than 159,000 jobs were being advertised around Australia, yet 712,000 Australian were officially unemployed and a further 1.2 million didn't have a job but said they would like one.

The public are not angry about inequality per se, but rather with an economic system that appears to be allocating extreme rewards to small groups that bears little relationship with the intrinsic contribution of those groups. Senator Pauline Hanson was right, for instance, to question the salary of the ABC managing director, which was almost $1 million.

But that's just one example of a phenomenon that extends throughout the public sector, where eye-popping salaries are the norm, easily outstripping those offered in other countries with equally high costs of living.

The author Nassim Taleb in his recent book *Skin in The Game* explains how this is the sort of inequality voters loathe, where the subject 'appears to be just a person like you, except that he has been playing the system, and getting himself into rent-seeking, acquiring privileges that are not warranted, and although he has something you would not mind having (maybe a Russian girlfriend), you cannot possibly become a fan. This category includes bankers, bureaucrats who get rich, former senators shilling for [evil firms] and clean-shaven chief executives who wear ties'. In effect, this includes the proliferating managerial class who are paid increasingly extraordinary sums for overseeing large corporations with little real personal risks.

The quickest way to wealth in Australia is to join the swollen ranks of the political, financial and managerial class, who support each other despite feigned disagreement. For all the gnashing of teeth about the findings of the royal commission, reforms that actually affect the sector's revenues in a meaningful way haven't emerged. Indeed, despite the biggest global financial crisis since the 1930s in 2008 and after, regulation of banks barely changed, their political power and size in fact increased.

If the right wants to remain electorally appealing, it must recognise that a lot of what it championed before the crisis were not genuinely free markets, but rent-seeking by corporations with considerable monopoly power, enjoying significant implicit or explicit state subsidies. Support for free markets isn't meant to be knee-jerk defence of the rich.

Unfortunately, there's a real risk voters blame 'free markets' or 'capitalism' for developments they instinctively recoil from, be it what happened in the financial crisis, the royal commission findings, or conspicuous gouging by privatised airports and electricity providers.

In the rest of this chapter I want to focus on three areas where people on the right, in my view, need to go back to the drawing board.

The Corporate Veil

For-profit, limited liability companies are not the embodiment of the free market. In fact, limited liability companies are a gift and construction of government.

Companies emerged in the 18th century to promote risky

ventures whose success could bring wider benefits. Companies allowed a pooling of capital on an unprecedented scale, and the easy trading of ownership on the stock market. The limited liability that went with them — the guarantee owners could only lose what they put in, creditors having recourse only to the company's assets — encouraged risk-taking that could ultimately benefit everyone.

Columbia University president Nicholas Butler famously said in a 1911 speech that the limited liability corporation was the greatest single discovery of modern times. 'Even steam and electricity are far less important,' he insisted.

Until recently they had been a boon for western civilisation, although it is less clear now. The larger they become, the more important it is for their managers to exercise prudence and restraint, especially in the banking sector where limited liability for shareholders, and zero liability for bankers, has caused great harm. Adam Smith himself highlighted serious problems with companies in 1776, when he observed the behaviour of the East India Company's management first hand:

> being the managers rather of other people's money than of their own, it cannot well be expected that they should watch over it with the same anxious vigilance with which the partners in a private partnership frequently watch over their own. ... Negligence and profusion, therefore, must prevail, more or less, in the management of the affairs of such a company.

The severance of ownership from control by way of a legal fiction encourages waste just as much as it does when the government is spending other peoples' money. In fact, the waste is perhaps even greater in large companies because there is less accountability than in government. There is little moral dimension in the expenditure of shareholders' funds – witness the extravagance of boards and senior managers. Whereas the misuse of a few hundred dollars of taxpayers' funds by an MP or civil servants would probably destroy their career.

The artificial nature of companies extends to the rules that govern them, in Australia *The Corporations Act 2001*. The Act mandates that a company has the legal capacity and powers of an individual, reflecting legal principles going back more than a century.

Because the very existence of private companies depends on an act of parliament, in this sense, governments have the right to set whatever rules they deem politically and economically expedient. From rules related to salaries, to board composition. Don't like the rules? Be a sole trader or a partnership.

The explosion of companies has gone way beyond what's socially and economically useful. The number of companies has increased by 70 per cent to 914,000 over the 20 years to 2015, while the human population has increased only 28 per cent.

In contrast, the number of public companies (typically listed on stock exchanges) has collapsed by two-thirds to a little more than 9000 in 20 years. The number of companies that are non-profit or co-operatives has fallen to 4,300 from more than 28,000. The big increase has been in private 'micro' companies (those with revenues up to $2 million), of which there are now 707,000, particularly in the financial services sector.

Labor's plan to introduce a 30 per cent tax on trust distributions touched on a bigger and broader problem: the use of artificial structures to avoid tax rather than boost genuine economic activity.

This probably isn't what Butler had in mind. Does anyone seriously think this growth in companies has underpinned genuine innovation? Or isn't simply an exercise in tax avoidance and supporting the so-called professional services industry. Companies don't require roads and schools. But they do need lawyers, accountants and the attention of tax officials, diverting scarce resources away from more productive activities. The number of accountants and solicitors has roughly doubled as a share of Australia's rapidly growing workforce since the late 1980s.

Whatever lawyers might say, companies aren't people; they don't pay tax; they don't innovate. Ultimately, only humans can do these things.

As Smith forewarned, companies pay their executives lavish sums, which are justified by 'market rates', as if any arrangement deserves the 'free market' label if the government isn't directly involved.

The market for executive pay isn't a market in any meaningful sense of the word. Buyers of management services, shareholders, have no practical say in the amounts being paid. In a genuine free market buyers and sellers negotiate on behalf of themselves, and rival buyers and sellers can readily join in. People's own money is being spent.

The wage a corner shop owner pays his assistant is set in a free market. The so-called market for executive pay is anything but. Executives and their boards more generally, the sellers of management services, in effect set their price because the shareholders, the buyers, have no control over the sums paid.

The managerial class that profits from this structure perpetuates the myth that managers possess rare and extreme talents that justify obscene rewards, often by hiring new chief executives from overseas who have no knowledge of Australia or the company they are about to lead. AMP did exactly this in 2018. Remuneration consultants, incentivised to recommend 'above average' pay, add fuel to the fire, and help perpetuate the myth that good managers must cost a fortune.

The idea that the prestige or importance of senior management roles would be enough to motivate a person to carry them out with integrity is now considered laughable. The widespread use of complex short and long term bonus payments tied to financial outcomes tacitly presume money is the only thing that motivates anyone, which might be a narrow view of human nature.

The Banks Really Are That Bad

Perhaps no area of the economy is more poorly understood in Australia than banking. Modern banks are a crucial part of any economy, overseeing the payment system and transforming savings into credit, but they have more in common with government departments than they do with freewheeling engines of innovation.

Banks spend a lot of money trying to convince customers that they are innovative, dynamic and competitive — remember National Australia Bank's 'breaking up' campaign? — but they are all very similar. Their inputs and outputs are money and loans. 'Banks' are legal entities with unique government-sanctioned rights. Their business is to produce and manage sets of contracts and claims — which amount to dots on a computer screen — among depositors, borrowers and governments.

The monetary system is a deliberate choice of the state. The structure of the banking system in advanced countries such as Australia has very little to do with a free market. 'Modern banking is best thought of as a partnership between the government and a group of bankers, which is shaped by the institutions that govern the distribution of power in the political system,' writes Charles Calomiris, a professor of banking at Columbia University (and strong supporter of free markets) in his book *Fragile by Design* (written with Stephen Haber).

Government also limits the number of banks by law, which boosts their profits. Banking licences are licences to create money (as banks simultaneously enter a loan and a deposit on their balance sheet). Banks do not 'lend out deposits' as many mistakenly believe. It's no surprise then that the highest paid jobs are in finance: that's literally where the money is created.

Commissioner Hayne appears to understand this. 'Banks have a special position in the economy. They are licensed under Commonwealth statute ... To carry on any banking business in Australia without authority is an indictable offence. Others can therefore enter the market only with permission... Competition within the banking industry is weak. Barriers to entering the industry are high. To participate in the economy, to participate in everyday life, Australians need a bank account,' he wrote in the interim report.

The government also puts limits on how and what banks can sell (via various consumer credit codes) and it precisely lays out (via the banking regulator) the prudential rules that constrain their balance sheets. Indeed, extraordinarily lax prudential regulation, which permits banks to leverage themselves more than 20 times, ensures very high returns on equity for shareholders, and big bonuses for bankers. Given such slender minimum equity buffers, it also means the tail risk of any crisis sits squarely with the taxpayers.

The Reserve Bank provides banks loans at very cheap rates and the federal government guarantees pretty much all their liabilities — a remarkable combination. If banks can have deposits at the Reserve Bank, why shouldn't ordinary Australians also be able to keep their funds on deposit there?

This close relationship with government creates enormous rents or 'super profits', which aren't eroded by competition. In the same way government departments behave, these rents support a large number of socially useless jobs, like 'chief of staff', innovation officers, agile transformation agents, etc., naturally all with bizarrely-high levels of remuneration. Sociology, not economics, is a better guide to their existence. The roles could vanish without any impact on customers.

To think banks can exist independently of government is a fantasy. Governments look to banks to fund their budget deficits, while banks look to governments to create and enforce the contracts that govern their relationships with depositors and borrowers. The big four banks hold about half the state government bonds and about a quarter of the federal government's, for instance.

Calomiris says 'the property-rights system that structures banking is not a passive response to some efficiency criterion' that has emerged in the free market, but rather the result of political deals and laws. 'These deals are guided by the logic of politics, not the logic of the market,' he writes. Among the world's foremost banking authorities, Calomiris in his book explains how banking has become a honey pot for bankers and a periodic disaster for everyone else.

'When losses are borne by taxpayers, the incentives of stockholders and depositors to discipline bankers are much weaker ... as a result after 1945 banks in the world's most developed economies became more highly leveraged and maintained a smaller amount of low-risk assets,' says Calomiris. Australia's banks have followed this trend, with liabilities about 20 times the value of their equity. Their incentives, to create as much credit as possible to boost revenue and profits, don't necessarily align with what's best for the wider economy. When banks create credit, there are consequences far beyond the lender and borrower.

Banks haven't been especially innovative either, at least in ways that help consumers. Paul Volcker, former chairman of the Federal Reserve, famously said the ATM was about the only useful innovation in finance in a generation. 'I wish that somebody would give me some shred of neutral evidence about the relationship between financial innovation recently and the growth of the economy, just one shred,' he said in 2009, suggesting the bulk of innovation had been about obfuscating and gaming prudential rules to boost bonuses.

Despite significant improvements in digital and mobile technology, Australian banks' fee income from households and businesses rose 10 per cent from 2011 to 2015, to $12.5bn, for instance. In a real free market fees would bear some relationship to the underlying costs, which have decreased due to technological improvements. The new open banking regime, whereby new fintech firms will be able to access bank customers' data, might help bring downward pressure on these fees.

The Coalition's controversial bank levy, which imposes a small tax on the majors' non-deposit liabilities was vigorously resisted by the sector, and laughably branded as an 'attack on free markets' in the financial press. As if anything at all about banking is a free market! It might be the beginning of the end of the comfortable contract between the Australian government and bankers. The levy could be a sign that the negotiated division of spoils created by banking licenses will be rewritten and divided differently.

Apart from Calomiris, readers interested in understanding how banking really works and the incentives that pervade it should read John Kay's masterful *Other People's Money*, which chronicles how a humble, boring industry that used to serve industry for most of the 20th century, transformed into an excrescence that has come to dominate and harm the economy. Mervyn King's equally insightful *The End of Alchemy* proposes practical solutions that would keep the banking system in private hands but dramatically curtail its power and scope to create money.

When 'private' isn't private

Drawing the line where the public sector ends and the private sector begins is a third area where misunderstandings are common. The push to privatise state assets is meant to create competition and lower prices, but has often done the opposite. Electricity prices have been rising, airports are charging passengers more, banks are bigger and more profitable than ever.

While politicians trumpet the high price tags they obtain from selling ports and roads, they play down the impact on their long-term financial position. Asset recycling, a friendlier term than 'privatisation', is all the rage, and it has been a good way to accelerate development. But the assets being swapped by state governments aren't always like-for-like.

In its assessment of the NSW budget in 2018, ratings

agency Moody's pointed out that 'health' and 'education' were earmarked to receive $8bn and $6.4bn, respectively, in capital spending across the forward estimates, funds available from various asset sales including ports and electricity assets. You can bet the financial return on those 'investments' will be zero.

The state has sold electricity poles and wires, ports, land registries and the Snowy Hydro scheme, all of them generating cash to varying degrees, and put the money towards hospitals, schools, roads and trains, which don't. Selling income-earning assets to buy assets that lose money might be costlier in the longer run.

The economy-wide dividend from privatisations, especially natural monopolies such as airports, can be debated if they aren't regulated properly. Is the $4.50 gouge of every passenger who gets a taxi at Sydney airport justified? No wonder Sydney Airport Corporation's share price has soared sevenfold since 2002. Service doesn't appear to have changed much in that time.

In theory, brilliant, unbiased regulators step in to make sure privatised assets purr along, stamping out gouging. Yet the reality isn't like the textbooks. The regulation of the poles and wires, for instance, has been one of the biggest policy failures of the past 20 years, leading to a gold-plating that has ratcheted up power bills. 'Regulation' of the finance sector led to the biggest financial crisis since the 1930s.

It's a little bizarre when governments brag about how much they've sold utilities for because the sale price, obviously, reflects how much the new owners think they can get away with squeezing out of customers.

In fact, there's a greater intellectual case for keeping

things such as airports and land titles offices in state-run hands and selling off swathes of the ABC, which has many viable competitors.

Sometimes it can be better to run essential services cheaply, at cost, leaving consumers with more money to spend in areas where genuine competition can function. Selling the Sydney Harbour Bridge might net a tidy sum for the government but the ensuing massive tolls sure to emerge would throttle commerce.

In the economic sphere never have we been so regulated. Parliaments spew out ever longer reams of regulations every year, from stipulating the amenities at childcare centres to the fraction of our incomes that must be saved for retirement. The superannuation system is a creation of the state, yet it is 'privately managed'.

Government regulations affect construction, competition, corporate governance, insurance and financial services, education, industrial relations, safety, and permeate every facet of commerce. Such pervasive influence would have been unthinkable even 50 years ago.

Every page of regulation upsets the natural economic order somehow, furnishing an implicit subsidy here or there, diverting scarce resources from some alternative use. While not a line item in the national accounts, the defining industry of our era is not mining or health care, but compliance. It is difficult to think of a single transaction that can occur without direct or indirect government influence.

If free market prices and wages are those free of government interference, then it is difficult to find many examples. Public sector pay sets a benchmark, a comfortable floor, against which private companies must compete, for both low and high skilled workers. And it is tough competition given that government, which doesn't have to worry about bankruptcy, typically doesn't lay off staff or cut pay in downturns.

If there are no free market prices because regulation has twisted the free market outcomes so much, what sort of economic system do we have? It's common to say in the West we have a 'free market' system, yet in Australia the government consumes almost 40 per cent of national income, and it's as high as 55 per cent in France.

Trade unions are often considered grit in the wheels of free markets, and they were illegal throughout Europe until the late 19th century, but workers' desire to organise is a natural, even 'free market', impulse. By contrast, as discussed earlier, limited liability companies are creations of government.

Are we prosperous despite or because of this pervasive regulation? I think the level of regulation is too high, but it is dishonest to hold up Western prosperity as the result of free markets when the scope of government broadly defined has reached unprecedented levels and continues to expand. Apologists for communism say we've never tried it; but it's not clear we've tried unfettered free markets either.

The best paid jobs are increasingly ones that game or administer complex regulations, or are in financial services, which is meant to be an intermediary but at 9 per cent of GDP, it has become the largest industry in the economy.

Contractors for government are nominally 'private sector', but if the bulk of their work arises from government, is it really a genuine market, especially if the expenditure is patently wasteful, such as hundreds of millions spent on consultants.

We could have a clearer idea of the damage excessive regulation does if our statistics were more discerning. Gross domestic product, for instance, includes all output equally, but perhaps some are less valuable than others. The costs of compliance, sickness, war, family breakdown, for example, all enter as positive contributions. We might not be as prosperous as it suggests.

Conclusion

The alliance between government and business is vast and underappreciated. Too often 'free market' businesses are dependent on government for work or for their position. The idea they are antagonists, the popular view in the media, is false. Big business and regulators need each other to maintain their jobs and incomes. Indeed, much regulation is in the interests of the regulated, as Goldman Sachs chief Lloyd Blankfein explicitly said in the wake of the US Dodd-Frank Act of 2012. Financial regulation was, and despite all the rhetoric to the contrary, lax. Absence of a 'crisis' is hardly evidence of an efficient or reasonable financial system.

Companies are a legal fiction whose original purpose has been lost. Their use has spiralled out of control, and corrupted what's left of the 'free market'. What anthropologist David Graeber has termed 'bullshit jobs' have proliferated. The biggest sector in the economy by far, finance, is in reality an extension of the state. The political settlement propping up banks undermines the assumption that we live in a free market economy. The sale of state assets has angered people when they see prices increase and top managers on huge bonuses with little appreciable improvement in services (or actually diminution, in the case of Sydney airport).

The right's championing of big business and regulated monopolies rather than genuine competition has undermined its appeal and its integrity.

THE REAL ADAM SMITH[1]

*Labelling him the poster boy for free-market economics
distorts what Adam Smith really thought.*

Paul Sagar

If you've heard of one economist, it's likely to be Adam
Smith. He's the best-known of all economists, and is typically hailed as the founding father of the dismal science
itself.

Furthermore, he's usually portrayed as not only an early champion of economic theory, but of the superiority
of markets over government planning. In other words,
Smith is now known both as the founder of economics,
and as an ideologue for the political Right.

Yet, despite being widely believed, both these claims are
at best misleading, and at worst outright false.

Smith's popular reputation as an economist is a remarkable twist of fate for a man who spent most of his life as a
somewhat reclusive academic thinker. Employed as professor of moral philosophy at the University of Glasgow,

---

[1]   This essay was originally published in Aeon: aeon.co.

the majority of Smith's teaching was in ethics, politics, jurisprudence and rhetoric, and for most of his career he was known for his first book, *The Theory of Moral Sentiments* (1759). His professional identity was firmly that of a philosopher – not least because the discipline of 'economics' didn't emerge until the 19th century, by which time Smith was long dead. (He died in July 1790, just as the French Revolution was getting into full swing.)

Admittedly, Smith's reputation as an economist isn't entirely mysterious. His oft-quoted *An Inquiry into the Nature and Causes of the Wealth of Nations* (1776) was undoubtedly important in the eventual formation – in the next century – of the discipline of economics. But even here things are not as straightforward as they appear. For *The Wealth of Nations* – a 1,000-page doorstopper that blends history, ethics, psychology and political philosophy – bears little resemblance to the ahistorical and highly mathematical nature of most current economic theory. If anything, Smith's best-known book is a work of political economy, a once-prevalent field of enquiry that suffered a striking decline in the latter half of the 20th century.

Smith's reputation, however, began to get away from him early on. Shortly after publication, *The Wealth of Nations* was fêted in the British Parliament by the Whig leader Charles James Fox. Ironically, Fox later admitted that he had never actually read it (few subsequent non-readers of the book have showed such candour, despite plenty of them citing it). Indeed, Smith suspected that those quickest to sing his praises had failed to understand the main arguments of his work. He later described *The Wealth of Nations* as a 'very violent attack ... upon the whole commercial system of Great Britain'. Despite this, his vocal political cheerleaders in Parliament continued to prop up the very system that Smith was railing against.

Yet if Smith was disappointed by his work's immediate reception, he would likely have taken even less cheer from the future uses to which his name would be put. For it has been his fate to become associated with the strain of Right-wing politics that rose to dominance in the early 1980s, and which continues to exert a strong influence on politics and economics today. Usually known as neoliberalism, this development is most famously associated with Ronald Reagan and Margaret Thatcher. But it is in fact a movement with deep intellectual roots, in particular in the mid-century writings of the economists Friedrich Hayek and Ludwig von Mises. Later, the Chicago economist Milton Friedman and the British policy adviser Keith Joseph championed it during the 1980s, as did the extensive network of academics, think tanks, business leaders and policymakers associated with the Mont Pelerin Society.

Neoliberals often invoke Smith's name, believing him to be an early champion of private capitalist endeavour, and a founder of the movement that seeks (as Thatcher hoped) to 'roll back the frontiers of the state' so as to allow the market to flourish. The fact that there is a prominent Right-wing British think tank called the Adam Smith Institute – which since the 1970s has aggressively pushed for market-led reforms, and in 2016 officially rebranded itself a 'neoliberal' organisation – is just one example of this tendency.

It is certainly true that there are similarities between what Smith called 'the system of natural liberty', and more recent calls for the state to make way for the free market. But if we dig below the surface, what emerges most strikingly are the differences between Smith's subtle, skeptical view of the role of markets in a free society, and more recent caricatures of him as a free-market fundamentalist avant-la-lettre. For while Smith might be publicly lauded by those who put their faith in private capitalist enterprise, and who decry the state as the chief threat to liberty and prosperity, the real Adam Smith painted a rather different picture. According to Smith, the most pressing dangers came not from the state acting alone, but the state when captured by merchant elites.

The context of Smith's intervention in *The Wealth of Nations* was what he called 'the mercantile system'. By this Smith meant the network of monopolies that characterised the economic affairs of early modern Europe. Under such arrangements, private companies lobbied governments for the right to operate exclusive trade routes, or to be the only importers or exporters of goods, while closed guilds controlled the flow of products and employment within domestic markets.

As a result, Smith argued, ordinary people were forced to accept inflated prices for shoddy goods, and their employment was at the mercy of cabals of bosses. Smith saw this as a monstrous affront to liberty, and a pernicious restriction on the capacity of each nation to increase its collective wealth. Yet the mercantile system benefited the merchant elites, who had worked hard to keep it in place. Smith pulled no punches in his assessment of the bosses as working against the interests of the public. As he put it in *The Wealth of Nations*: 'People of the same trade seldom meet together, even for merriment and diversion but the conversation ends in a conspiracy against the public, or in some contrivance to raise prices.'

The merchants had spent centuries securing their position of unfair advantage. In particular, they had invented and propagated the doctrine of 'the balance of trade', and had succeeded in elevating it into the received wisdom of the age. The basic idea was that each nation's wealth consisted in the amount of gold that it held. Playing on this idea, the merchants claimed that, in order to get rich, a nation had to export as much, and import as little, as possible, thus maintaining a 'favourable' balance. They then presented themselves as servants of the public by offering to run state-backed monopolies that would limit the inflow, and maximise the outflow, of goods, and therefore of gold. But as Smith's lengthy analysis showed, this was pure hokum: what were needed instead were open trading arrangements, so that productivity could increase generally, and collective wealth would grow for the benefit of all.

Even worse than this, Smith thought, the merchants were the source of what his friend, the philosopher and historian David Hume, had called 'jealousy of trade'. This was the phenomenon whereby commerce was turned into an instrument of war, rather than the bond of 'union and friendship' between states that it ought properly to be. By playing on jingoistic sentiments, the merchants inflamed aggressive nationalism, and blinded domestic populations to the fact that their true interests lay in forming peaceful trading relationships with their neighbours.

The peace and stability of the European continent was imperilled by the conspiracies of the merchants, who goaded politicians into fighting wars to protect home markets, or acquire foreign ones. After all, being granted militarily-backed private monopolies was far easier than having to compete on the open market by lowering prices and improving quality. The merchants in this manner constantly conspired to capture the state, defrauding the public by using political power to promote their own sectional advantage.

Indeed, Smith's single most famous idea – that of 'the invisible hand' as a metaphor for uncoordinated market allocation – was invoked in precisely the context of his blistering attack on the merchant elites. It is certainly true that Smith was skeptical of politicians' attempts to interfere with, or bypass, basic market processes, in the vain hope of trying to do a better job of allocating resources than was achievable through allowing the market to do its work. But in the passage of *The Wealth of Nations* where he invoked the idea of the invisible hand, the immediate context was not simply that of state intervention in general, but of state intervention undertaken at the behest of merchant elites who were furthering their own interests at the expense of the public.

It is an irony of history that Smith's most famous idea is now usually invoked as a defence of unregulated markets in the face of state interference, so as to protect the interests of private capitalists. For this is roughly the opposite of Smith's original intention, which was to advocate for restrictions on what groups of merchants could do. When he argued that markets worked remarkably efficiently – because, although each individual 'intends only his own gain, and he is in this, as in many other cases, led by an invisible hand to promote an end which was no part of his intention' – this was an appeal to free individuals from the constraints imposed upon them by the monopolies that the merchants had established, and were using state power to uphold. The invisible hand was originally invoked not to draw attention to the problem of state intervention, but of state capture.

Smith was, however, deeply pessimistic about the stranglehold that the merchants had managed to exert over European politics, and despaired of it ever being loosened. Accordingly, he labelled his preferred alternative – of liberal markets generating wealth to be passed on to all members of society – a 'Utopia' that would never come to pass. History has to some extent proved him wrong on this score: we now live in an era of comparative market freedom. But nobody should deny that merchant conspiracy, and the marriage of the state to what we now call corporate power, remain defining features of our present-day political and economic reality.

In any case, Smith's hostility to the merchants is a long way removed from a Reagan-style championing of the entrepreneurial capitalist hero, she who needs only to be released from the constraints of the state to lead us to the sunlit uplands of economic growth. On the contrary, Smith's analysis implies that a free society with a healthy economy is going to need to put fetters on economic elites if the invisible hand is to have any chance of doing its paradoxical work.

Does this, then, make Smith an early proponent of the political Left? No, and it would be a serious mistake to draw that conclusion. The truth is both more complex, and more interesting, than that.

Although Smith was deeply critical of the way that the merchants conspired to promote their own advantage at the expense of the rest of society, he was under no illusion that political actors might successfully replace private merchants as the necessary conduits of economic activity.

Certainly, when merchants were allowed to rule as sovereigns – as the British East India Company had been permitted to do in Bengal – the results were disastrous. 'Want, famine and mortality', themselves the results of 'tyranny' and 'calamity', had been unleashed on India, all products of an 'oppressive authority' based on force and injustice. Under absolutely no circumstances, Smith thought, should merchants be put in charge of politics. Their monopolistic conspiracies would be 'destructive' to all countries 'which have the misfortune to fall under their government'.

Nonetheless, something like the reverse was also true: politicians made for terrible merchants, and ought not to attempt to take over the systematic running of economic affairs. This was a product of the structural predicament faced by political leaders, whom Smith claimed have 'scarce ever succeeded' in becoming 'adventurers in the common branches of trade', despite often having been tempted to try, and often from a genuine desire to better their nation's condition.

Politicians, according to Smith, were much poorer judges of where and how to allocate resources than the aggregated outcome of individuals spontaneously undertaking free exchange. As a result, in matters of trade it was usually folly for politicians to try to replace the vast network of buyers and sellers with any form of centralised command. This, however, included precisely those networks structured around the profit-seeking activities of merchant elites.

On Smith's final analysis, the merchants were a potentially pernicious, but entirely necessary, part of the functioning of large-scale economies. The true 'science of a statesman or legislator' consisted in deciding how best to govern the merchants' nefarious activities. Effective politicians had to strike a balance between granting economic elites the liberty to pursue legitimate commercial activities, while also applying control when such activities became vehicles for exploitation. In other words, Smith was very far from asking us to put our faith in 'entrepreneurs', those supposed 'wealth-creators' whom neoliberalism looks to as drivers of economic prosperity. On the contrary, giving the entrepreneurs free reign would be rather like putting the foxes in charge of the chicken coup.

Crucially, however, Smith did not offer up any kind of premeditated plan regarding how to strike the right balance between commercial freedom and watchful political control. On the contrary, he pressed home the deep underlying difficulties of the situation that commercial societies found themselves in.

Political actors, Smith claimed, were liable to be swept up by a 'spirit of system', which made them fall in love with abstract plans, which they hoped would introduce sweeping beneficial reform. Usually the motivations behind these plans were perfectly noble: a genuine desire to improve society. The problem, however, was that the 'spirit of system' blinded individuals to the harsh complexities of real-world change. As Smith put it in *The Theory of Moral Sentiments* in one of his most evocative passages:

> [The man of system] seems to imagine that he can arrange the different members of a great society with as much ease as the hand arranges the different pieces upon a chessboard. He does not consider that the pieces upon the chessboard have no other principle of motion besides that which the hand impresses upon them; but that, in the great chessboard of human society, every single piece has a principle of motion of its own, altogether different from that which the legislature might choose to impress upon it. If those two principles coincide and act in the same direction, the game of human society will go on easily and harmoniously, and is very likely to be happy and successful. If they are opposite or different, the game will go on miserably, and the society must be at all times in the highest degree of disorder.

Smith's point is easily misunderstood. At first glance, it can look like a modern Right-wing injunction against socialist-style state planning. But it is much more subtle than that.

What Smith is saying is that in politics any preconceived

plan – especially one that assumes that the millions of individuals composing a society will just automatically go along with it – is potentially dangerous. This is because the 'spirit of system' infects politicians with a messianic moral certainty that their reforms are so necessary and justified that almost any price is worth paying to achieve them.

Yet it is a short step from this to discounting the very real harm that a plan can unleash if it starts to go wrong – and especially if the 'pieces upon the chessboard' act in ways that resist, or subvert, or confound, the politician's scheme. This is because the 'spirit of system' encourages the sort of attitude captured in such cheap sayings as 'You can't make an omelette without breaking eggs'. In other words, that inconvenient opponents and bystanders can be sacrificed to an overriding moral vision.

Smith was warning against all abstract plans alike. Certainly, his outlook urges skepticism about such strategies as taking over the industrial base of a state, presuming to know what goods citizens will want and need over the next five years, and thereby trying to eliminate the market as a mechanism for resource allocation. But it likewise views with deep suspicion a plan to rapidly privatise previously state-owned industries, exposing millions of citizens to the ravages of unemployment and the attendant destruction of their communities. In other words, while she certainly didn't realise it, Thatcher's violent restructuring of the British economy during the 1980s was as much a product of the 'spirit of system' as any piece of top-down Soviet industrial strategy.

The message that Smith conveys cuts across party and ideological lines, and applies to both Left and Right. It is about a pathological attitude that politicians of all stripes are prone to. If not kept in check, this can be the source not just of disruption and inefficiency but of cruelty and suffering, when those who find themselves on the wrong side of the plan's consequences are forced by the powerful to suffer them regardless. Smith in turn urges us to recognise that real-world politics will always be too complex for any prepackaged ideology to cope with. What we need in our politicians is careful judgment and moral maturity, something that no ideology, nor any position on the political spectrum, holds a monopoly on.

In the fraught times that we now occupy, it is hard to believe that the careful and responsible political judges that Smith envisaged have much chance of emerging. (Does anybody in Western politics currently measure up?) Much more likely will be new men and women of system, with alternative abstract plans, seducing desperate electorates before attempting to impose their own forceful reforms, regardless of what the pieces on the chessboard happen to think or want.

Whether these reforms come from the Left or the Right might not, in the end, matter much. As Western economies continue to struggle, and politics becomes increasingly polarised, the results could yet be catastrophic. But if so, we should certainly not consign Smith to any parade of blame. On the contrary, he tried to warn us of the dangers that we face. It is time that we listened, a little more carefully, to what the real Adam Smith had to say.

Part IV.
God, Beauty
& Virtue

BEAUTY AND THE WEST

Modern conservatism imperfectly recalls a wisdom far more ancient.

James Matthew Wilson

Every intellectual tradition, and the disposition or sensibility that comes into being through it, consists of an unstable mixture of remembering and forgetting.[1] This was true of the conservatism of Burke, and no less true of that of the great lights of modern intellectual conservatism, including John Henry Newman, T.S. Eliot, and Russell Kirk. The flourishing of a tradition depends not, therefore, on whether *any* elements of it have in some way been forgotten, for they always will have been, but rather on the particular kind of forgetting.

I propose that the particular Enlightenment age in which conservatism first appeared was one unpropitious to a proper kind of remembering. If conservatism affirmed

---

[1]   'On Poetic Traditions: T.S. Eliot, Alasdair MacIntyre, and the Practice of Reason,' in *Communio* 44.4 (Winter 2017): 747-786.

great truths and defended genuine goods as its ends, such 'orthodoxy' was typically defended by heterodox means; men of good conscience defended sound conclusions by unsound arguments.[2] Conservatism, from the beginning, had a philosophical basis inadequate to vindicate the insights about man and the universal and political order it nonetheless continued to profess against the rising tide of liberalism.

This forgetting proved of long term consequence particularly for conservatism's understanding of human nature. The hard-won insights of the ancients about what it means to be a person, specifically as one outfitted by nature to the contemplation of being as a beautiful order, was retained in principle by modern conservative thought, but also distorted in its interior contents or meaning. This smudging out of the meaning of beauty has, in time, led to an obscuring of our understanding of human nature. Conservatism is a disposition to defend the truth about human beings and the political order that makes a decent life possible. This can hardly be done if sound judgments are untethered from the reasoning that first arrived at them; principles become platitudes, conclusions mere items of dogma, convictions mere assertions, drained of the understanding that can make them fully compelling and which could justify their role in our political life.

In the reflection that follows, I want to consider, first, the particular combination of remembering and misremembering we find in the conservative tradition. I shall then turn, second, to the misremembering involved in modern conservative thinking on the relation of beauty to being and its role in the formation of the human person. Our

---

[2]   An instance where this was done consciously, if a bit clumsily, would be John Crowe Ransom's *God without Thunder: An Unorthodox Defense of Orthodoxy* (Harcourt, Brace and Company, 1930).

age, having seen the partial success and final failure of the conservative response to the ideologies of liberalism, requires not that we abandon the general goods to which conservatives have historically been devoted. Rather, it requires that we remember the philosophical basis that once lay behind the conception of those goods.

It will become clear in what follows that I believe conservatism, from Burke onward, ceded too much to the impoverished philosophical vision of the modern age, thereby depriving itself of the genuinely permanent insights of the classical, or what I shall call the Christian-Platonist, tradition. Under a third heading, then, I shall summarize the chief claims of that tradition, before, fourth, arguing for a renewed philosophical and political commitment to a non-liberal, genuine vision of personhood that understands human dignity in light of our capacity to contemplate being's beauty, what Plato called the Good, and what Christians know to be the very light or splendor of God.

With the full strength of that tradition behind us, we can better understand what it means to be human and what goods our intellectual, social, and political order ought to pursue if we are to live—as we are called—in a communion of persons, rather than, as it were, in a petri dish merely containing innumerable, atomized individuals subject to their private, flagellating wills. That tradition, in brief, tells us that human beings, as persons, are ordered, as their good, to the contemplation of the beauty of being, which forms the world but also transcends the world. Whereas liberalism, following Thomas Hobbes, sought to evade every reference to goodness as anything other than the ever-varying object of one's private will, the Christian-Platonist tradition gives us reason to see that the Good orders all things and that political life is the preparation for the human person to become capable of contemplation of the Good in the fullness of its light, that is to say, its beauty.[3]

Decadence and Remembering

Russell Kirk used to quote the English Christian socialist C.E.M. Joad by saying that 'decadence' was the 'loss,'
or forgetting, of the 'object.'[4] Joad's meaning was quite
specific: when man misreads 'his position in the universe'
and fails 'to acknowledge the non-human elements of
value and deity to which the human is subject,' man has
lapsed into decadence.[5] Kirk's use was more general; decadence was any condition in which a cultural practice or
way of life ceased to be ordered to its proper end.

Conservatives, from Burke to Kirk, have sought to recall
man to the proper ends of human life. In doing so, however, their efforts have often suffered from a distinct but
related kind of forgetting. They may recall human beings,
and society as a whole, to their proper ends, but they have
done so without properly expressing the reasons for those
ends. Like Immanuel Kant, on Alasdair MacIntyre's account of him, they saw the goodness of some principle or
maxim, and then proceeded to fill in beneath it poor rational arguments in favor of its truth.[6] This is another sort
of decadence, one in which we may continue to affirm the
goods at which our activities aim—in that sense we know

---

[3]   Cf. Remi Brague, 'The Necessity of the Good,' *First
      Things* 250 (February 2015): 47-52. My language here
      has vacillated between the good and the beautiful, but
      it will become clear that Christian-Platonism accords a
      certain ultimacy to beauty as the splendor or excess that
      makes truth and goodness ends in themselves in which
      the mind may rest in contemplation.

[4]   Bradley J. Birzer, *Russell Kirk: American Conservative*
      (Lexington, KY: University Press of Kentucky, 2015), 397.

[5]   Ibid.

[6]   Alasdair MacIntyre, *After Virtue* 3rd Edition (Notre Dame,
      IN: University of Notre Dame Press, 2007), 46-50.

why we act, we know our ends—but where we have ceased to understand how we determined or came to understand those goods *as good* in the first place: we lose an interior sense of *why* our ends are what they are.

Eliot recalls both these forms of decadence in his Choruses from *The Rock,* when the Seventh Chorus recounts the rise of human civilization as the story of man's search for God, and God's search for man. Lamenting the present age of secular liberalism, the Chorus states,

> But it seems that something has happened that has
> never happened before: though we know not just
> when, or why, or how, or where.
>
> Men have left GOD not for other gods, they say, but for
> no god; and this has never happened before
>
> That men both deny gods and worship gods, profess-
> ing first Reason,
>
> And then Money, and Power, and what they call Life,
> or Race, or Dialectic.[7]

The Chorus's potted account interprets history specifically as the coming together of God and man, whose fulfillment is realized in the Incarnation, the coming of Christ into the world. Our age, idling on two thousand years afterward, has become decadent insofar as it has lost its proper end—union with God—and so flails about ignorantly searching for other objects to fill in for the true one that has been lost.

Eliot's claim that men 'deny gods' and yet end up worshipping new ones, however unacknowledged, by default, is perceptive, but not as perceptive as an observation made earlier in the same Chorus. Of late antique religions, Eliot

---

7   T.S. Eliot, *The Poems* Vol. 1 (Christopher Ricks and Jim
      McCue, eds. Baltimore: Johns Hopkins UP, 2015), 169.

writes,

> But their light was ever surrounded and shot with
> darkness
>
> As the air of temperate seas is pierced by the still dead
> breath of the Arctic Current;
>
> And they came to an end, a dead end stirred with a
> flicker of life,
>
> And they came to the withered ancient look of a child
> that has died of starvation.
>
> Prayer wheels, worship of the dead, denial of this
> world, affirmation of rites with forgotten mean-
> ings.[8]

Here is another decadence, another 'withering,' of what once had flourished. The forms and actions of civilization persist, the object has not been lost sight of, but the meaning of it has been eviscerated or become opaque to those who nevertheless persist in the observance.

MacIntyre discusses his form of decadence with reference to the Polynesian idea of taboo:

> taboo rules often and perhaps characteristically have a history which falls into two stages. In the first stage they are embedded in a context which confers intelligibility upon them . . . Deprive the taboo rules of their original context and they at once are apt to appear as a set of arbitrary prohibitions, as indeed they characteristically do appear when the initial context is lost, when those background beliefs in the light of which the taboo rules had originally been understood have not only been abandoned but forgotten.[9]

By its very definition, conservatism comes into being as

---

[8]   Eliot, 168.

[9]   MacIntyre, 112.

a reaction *against* a loss of the object threatened by the rise of liberal or leftist ideologies; it is always a movement against forces of dissolution and decadence. But, as often as not, in its effort to shore up a vision of what is good and the order that follows from it, in its effort to recall us to some good, it nonetheless forgets the meaning, the interior reason, that explains or justifies that good as good.

What is worse, in defending a position that a tradition has previously arrived at by one pathway, it often adopts the assumptions, the philosophical framework, and arguments that initially gave rise to the doctrines of the left. The good, as understood by a non-liberal tradition, cannot be adequately defended by means of liberal premises. Conservatism, I am proposing, has typically defended what is good, but has done so from an impoverished philosophical framework. It recalls the *end*, but not the *why*. It would compel us to accept its conclusions as true, but argues for them by means external and alien to the tradition of reasoning that first drew those conclusions and, generally, does so by means of shoddy equipment that is unlikely to prove compelling.

This, of course, has further consequences. Affirming an end, but failing to explain adequately and coherently why it should be *our* end, will in short order and often invisibly transform a tradition of reasoning and argument such that it itself becomes incoherent to those who live within it. To be in such a condition is to be like Eliot's practitioners of traditional religions, who observe the rites, but now lack the tradition of reasoning necessary if they are to remain intelligible, their meaning still to be understood.

One senses this kind of decadence from Year One of the conservative resistance to the new world being brought into being by the liberalism of the French Revolution. Burke seems to be inventing his political philosophy as he composes his letter to Depont. That is not quite what he is doing; he is drawing extensively on English constitutional theory and on whatever information is available to his wide-ranging intelligence, but he synthesizes this all, by the way, with moral theories of sentiment and sensation that not only were products of his Enlightenment age, but which had themselves helped lead to the rise of the intellectuals behind the Revolution. If, as J.C.D. Clark argues, most of his arguments 'were eighteenth-century commonplaces' marshalled in favor of institutions far older and more mysterious in historical origin, we may expect the rhetoric, however rich, to seem a bit like a foreign imposition on a native body.[10] At their heights, we may justly contrast Burke and Jean-Jacques Rousseau, for instance, but I think we should find them a bit tangled at their roots.

This bricolage of intellectual resources is uneven and only as coherent as the occasion allowed, which explains in part why Burke has been subject to such a wide range of interpretations over the centuries, and why the adoption of him as the founding figure of modern conservatism is a relatively belated, various, and unsatisfactory phenomenon.[11] Eliot defined conservatism as 'a fusion of Tory and Whig elements, due largely to the effect of the French Revolution upon the mind of Burke,' and he certainly was correct in referring to assorted elements, though not quite as just in proposing they ever became wholly fused into a coherent whole.[12]

---

[10] Edmund Burke, *Reflections on the Revolution in France* (J.C.D. Clark, ed. Stanford: Stanford University Press, 2001), 85.

[11] See, Burke, *Reflections on the Revolution in France*, 105-111

[12] T.S. Eliot, *To Criticize the Critic* (New York: Farrar, Straus & Giroux, 1965), 138.

Something similar may be said of that superior Burkean mind, John Henry Newman. His many historical investigations of the early Church in order to characterize and crystalize what is properly its *Catholicity*, proceed by several tacks. He is at his finest when simply re-narrating episodes from Church history, though it seems no act of imaginative sympathy will overcome his position as a latter-day outsider straining to look backward and within. He is, in one sense, a weaker guide, when he engages in a philosophical justification for Christian faith itself. In the *Essay in Aid of a Grammar of Assent*, we find great ingenuity and a fascinating, novel account of the psychology of belief and truth. But, it is hard wholly to resist the common criticism that this brilliant defense of religious faith in a rationalist age has not simply begun with the principles of John Locke's rational empiricism and sought to carve out a place for conclusions that predate Locke and at which one would not normally arrive, if beginning from Locke's principles, did one not already have them in mind.[13]

Newman, with the greatness of his mind, must have sensed this weakness. When he came to Rome, as a new convert, he found the intellectual life of the place a 'gloomy' one, asking again and again whether either Aristotle or Aquinas were read, and finding that they were not.[14] And yet, within his lifetime, the neo-Scholastic revival would begin to bear substantial fruit, reestablishing old doctrines in sound reasoning. Could he have found the support he needed from the tradition, he might not have had to improvise with inadequate materials.[15]

---

[13] John Henry Newman, *A Grammar of Assent* (Notre Dame, IN: University of Notre Dame Press, 1979).

[14] Ernest L. Fortin, "Sacred and Inviolable': *Rerum Novarum* and Natural Rights,' *Theological Studies* 53 (1992), 330.

[15] Newman's *University Sermons*, which contain short outlines of nearly all his major ideas, and were written

A great quantity of modern thought seems as if it were shaped by some such compound of conservative moral instinct and special pleading. Burke anticipated the idealism of Immanuel Kant, while Newman followed indirectly upon it, but in all such cases we hear an echo of Kant's, 'I had to deny knowledge in order to make room for faith.'[16] Goods that had once been known—understood in the strict sense of having been seen from their intellectual foundation—could now be defended only as claims of faith.

Because all traditions are, again, unstable compositions of remembering and forgetting, such faith claims could sustain a civilization and for long—but not forever. It is to this, in part, that others refer when they speak of the present age spending the collective social capital of the past. But the capital is now spent. The acidic properties of liberalism have eaten their way through every institution—with some help, if my thesis is correct, from the misremembering arguments of conservatives. Hence, Eliot's despairing defiance, when he hectored an audience of Virginians with the words, 'In a society like ours, worm-eaten with Liberalism, the only thing possible for a person with strong convictions is to state a point of view and leave it at that.'[17] Mere statement will not suffice and never should have; we have rather to remind ourselves why, what was

---

in the years before his conversion, were made 'with no aid from Anglican, and no knowledge of Catholic theologians.' I detect a trace of melancholy in this retrospective statement directed not only at his Anglican training in divinity but the failure of the Church to furnish him with the aid he required (*Fifteen Sermons* (Notre Dame, IN: University of Notre Dame Press, 2003), ix-x).

[16] Immanuel Kant, *Critique of Pure Reason* (Paul Guyer and Allen W. Wood, trans. Cambridge: Cambridge University Press, 2007), 117.

[17] T.S. Eliot, *After Strange Gods: A Primer in Modern Heresy* (New York: Harcourt, Brace and Company, 1934), 12.

once known as good, should still be thought such. And this we can do.

Goods Misremembered

Let us list four claims about man and the good enounced by the conservative figures I have mentioned so far and consider the ways in which they attest to the kind of forgetting I have described as decadence. We shall proceed in reverse chronological order, ending with Burke, whose particular kind of forgetting is in a double sense foundational, as it illustrates conservatism's effort to stand against the rising liberal tide and its susceptibility to that tide. The claims taken together, however, constitute a complete vision, a conservative vision, of man and reality.

The great historical account of conservatism is, of course, Kirk's book, *The Conservative Mind*. In the first chapter, he lists six 'canons of conservative thought,' only the first of which touches on human nature as such. The conservative affirms a

> Belief in a transcendent order, or body of natural law, which rules society as well as conscience. Political problems, at bottom, are religious and moral problems. A narrow rationality, what Coleridge called the Understanding, cannot of itself satisfy human needs . . . True politics is the art of apprehending and applying the Justice which ought to prevail in a community of souls.[18]

I repeat this principle not to dissent from it. Rather, I would simply point out how anodyne is its first sentence; how abstracted from any actual religion is its second; and how dependent on a modern theory of knowledge—that is, specifically, Kant's as interpreted by S.T. Coleridge—

---

[18] Russell Kirk, *The Conservative Mind* Seventh Revised Edition (Washington, D.C.: Regnery Publishing, 2001), 8.

is its argument. In a time when the need to subordinate the individual will to a transcendent, lawful (and therefore rational) order seemed almost a self-evident good, nothing more needed to be said. But, of course, Kirk was not writing in such an age; to the contrary, he was writing during a time when such belief could not be viewed as self-evidently true, but was still generally seen as good, and so, he hoped to shore up desire for that good simply be describing it.

Something similar occurs in a late address of Eliot's on the purpose of education, which culminates as follows:

> I do not suggest for a moment that we should abandon the attempt to define the purpose of education (and the definition of the purpose is an inevitable step from the definition of the word itself). If we see a new and mysterious machine, I think that the first question we ask is, 'What is that machine *for*?' and afterwards we ask, 'How does it do it?' But the moment we ask about the purpose of anything, we may be involving ourselves in asking about the purpose of everything. If we define education, we are led to ask, 'What is Man?'; and if we define the purpose of education, we are committed to the question 'What is Man for?' Every definition of the purpose of education, therefore, implies some concealed, or rather implicit philosophy or theology.[19]

Eliot is conscious here, as he was in the Chorus quoted above, that modern decadence regarding such goods as education can be seen in our continuing to do something whose meaning we have long since forgotten. Everyone shall be schooled, we insist, but we have but little idea what a school should be. Eliot makes this fine insight—education involves the fundamental purpose of man, the *why* implicit in the *what* of human nature—only in the

---

[19] T.S. Eliot, *To Criticize the Critic*, 75.

first of a series of addresses on education. He does not hesitate to suggest that to answer this question involves what Kirk blandly calls a 'transcendent order,' and thus it touches on 'philosophy or theology.' But the lectures that follow never actually answer the question.

Eliot's procedure will be familiar to everyone. In a liberal society, we often warm to talk of 'asking the big questions.' Education is about big questions; life itself is an experiment in living, a sweet mystery that we have the 'right' to define for ourselves. But if you dare to advance a big answer to the big question, if you claim to have some purchase on the mystery, or to have drawn a conclusion on the experiment that binds anyone with the bonds of truth, you are liable to be called a fascist.[20]

Despite the politicized language, this aversion to admitting answers to the 'big questions' is not fundamentally political in nature, nor is it a product of suspicion or skepticism (in which case, merely to claim a question was 'big,' whatever that may mean, would itself be dubious). It is rather a consequence of the modern philosophical turn first taken by Kant and which gave rise to a romantic and liberal vision of human nature. As Jacques Maritain rightly argued nearly a century ago, Kant feared that what we would call judgments of fact regarding the intellectual and spiritual life of human persons would amount to an assault upon human dignity. To say, education serves such-and-such a purpose and man has such-and-such an end appeared, in Kant's view, as if to subordinate the spiritual reality of the mind to the determinate conditions of merely physical forces.[21] The laws of things seemed to

---

[20]   Cf. T.S. Eliot, *Essays Ancient and Modern* (New York: Harcourt, Brace and Company, 1936), 107-108.
[21]   Jacques Maritain, *The Degrees of Knowledge* (Gerald B. Phelan, trans. Notre Dame, IN: University of Notre Dame Press, 1995) 115-116.

impose upon the freedom of spirit.

Eliot senses as much in his lecture, as have so many since him, and so raises questions—which are invitations to freedom—but dares not to pose an answer, which would seem, on Kant's theory, to conclude and extinguish that same freedom. It would be, in the modern view, illiberal of itself to answer the question.

Eliot came by this honestly, having studied, at Harvard, with the Kantian idealist Josiah Royce and, more importantly, the conservative new humanist, Irving Babbitt.[22] Babbitt's view of education entailed study of the 'classics' without affirmation of the truth of any of them.[23] The positive end of such education remained unstated, but what we might call the negative one, a Kantian moral self-control, an 'inner-check,' could be expressed, as it did not finally specify an answer to what man *is*.[24] It merely laid claim to his spiritual freedom and the need for moral discipline.

Kirk's canon affirms belief in a transcendent order; Eliot's circumlocutions on education suggest that education is involved in arrival at knowledge of that order and that this

---

[22] On Royce, see Allen C. Guelzo, 'Dissenter for the Absolute,' *First Things* 259 (January 2016).

[23] Irving Babbitt, *Literature and the American College* (Washington, D.C.: National Humanities Institute, 1986), 96.

[24] There is much to be said in favor of Babbitt, though Eliot criticized the same features I propose he *maintained* from his teacher (See, James Matthew Wilson, 'The Rock against Shakespeare: Stoicism and Community in T.S. Eliot' (*Religion and Literature* 43.3 (Autumn 2011), 49-81). The most perceptive early criticism of Babbitt's merely negative account of education comes from his colleague George Santayana, *The Genteel Tradition at Bay* (New York: Charles Scribner's Sons, 1931).

is both definitive and formative of the human soul. New-man's writings are more vast and varied in their touching on these matters, but I shall mention three points in passing. He understood that reason as defined under modern rationalism did not allow one to arrive at knowledge of that order, therefore he conceived of the 'illative' sense to suggest that there were other means of knowledge besides pure reason.[25] Liberal education was itself a kind of initiation into other ways of knowing, and the gentleman was just that character who had been formed by the daily, civilizing, practice of those modes, not to any substantive end and not by any one method but by a universal diet intended to cultivate a disinterested liberality of spirit.[26] The gentleman's was primarily an *aesthetic* kind of perception as opposed to a *logical* one. But, Newman viewed beauty in a typically modern way, to wit, as an experience of sensible forms of perfection as had by our sentiments and emotions.[27] Beauty is somehow involved in what makes us human and in fulfilling our purpose, but it is also an eviscerated reality: deceptive because superficial, subjective in nature, misleading because a matter of feeling rather than intellect, and to be found in rare feats of culture (as a perfection) rather than as a feature of reality as a whole (as, we shall see, the ancients held).

Newman's understanding of beauty was typical of his age, and of ours as well. One finds a similar account in Kant, as one might expect, in part because Kant and Newman alike knew Burke. Burke's early treatise, the *Enquiry into*

---

[25] John Henry Newman, *An Essay in Aid of a Grammar of Assent* (Notre Dame, IN: University of Notre Dame Press, 2001), 270 ff. Cf., Newman, *Fifteen Sermons*, 55.

[26] John Henry Newman, *The Idea of a University*, (Notre Dame, IN: University of Notre Dame Press, 1986), 159.

[27] Matthew Muller, 'The False Idol of Beauty: Bl. John Henry Newman's Critiques of Aesthetics and the Challenge of Evangelization,' *Logos* (Fall 2017): 54-65.

the Sublime and the Beautiful (1757), defines beauty as a material form, a certain defined proportion and perfection, that triggers in the divinely constituted machine of the human body a particular response:

> The head reclines something on one side; the eyelids are more closed than usual, and the eyes roll gently with an inclination to the object, the mouth a little opened, and the breath drawn slowly, with now and then a low sigh: the whole body is composed, and the hands fall idly to the sides.[28]

The French Revolution thrust a more robust understanding of beauty upon Burke, a classical and ontological rather than a modern and subjective one. The language of the *Reflections* itself reflects something of the sort, though Burke never accounts for it. The early treatise on beauty would be insufficient to justify the aesthetics behind Burke's claim, by way of Cicero, that 'There ought to be a system of manners in every nation which a well-formed mind would be disposed to relish. To make us love our country, our country ought to be lovely.'[29] For, the *Reflections* as a whole trusts that the perception of beauty elicits not just a fine aesthetic, but a good, moral feeling from us, and that the form of a sound polity—an order—is based on principles of proportion, form, and the fitting that exceed the dainty ideas of his early writing. His treatise requires beauty in some sense to contain truth and goodness within it; if so, it must be greater than a fine form that makes the 'eyes roll.' From the beginning, therefore, modern conservatism has remembered sound principles but failed to recall how they are to be understood.

These conservatives have suggested that their tradition

---

[28] Edmund Burke, *A Philosophical Enquiry and Other Pre-Revolutionary Writings* (London: Penguin Books, 1998), 177.

[29] Burke, *Reflections*, 241.

defends a transcendent order, formative of reality as a whole and of the human person in particular, and that the point of contact between, as it were, macrocosm and microcosm, is the formal one of beauty. The principles are there, but they can hardly be said to be held together by the understanding. They are defended, but in various ways, some of them weakly argued, some not argued at all. In our day, we need to do better and we can do better.

Conserving Christian-Platonism

Much of what I have said here was at least hinted at by Richard Weaver, more than seventy years ago, in *Ideas Have Consequences*. There, Weaver judges the 'dissolution' of the modern West as a consequence of medieval scholasticism's decline from metaphysical realism to nominalism.[30] Among other things, beauty as property of reality was dissolved into a subjective concept. The power of his book lies in just this lamentation for the loss of a Christian-Platonist metaphysics, but he can only describe it with the vocabulary of Burke, as he refers to 'the unsentimental sentiment' and man's 'metaphysical dream of the world,' filtering one tradition's ideas through the language of another.[31]

Conservatism is the defense of the intellectual tradition of the West, and the intellectual tradition of the West is Christian-Platonism; what require conserving are not only the conclusions that tradition draws, but the rational account of things it, over time, advanced. That account, in its broadest features, is easily summarized in what I call the six great insights of the West:

1) that man is an intellectual animal;

---

[30] Richard Weaver, *Ideas Have Consequences* (Chicago: The University of Chicago Press, 1984), 3.

[31] Weaver, 18.

2) that his nature is founded on a prior or foundational intelligibility in the world and that he is intellectually and erotically oriented toward a transcendent knowledge of it;

3) this dual orientation proceeds by way of reason towards an intellectual vision perceptive of Beauty Itself, which is the splendor of truth;

4) that the world is itself ordered by and to Beauty;

5) that human dignity specifically consists in our capacity to perceive and contemplate that splendorous order, and, thus, the most excellent form of human life is that which is given over to such contemplation;

6) and, finally, this contemplation realizes itself in what we may call happiness or salvation, and it is characterized by an activity that resembles passivity, that is to say, not simply the absence of motion but a fullness of activity that is called peace and freedom.[32]

These insights result from several things we may discover about the nature of reality, which I have argued for elsewhere, and which I can no more than mention here. While sensation is bodily and material, the knowledge of being and truth is necessarily spiritual and intellectual. Our intellectual natures define what it means for human beings to be persons—beings having intellects and so capable of knowing reality. Reality, for its part, down to its simplest,

---

[32]   James Matthew Wilson, *The Vision of the Soul: Truth, Goodness, and Beauty in the Western Tradition* (Washington, D.C.: Catholic University of America Press, 2017): 73.

most material element, is constituted in existence by way of intellectual form. Reality is put in being by the creative intellect of God, each being is conferred *as a being* by having an intellectual form; in consequence, the world is eminently knowable or intelligible.

The capacity of existent form to share itself, to enter into relation with other beings, whether by way of knowledge or love, or by way of some other formal proportion, is what the Christian-Platonist tradition intends by the word beauty. Beauty is not a rare perfection, but a fundamental property of being: everything that exists is beautiful to the degree that it has being.[33] As such, beauty is no mere superficial ornament, but the glimmer, the light that gives shape to reality as a whole and which, in drawing the attention of man's intellect, gives form or shape to human life.[34]

To perceive beauty is to see the form of reality; beauty exists in the world as the very shape of that world, communicating its myriad relations. The perception of beauty is an intellectual (rather than a sentimental) one, though vastly more comprehensive than the narrow modern reason that Burke and Newman rightly decried. The effort of modern thinkers to preserve the freedom of the human spirit by denying it has any particular end was at once preposterous and unnecessary; that freedom is specifically preserved in our intellects' having the contemplation of beauty, the splendor of truth, as their end. This is the truth about reality and about man that conservatism

---

[33] See, Wilson, *The Vision of the Soul*. Cf. James M. Jacobs, 'Beauty as Excess of Intelligibility,' *Logos* 19.2 (Spring 2016): 18-32.

[34] Joseph Pieper, *Leisure the Basis of Culture* (San Francisco: Ignatius Press, 2009), 94-99. Cf. Hans Urs von Balthasar, *The Glory of the Lord* Vol. 1 (San Francisco: Ignatius Press, 1998), 19.

dares to defend against the depredations and impoverishments of every species of liberalism.

Renewing 'Statescraft as Soulcraft'

But what difference does it make?

Burke's *Reflections* was no philosophical exercise, but the first movement in his effort to rouse resistance to revolutionary France. Newman was trying to safeguard the prerogatives of the Church in a secularizing England. Eliot and Kirk attempted to soften the post-War order with its tendencies toward utilitarianism in morals, remediation in education, and technocracy in government. Why, now, do we need to recover such an ostensibly rarified—and beyond dispute ancient—vision of man and the world?

The answer is simple. The advance of liberalism has put everything not merely into question but into an entirely listless state of impoverishment. Man is understood only in terms of his desires and capacity for 'expressivity,' by which is meant, his assertion of a weak, unprincipled, but insistent will. The world is viewed as particulate, disintegrated and dead, and entirely subject to the movements of that will.[35] That either should have a purpose, and that purpose be subject to our understanding rather than the bald appeal of sincerity and emotion, has become almost unintelligible to those who shape our public discourse.[36]

Our political life has decayed from the search for a just order to a craven pursuit of emolument for the few and

---

[35] Karl Barth, *Protestant Theology in the Nineteenth Century* (Brian Cozens and John Bowden, trans. Grand Rapids, MI: Eerdmans, 2002), 23-24

[36] See, MacIntyre, *After Virtue*, 11-12.

an extension of the lifespan for the many. Our age is brutal not because brutal acts are performed (violence and war are part of the order of things and not without their share of beauty), but because its fundamental vision of reality, such as it is, is in itself brute and brutalizing.

A renewal of the insights of Christian-Platonism, advanced by clear argument rooted in its tradition, rather than by the modern 'fusions' that only somewhat sufficed in the past, could do much to reverse these trends. It would lead us to strengthen institutions that support self-government, whose founding principle is necessarily that citizens are first and foremost persons ordered to the knowledge of truth and goodness and to live in a manner responsive to those realities. Democratic and representative governments are not justified by their pretentions to equality, but by their insistence that persons practice the virtues proper to their intellectual natures. Our civil and cultural institutions, especially the schools, but also those charged with the preservation and advancement of culture, such as museums, would see the need to restore the disciplines of contemplation proper to liberal education, so that the young may be formed through their own free study of the beautiful. And, finally, our public law, which has over the last five decades sought to clear the public square of every substantive form to afford the private will as much license as possible to pursue its errant ways, will regain a sense of its true aim. Law does not serve to set the limits of acceptable deviance; rather, it cooperates in the formation of persons capable of practicing intellectual and moral virtues and of attaining their destiny: the knowledge of God's truths in this world and their free contemplation in the next.[37]

---

[37] Thomas Aquinas, *Summa Contra Gentiles* (Vernon J. Bourke, trans. Notre Dame, IN: University of Notre

In brief, a society fit for persons must first know what it means to be a person; Christian-Platonism gives us the 'big' answer. The person, by nature is ordered to the contemplation of the world and what transcends it, the beautiful order of things, processing from and returning to the divine beauty. Any denial of that nature brutalizes; every time it is acknowledged, however modestly, a part of the world is saved.[38]

Dame Press, 2001), 3.37-40.

[38] Cf. Jacques Maritain, *The Person and the Common Good* (John J. Fitzgerald, trans. Notre Dame, IN: University of Notre Dame Press, 2006), 15-16. The name for this vision of the person has variously been called, by Maritain among others, 'personalism,' 'integral humanism,' and 'Christian' or 'Christocentric humanism.'

THE RELIGION OF HUMANITY

The religion of humanity and its liberal origins – how man became a limitlessly relativistic and limitlessly moralistic god.

Daniel J. Mahoney

In his remarkable new book *Protestant Nation: The Fragile Christian Roots of American Greatness* (St. Augustine's Press, 2019), the distinguished French philosophic historian (and amateur theologian) Alain Besançon argues that the coterminous crises of the Catholic Church and Protestantism have been accompanied by 'the global emergence of a substantially different religion,' 'the religion of humanity.' Besançon argues (as I have in my recently published *The Idol of Our Age: How the Religion of Humanity Subverts Christianity*) that 'this religion encompasses Christian elements and gives them a different meaning.' It emphasizes doctrinaire egalitarianism and the endless expansion of rights whose precise ground or support is extremely difficult to discern. 'It is now possible to speak of a sacralized doctrine of human rights,' linked to a democratic civil religion that ignores the beliefs and traditions that have long prevented democracy from becoming a vague and empty abstraction at the service of negating the traditional moral contents of life. As Besançon observes, 'the religion of humanity is relativistic. It is convinced that there is no established truth and that all religions are equivalent, equal in dignity, and worthy of respect, and that a person can find his spiritual good, his salvation, in any one of them,' or none of them. Such a position quickly leads to theological and moral indifference, and a contempt for those who dare to pursue the truth.

Pope Benedict XVI 'opposed relativism with all his strength, but the movement appears to be irresistible.' I might add that his successor confuses the mercy of the Christian God with democratic compassion (the latter inclines more and more towards pure relativism) and a deep reticence, a quasi-silence, on the permanent imperative of repentance in the life of souls. Besançon and I have both argued that pacifism is a logical consequence of the religion of humanity. The West—marked by 'crusades, persecutions, and discrimination'—is on this account inherently culpable, guilty of massive injustices like no civilization before or after it. It is thus unworthy of defense. Some Christians have thoughtlessly imbibed this religion of humanity and accepted its problematic premise—so central to pacifism and relativism alike—that 'there are no enemies and it is intrinsically evil to have any' (something, of course, Christ never said or suggested). But our humanitarian relativists (and their Christian fellow travelers) are, at the same time, filled with nearly limitless moralistic indignation, especially at those who believe that the remnant of Christian civilization is worth defending.

The religion of humanity is not new and it took on farcical dimensions with the formalized 'religion of humanity' promoted by August Comte and John Stuart Mill in the middle of the nineteenth century. Mill was somewhat more circumspect in making his unbounded hostility to traditional Christianity known, no doubt out of deference to the power of public opinion. Still, he, too, advocated

a 'religion of humanity.' But Comte lauded the birth of a
new 'Occidental Republic' where war would become ob-
solete and the 'unity' of the human race would be fully
manifested. He combined positivism, a deep aversion to
theology, metaphysics, and traditional philosophy, with
a new morality where 'Humanity,' as a self-subsistent
Whole, would become the Grand-Etre, the new deity,
to be worshipped by limited and fallible human beings.
Comte was the great prophet of human self-deification
even as he aped and appropriated Christian rituals and
ceremonies. In the early 1850s, he even declared himself
the 'High Priest' of the new religion of humanity. He for-
got, as the great Hungarian Catholic moral and political
philosopher Aurel Kolnai (1900-1973) once put it, that
nobility and human dignity both entail 'the subordination
of everything human to what is above man.' Comte woe-
fully underestimated the staying power of the old nations
and the old religion. But over time, his religion of humanity took on a more diffused but still quite influential form.

As for today, as Besançon suggestively remarks, for secular humanitarians and Christian progressivists alike, the
Old Christianity 'is everywhere the object of mockery and
indignation.' And some *soi-disant* Christians are deeply
committed to subverting it from within. As Philip Lawler
has recently pointed out, the Honduran Cardinal Oscar
Maradiaga has endorsed 'Modernism' as a necessary reaction against 'injustices and abuses.' As Lawler notes: Not
some aspects of Modernism, but all of it. Maradiaga, so
close to the Holy Father and head of his advisory council, is filled with utopian rage against the very idea of authoritative institutions, the Church included. In his case,
the cosmic struggle against 'injustice,' real or imagined,
substitutes for the life of faith and reason. There is no so-
briety or measure in such an ill-considered rejection of
enduring realities and authoritative institutions. Utopia
takes the place of the Real.

Central to the task of both classical philosophy and biblical religion is the notion of 'mediation.' God chose his people Israel who were to be a light unto the nations. Jesus, the incarnate Lord, allows humanity to *see* the face of God. God is no longer completely hidden, Wholly Other. In classical Aristotelian-Thomistic thought, human beings live in plural political communities which are the only home for common life and for the fulfillment of meaningful conceptions of the Common Good. But today, bishops and popes speak of a 'world governing authority,' and ignore the mediation that gives political expression to our humanity. As Pierre Manent has argued, we human beings have no 'immediate' access to the universal except through the concrete communities in which we live. But Church elites, humanitarian to the core, reject mediation, temporal and sacred, and respond to the elementary requirements of self-governing nations, including secure borders, with something like what Manent calls 'sacred indignation.' There is nothing specifically Christian about their attitudes or their fashionable contempt for the nation.

They have become partisans of an abstract humanity and not of the political common good manifested in concrete human communities. They show little or no awareness of what Christopher Lasch in his famous 1995 book *The Revolt of the Elites* called 'the darker sides of cosmopolitanism.' Without particular attachments, and that includes national attachments, 'people have little inclination to make sacrifices or to accept responsibility for their actions.' Humanitarians speak the language of the poor and disadvantaged (see the Church's much vaunted 'preferential option for the poor') while siding in practice with 'a class of cosmopolitans who see themselves as 'world citizens, but without accepting...any of the obligations that citizenship in a polity normally implies.' Christian progressives, half-adherents of the religion of humanity, share the professional classes' 'scorn and apprehension' towards what used to be called 'Middle America': Those who suffer from unmitigated free trade, who defend the 'traditional family,' love their country as old-fashioned patriots do, who are suspicious of new sex roles and 'genders,' and are insufficiently knowledgeable about the latest antinomian intellectual trends. Many Churchmen side with what Charles Péguy called 'the intellectual party,' the party that cares for neither religion nor country, heroes nor saints, even though the purists in the intellectual party have nothing but contempt for authentic or orthodox Christianity. Knowingly or unknowingly, they are adherents of a new religion which is committed to dispensing with both transcendental religion and concrete familial, local, and national attachments. Members of a Church that gave life to the West as the West, they belong to the intellectual party that yearns to depoliticize and de-Christianize what is left of Western civilization. They affirm the truth of the Gospel (at least in a modernist, historicist, or progressive manner) *and* the pressing requirements of the religion of humanity. This incoherent double allegiance cannot be sustained for long.

Our half-humanitarians in the Church are blind to the stupefying incoherence of contemporary humanitarianism and cosmopolitanism. They are silent about the grace and goodness of God, completely ineffectual in responding to ever more strident affirmations of individual and collective autonomy that pass for morality today, and overlook the capacity of self-governing nations, and Churches with conviction, to speak to the human capacity for action in the service of truth, liberty, and human dignity. Instead, they speak endlessly about an ill-defined social justice (what does the adjective add to the noun?), mistake undemanding sentimentality for the *caritas* of Scripture, and have long forgotten the theological (faith, hope, charity) and cardinal virtues (fortitude, justice, temperance, and prudence) that are at the heart of human and political life properly understood. As I argue in *The Idol of Our Age*, humanitarianism is neither politically nor morally demanding. It makes modern men and women feel smug and self-satisfied, needing neither divine grace nor the cardinal virtues heralded by Aristotle and Cicero. Modern man is left bereft of magnanimity, greatness of soul—so evident in Plutarch's heroes or in a Churchill or de Gaulle, to mention exemplars of this virtue closer to home, or humility before our friend and Father, the Creator God. This was the defining trait of St. Mother Teresa or St. Francis of Assisi. Secular humanitarians and Christian progressives are seemingly content with a world without heroes or saints, a world in which the capacity to admire what is truly admirable is deeply undermined.

As Besançon has argued, Pope Benedict XVI was the only prominent modern Churchman to fully appreciate what was at stake in the humanitarian subversion of Christianity and of free and decent political life. He repeatedly insisted that the Christian's 'program'—the program of the Good Samaritan—should not be confused with the revolutionary agenda of *The Communist Manifesto,* centered as it is on four inhuman 'abolitions,' those of private property, the family, the nation, and religion (see part 2 of the *Manifesto*). Our religion, in contrast, centers first and foremost around 'care of the soul' even as it ministers to the wounds of the body.

The humanitarians and Christian progressives have learned nothing, absolutely nothing, about the dire evil that was totalitarianism in the twentieth century. In a sermon delivered in Bonn on November 26, 1981, addressing 'Christians Faced With Forms of Totalitarianism,' the then Cardinal Ratzinger spoke nobly and eloquently about how 'the hope of faith' must inform 'political reason and its sense of proportion.' There is no place in authentic Christianity for an 'authority-free society' or for 'the mythical hope of a man-made paradise' (a cheap and illusory, not to say inhuman, substitute for God's eschatological Kingdom). Christian political witness, the future Pope Benedict wisely concludes, has nothing to do with 'adventurous' and utopian moralism. It 'accepts man's limits' (one might add his 'nature') and 'does man's work with them.'

Unlike our neo-totalitarian 'Social Justice Warriors,' finding victims and victimizers everywhere in a new and terrible Manicheanism wrecking our campuses and public life, Benedict reminds us that 'compromise is the true morality in political matters.' Morality, of course, is not a private matter, 'it has public significance.' But it has nothing to do with a utopian moralism that has come to despise the very structure of Reality. Christianity must respect political reason in its own sphere and reason needs the truths revealed by biblical religion and discerned by classical philosophy so that reason does not forget humanity and succumb to a technological rationality, 'the objectivity devoid of values, the objectivity of statistics and mere social dynamics.' Rejecting both the totalitarian negation of man and technocratic illusions, the Church stands for the common good, human liberty, and political reason against 'the myth of the divine state (DM: note to integralists everywhere), the myth of the earthly paradise or utopian state and of a society without rule.' Here is a 'program' bereft of all ideological thinking and refusing to take its bearings from a fashionable but self-destructive *zeitgeist*. Against the religion of humanity, torn as it is between utopian fanaticism and the negation of the moral law, Benedict recovers Christian humanism, rooted in natural law and practical reason. Christian political wisdom may not be unambiguously 'liberal' (given liberalism's increasingly open contempt for divine and natural limits) but it is firmly and irrevocably anti-totalitarian. It is full of hope precisely because it sees through false and debilitating promises of Utopia.

In a recent interview with *The Catholic World Report*, Cardinal Gerhard Muller, the former prefect of the congregation of the Faith who was dismissed by Pope Francis in the summer of 2017, spoke eloquently and forcefully about 'growing confusion in the Church.' It should be noted that Muller is not a political conservative, works each summer with the poor in Peru, and is a friend of the liberation theologian Gustavo Gutierrez (who, it seems, has now wisely repudiated Marxism). In the *CWR* interview, Muller reminded his readers of the theology of the cross, and of the assault on the Church on the part of those who remain largely silent about sexual crimes in other social institutions. According to Muller, the grave crimes and sins in the Church are not the result of some ill-defined clericalism but rather of an open contempt for God's law in the form of 'unmastered desire, which leads to the sin of lust and dehumanizes the victims.' This is the language of moral and theological clarity, and not of relativistic therapeutic categories.

Cardinal Muller notes that the media 'only praise the Pope when they can make use of him for their agenda.' But, above all, he speaks against Maradiaga's endorsement of full-fledged Modernism without mentioning this papal acolyte by name. Reform, Christian reform worth its salt, can only mean 'spiritual and moral renewal in Christ and not the dechristianization of the Church or her transformation into an NGO.' Muller takes aim at an ideologized Church, kneeling before the world, in Maritain's memorable phrase, 'where global warming is more important than the awareness that God is the source and goal of man and of the whole creation.' We have lost everything when in the name of meeting the modern world half-way, we succumb to the sophistry, at odds with God's eternal truth, that 'modern man can understand [Jesus] only as a moral preacher on environmental protection—not on sexual morality, of course.'

We began with Besançon's forceful critique of the religion of humanity and will end with Cardinal Muller's sobering call to affirm the true faith of the Church. Both remind us fearlessly, and in the spirit of truth, that *our* religion, the religion of Jesus Christ, is not the religion of humanity. When we Christians exercise our responsibilities as 'political animals,' we must do so firmly, soberly, courageously, guided by practical reason and the natural moral law. No misguided Church bureaucracy can supersede the requirement that we remain faithful to the full array of theological and cardinal virtues. Those who have joined in Christopher Lasch's 'revolt of the elites' have long left those cardinal and natural virtues behind. They are a lesson in what is to be avoided.

DUMB AND DUMBER

How the ideas of Jean-Jacques Rousseau and J.S. Mill take turns ruining our education system.

Blaise Joseph

Australia is now ranked behind Kazakhstan on international school tests. Something is going wrong.

More broadly, Australia's performance on international tests has declined significantly over the past 10 years despite substantial increases in government funding for schools,[1] and a growing and remarkably consistent body of research evidence on how to improve student outcomes.

Everyone has an opinion on the problem with today's schools. Many people on the right will instinctively blame political correctness, cultural Marxism, and identity politics for poor school results — and with good reason.

---

[1] Department of Education and Training. 2017. *TIMMS and PISA results: Answer to Question on Notice SQ17-000543.* Senate Committee: Education and Employment, Additional Estimates 2016 – 2017

But what are the right's answers? A practical, utilitarian efficiency? This also completely misses the mark. In fact libertarianism and utilitarianism are already two of the guiding philosophies of modern education policy.

Education should be about passing on knowledge to children and helping them to have a high quality of life. But is this possible when the starting point is a consideration of what the student seems to want? The simple idea that a teacher's role is to teach has become a controversial debate. There is now an unreasonable focus on the preferences of students in schools. Hence the modern tendency to condemn 'old-fashioned' education with a focus on traditional teaching methods like direct instruction, or to lament rigid school discipline policies. The common view of teachers as 'learning facilitators' or the 'guide on the side rather than sage on the stage' is a manifestation of this underlying attitude.

The foundations of this approach are twofold. A belief in the absolute sovereignty of the individual, as well as an economic and reductionist approach to education which reduces schools to mere job factories. The purpose of schools has been degraded to simply giving students what they want or maximising their future wealth by preparing them for jobs.

Both the focus on student-centred creativity and the opposite extreme with a narrow utilitarian view of schools undermine the fundamentals of a good education. To avoid these extremes, there needs to be a return to academic rigour in schools, but ultimately to instilling in students virtue, wisdom, and understanding of tradition.

Rousseau and the natural learner

'Man is born free, and everywhere he is in chains.'

These famous words of Jean-Jacques Rousseau, the Enlightenment philosopher of the 18th century, have underpinned the progressive ideas which run rampant in modern education. Rousseau's unconstrained view of humanity — the idea that human beings are fundamentally good and it is unjust social structures which cause evil — has been widely applied to schooling for much of the 20th century. Today it is so widely accepted as to be taken as an unquestionable, obvious truth. His idea of the 'noble savage' means that children are inherently good, natural learners, and capable of discovering knowledge themselves if only given the right opportunities. Children do not need to be taught *per se*, merely encouraged. They certainly should not be hindered by rigid, teacher-led instruction.

The libertarian view of individuals as entirely autonomous and not just a part of a social system fits in with Rousseau's philosophy of student-centred education. But this view of humanity is disastrous when applied to schooling.

Assuming that kids do not need to be explicitly taught content because they will just simply 'pick it up' themselves is downright foolish. The idealistic view of children could be laid low by parental anecdotes, or a simple appreciation of the Christian doctrine of original sin. But it is simpler than that: it just does not work.

Decades of empirical research have repeatedly shown that in terms of student results traditional, teacher-led direct instruction is significantly more effective than enquiry-based, student-centred learning. Students tend to learn more about a topic when they are clearly and systematically taught new content by a teacher in a traditional education setting. A recent comprehensive meta-analysis — which analysed the findings of over 300 studies across 50 years — found direct instruction has significant positive effects on student achievement across all subjects and non-academic indicators.[2] Rejecting utopian ideas about children's learning abilities is simply sound evidence-based policy.

The dangers of the idealism of Rousseau in modern education are even more pronounced in the area of reading instruction. It would seem that the foundational role of a school is to teach children how to read. This should not be controversial, as all school subjects and possible employment paths require at least a basic level of reading ability. And yet it is in this area where education progressivism has arguably had the most dire consequences.

The early school years are vital for acquiring core reading skills. There is a well-established phenomenon called the Matthew Effect, which states that relatively small differences in reading ability in the early years of school lead to relatively large differences in achievement by the end of school and beyond, if not rectified early. This is why teaching children how to read at the start of primary school is so important.

The more traditional approach to reading instruction involves the use of phonics. Phonics-based instruction links sounds and letters, beginning with regular connections and gradually progressing to less regular connections. That is, children are explicitly taught the relationships between sounds and letter-symbols so they can decode (sound out) written words. Phonics instruction by itself is

---

[2] Stockard, J., Wood, T., Coughlin, C., & Rasplica Khoury, C. 2018. The effectiveness of direct instruction curricula: a meta-analysis of a half century of research. *Review of Educational Research*.

insufficient for teaching reading but it is a necessary component.

But what if children are natural learners, as educational progressivism maintains, and do not need teachers to explicitly teach them how to read? An alternative to phonics is known as whole-language instruction, which has a greater focus on immersing children in text so as to allow them to 'pick it up' by looking at whole words without generally breaking them down into connections. This often involves students being encouraged to guess unfamiliar words by looking at context.

It should be obvious which approach tends to be more effective. The evidence base from decades of research — confirmed by the findings of three separate government reviews done in the US, UK, and Australia[3] — clearly shows that phonics instruction is vital to the effective teaching of reading. Why? Largely because unlike speech which develops naturally and spontaneously with exposure to spoken language, reading is not something children will learn through exposure to print. They need someone to teach them.

Many proponents of enquiry-based learning and whole-language instruction will deny the validity of the education research literature, because they claim the metrics used to evaluate student achievement are too narrow. In other words, literacy and numeracy are only one part of a good education, and enquiry-based learning or whole-language instruction have other qualitative benefits for individuals which cannot be measured. But the

---

[3] Department of Education, Science and Training. 2005. *Teaching reading: Report and recommendations.* p.14; Rose, J. 2006. Independent review of the teaching of early reading, p. 70; National Reading Panel. 2000. *National Reading Panel: Teaching children to read.*

truth is almost all social, economic, and emotional out-comes are strongly correlated with success in school in terms of literacy and numeracy results — and emphasis-ing the importance of 'the 3 Rs' does not preclude learning other skills at school — so a traditional focus on measur-able academic achievement is entirely justified.

A necessary precondition for creating independent adults is that they leave school with core literacy and numeracy skills. It is impossible for young people finishing school to be fully autonomous if they were left to their own devices in the classroom and graduated with a low level of reading ability.

What about freedom for students?

It is often alleged that traditional schooling stifles chil-dren's creativity, natural development, and happiness. Children should be more free at school and education should be less rigid, it is argued. This is displayed by calls for more student play time, fewer tests, and less focus on discipline. Students like playing, dislike tests, and of course object to rigid discipline policies — so why impinge on their freedoms by forcing them to do things at school they do not like? But taking the student-centred approach on the issues of play, assessment, and discipline is unwise.

There is little reason to believe Australian children do not have enough time to play or be physically active. About one quarter of every school day is given to recess and lunch breaks, there is additional school time devoted to physical education and sport, and the school day typical-ly ends at about 3pm. Students can only benefit a limit-ed amount from more play time and outdoor activities, and there is potentially a large opportunity cost of more school time allocated for non-academic purposes.

Testing and assessment are an integral part of education. Tests followed by feedback is the most rigorous way to assess student learning and enable teachers to respond accordingly to improve student results in future. Of course, few people like doing tests — most students do not like preparing for or sitting tests, most teachers do not like administering and supervising them, and marking is an arduous process. But nothing worth doing is easy.

Standardised testing is a particular target of educational progressives. They say standardised tests like NAPLAN are too stressful for students, result in teachers just 'teaching to the test', and are generally counterproductive. But a recent OECD study found neither test anxiety nor test performance are related to the frequency of testing, for both teacher-developed and standardised national tests.[4] Rigorous testing is not an end in itself, but a means to improve student performance over time.

While Rousseau's view of humanity maintains that students are naturally good and will behave well unless negatively influenced by others, the reality is students have a tendency to play up and bully each other regardless. In order to manage student behaviour so that they can have a good education, school discipline is required. In fact, according to a recent paper from Macquarie University researchers, school discipline is far more important than school funding in determining a country's educational performance.[5]

---

[4] OECD. 2017. *Is too much testing bad for student performance and well-being?*

[5] Baumann, C., & Krskova, H. 2016. School discipline, school uniforms and academic performance. *International Journal of Educational Management*, 30(6), pp. 1003–1029.

Many education academics still maintain that the concept of 'behaviour management' is outdated, and insist teachers should instead focus on understanding the reasons for student behaviour. That is, a role of teachers is to understand what students are trying to communicate when they misbehave. This explains why many new teachers leave university without a solid grounding in effective classroom management techniques; and this is perhaps a cause of Australia's high levels of classroom misbehaviour compared to the top-performing OECD countries, according to the main international education datasets.[6]

Another consequence of the 'anti-behaviour management' approach is the growing tendency to criticise schools when they suspend or expel students for serious incidents of misbehaviour. The instinctive response to blame schools and teachers when students behave badly is endemic of the underlying philosophy that institutions (not individuals) are the cause of all problems. But this ignores the common experience of humanity that children often make irrational decisions, and take many years to acquire an adequate moral framework and impulse control. If discipline is too permissive, then misbehaving students will not learn to improve their conduct and will hurt the academic outcomes of other students at the school.

Expecting schools to treat students as if they are rational and autonomous adults is simply unrealistic.

---

[6] International Association for the Evaluation of Educational Achievement. 2016. *TIMMS 2015 International Results Report: School Discipline Problems – Principals' Reports*; Thomson, S., De Bortoli, L., & Underwood, C. 2017. *PISA 2015: Reporting Australia's Results*. Australian Council for Education Research. p. 278.

Schools as job factories: 21ˢᵗ century learning

John Stuart Mill, the utilitarian philosopher of the 19th century, has also had a substantial effect on modern education policy. For Mill, schools should produce an educated elite who can fulfil the principle of the greatest good for the greatest number in society.

Mill had a nuanced view of the purpose of education, but over time his broad philosophy has led to an economic reductionist approach to schooling, where schools exist merely to create citizens who can get jobs. It is argued that since the workplace has changed remarkably in recent times, so too must classrooms. It follows that school curricula and teaching practices should be guided by the job markets and technological advances of the day.

There is a growing push from both business and academics for schools to focus on the '4 Cs' (as opposed to the '3 Rs') of 21ˢᵗ century learning: critical thinking, communication, collaboration, and creativity — and some add computer coding as well to make it the '5 Cs'.

This line of thought has a lot in common with the education progressivism based on Rousseau's philosophy. They both suggest that measurable literacy and numeracy results are relatively unimportant because they are too narrow. And they both end up pushing now discredited pedagogies of enquiry-based learning and student-led instruction, to give students a broader education where they can either realise their natural ability to learn or be prepared for the jobs of the future with new skills. Ultimately, they both result in a less rigorous academic education.

For example, classrooms without desks or student rows or whiteboards may sound like a progressive education idea, but now people from the right of politics are endorsing this approach. The Trump-appointed US Secretary of Education, Betsy DeVos, once tweeted a succinct summary of this attitude with a photo of a traditional classroom lay-out: 'Does this look familiar? Students lined up in rows. A teacher in front of a blackboard. Sit down; don't talk; eyes up front. Wait for the bell. Walk to the next class. Everything about our lives has moved beyond the industrial era. But American education largely hasn't.' The problem with this argument is that alternative school policies and classroom structures which have 'moved beyond the industrial era' are either unclear or problematic. What is the alternative to a classroom with desks and student rows? How would schools work without children being asked to sit down and not talk? And how could school days be productive without timetables and classes?

Besides, this is just a historical fiction. The structure and layout of classrooms is much older than the industrial communities of the United States. Aristocratic children educated at Eton and the prestigious public schools in the United Kingdom were not being prepared for factory jobs.

The modern 'open collaborative learning spaces' — which involve flexible furniture, extensive group work, and very little direct instruction — are a nightmare for teachers trying to control student behaviour. And in the meantime students are likely to end up with lower levels of literacy and numeracy. Just because certain practices and approaches may be popular in workplaces does not mean they should be copied across to a school context. Is it really a good idea for businesses to tell schools what they must teach and how they must teach it? A narrow economic approach to schooling simply does not work, and more importantly it does an injustice to students by reducing their education to a mere means for future job prospects.

One of the most articulate proponents of a school system which focusses less on content knowledge and more on creativity is Sir Ken Robinson. His famous Ted Talk entitled 'Do schools kill creativity?' in 2007 has now received over 50 million views. It is engaging, entertaining, and thought-provoking; but it is fundamentally wrong and not evidence-based. Robinson claims that 'We don't grow into creativity, we grow out of it. Or rather, we get educated out of it.'

However, focussing on creativity and the other 'Cs' in school puts the cart before the horse. Children need to master the fundamentals of a subject before they can be creative or think critically about it, and too many students leave school without those fundamentals. Also, cognitive science research shows that creativity and critical-thinking skills are domain-specific skills, not generic skills.[7] This means rigorous subject knowledge is a prerequisite for 'higher-level thinking' in any area. For example, in order to be creative about physics, it is first necessary to have a good understanding of physics; and thinking critically about a classic novel is very different to thinking critically about maths problems.

Furthermore, there is very little evidence to suggest a focus on giving students high levels of literacy and numeracy is incompatible with developing creative students. The OECD regularly conducts international standardised tests in order to rank countries' education results, and while typically these tests focus on literacy and numeracy, more recently they have tested collaborative problem-solving ability. The results surprised many,

---

[7]   Willingham, D. 2007. Critical thinking. *American Educator*, 31(3), pp. 8–19.

because the country rankings were very similar for both test types. In both cases, the top-performing countries were in Asia: Singapore, Japan, Hong Kong, and Korea (all of which have very traditional approaches to schooling).[8] Concerns about traditional schooling resulting in 'rote learning' and 'killing creativity' are completely unwarranted.

Much of the discussion about the '4 Cs' is basically code for trying to get better student results without actually doing the hard yards in literacy and numeracy by using traditional teaching methods. There is no educational short cut that makes children get better grades and ready for the jobs of the future. The best way to help students be prepared for the 21st century is to ensure they leave school good readers, fluent writers, competent in maths, and with a sound and well-rounded knowledge of the core disciplines. These are the fundamental skills people will always need to be successful. Business will be doing itself no favours in the long-term if it continues to advocate a student-centred enquiry-based learning approach in schools.

There is an additional fundamental problem with viewing schools as just job factories: it takes away the responsibility of schools to help produce a virtuous citizenry. It is perhaps counterintuitive that advocates of 21st century learning — by suggesting that a traditional focus on literacy and numeracy is too narrow because the jobs of the future require much more — ultimately end up arguing for a narrowing of school curricula. For instance, there is no obvious way that studying poetry helps someone gain employment in the 21st century; and knowledge of history superficially seems much less important than coding in terms of future job opportunities.

---

8   Thomson et al. 2017 pp. 35, 112, 167; OECD. 2017. *PISA 2015 Results (Volume V).*

But in order to create virtuous citizens who are capable of participating in society beyond the workplace and creating a vibrant culture aware of its heritage, schools need to teach students more than a list of job criteria. Topics like poetry and history are important to a child's intellectual and moral development. As an old saying goes: 'Education without values, as useful as it is, seems rather to make man a more clever devil.'

The way forward in education

The idealism of Rousseau and the utilitarianism of Mill are both endemic in modern approaches to education and both degrade schools. Education has become too student-centred, with a naive belief in the innate learning abilities of children in addition to an unreasonable focus on getting them jobs after they leave school. Schools must move away from applying a belief in the absolute autonomy of the individual to children, and from the student-led learning that comes with it.

Aristotle maintained that virtue is a mean between two vices. In a similar way, schools need to find a way between the two extremes of being play centres with no focus on core academic outcomes and being job factories with a narrow focus on job skills.

On any measure, Australia's education system is underperforming, despite oscillating between viewing children either as innately creative geniuses on the one hand or as mere widgets in an economy on the other.

It is necessary for the right of politics to support the return to teacher-led learning which cultivates virtue in students and allows them to become good citizens, and enables students to leave schools with high levels of literacy and numeracy. Otherwise, the school system will continue to let down students by not giving them the education they deserve and let down taxpayers by not giving them a return on the more than $50 billion per year invested in schools.

For those who value an educated populace and realise that virtue is paramount, there is no more pressing policy issue than reclaiming the school system and returning to evidence-based education policy.

THE MERITS OF CAMPION COLLEGE

Campion College Graduation Ceremony
St Patrick's Cathedral, Parramatta
11 December 2018

What one liberal arts college reveals about the corruption of major universities.

Dyson Heydon

I cannot tell you how much pleasure it gives me to attend this ceremony. Everyone who has received a degree or diploma or both deserves the warmest congratulations. That view will be shared by parents, other family members and friends.

The conception underlying Campion College is to be admired. It seems to be unique in Australia and fairly rare outside Australia – a liberal arts college covering key aspects of Western languages, literature, history, philosophy and theology together with mathematics and science. These are vital elements of received Australian culture. As the Campion website says, the aim of the College 'is not the accumulation of knowledge but the cultivation of wisdom – not the filling of a pail, in WB Yeats' words, but the lighting of a flame'. The phrase is redolent of TS Eliot's view that education is 'the preservation of learning ... the pursuit of truth, and in so far as men are capable of it, the attainment of wisdom'. And the website rightly stresses the importance of developing the ability to think critically and argue rationally.

These are aspirations which the great Sir Owen Dixon, Chief Justice of the High Court of Australia, did not detect in the Australian universities of his mature years in the 1930s to 1960s. He made the wintry remark that in them, to copy out one book was plagiarism; to copy out two was diligent scholarship; but to copy out three was original research.

The reference to that great Irish poet Yeats on the website certainly highlights the desirability of openness to disciplines other than one's own. Yeats once met the great physicist, JJ Thomson, who ended his career as Master of Trinity College, Cambridge. The meeting took place at dinner in Trinity in the 1930s, when Yeats was at the height of his fame. At one point early in the meal Thomson turned to Yeats and said: 'Been writing many poems lately, Mr Keats?'

The President, in his introduction, pointed out in the kindest way that the length of my career has taken me into extreme old age. Many old people cease to care what others think. They wish just to say what they think. They share the demand of Yeats:

> Grant me an old man's frenzy,
>
> Myself must I remake
>
> Till I am Timon or Lear
>
> Or that William Blake

Who beat upon the wall

Till Truth obeyed his call.

To name an institution after Edmund Campion is to make a significant statement. He was born in 1540. He was executed in 1581. He was canonized in 1970. His biographer, Evelyn Waugh, said his career was that of scholar, priest, hero and martyr. Waugh also said that Campion's life was 'a simple, perfectly true story of heroism and holiness'. As a scholar – a fellow of St John's College, Oxford – Campion was both a theologian and a scientist. He thus illustrated the long connection between the Jesuits and experimental science. Indeed, at the age of 26 he achieved a brilliant success when on Queen Elizabeth's visit to Oxford in 1566 he addressed her on scientific subjects. He then fell under the patronage of Robert Dudley, Earl of Leicester. The Earl was a great man in the Elizabethan state. But his paternity revealed the precariousness of life in Tudor England. His grandfather, a high official under Henry VII, was executed by Henry VIII for extortion of taxes. His father, who was for a time supreme during the minority of Edward VI, was executed for supporting Lady Jane Grey's claim to the throne. The Earl himself had been sentenced to death for the same reason, perhaps ought to have been executed for murdering his wife, and concluded his career with a bigamous marriage.

Campion had been ordained as a priest of the Church of England. But he left England and became a Jesuit priest. He conceived the idea of returning as part of a Jesuit mission to convert England. The last year and a half of his life was spent on that mission. In the middle of that enterprise, Parliament enacted a statute in 1581 making it treason to convert the Queen's subjects to Rome. He was arrested. He was interrogated by his former patron, the Earl of Leicester, and other ministers. He was repeatedly subjected to very cruel tortures. But he made no significant confession of guilt by himself or implication of others. He was then tried for treason – not only under the 1581 statute, which he probably had breached, but also a statute of 1351 for allegedly seeking to raise rebellion, invoke foreign invasion and kill the Queen. Torture left him so ruined physically as almost to render him unfit for trial. That trial was flawed by perjured evidence, much of it hearsay. The trial concentrated on the more serious charges – the charges under the 1351 Act. As his brilliant conduct of his defence demonstrated, those charges had no evidentiary support at all. But he was convicted. At the gallows he was heckled and pestered and taunted – for the Elizabethan mob, like all mobs, loved a good execution, whether actual or metaphorical. He was then put to a brutal death by being hanged and then drawn and quartered. A Catholic witness of his death said he was 'an honour to our country, a glass and mirror, a light and lantern, a pattern and example to youth, to age, to learned, to unlearned, to religious and to the laity of all sort, state and condition of modesty, gravity, eloquence, knowledge, virtue and piety'. And in the ensuing centuries that view of him became general in all circles.

Now that is a sad tale. It is a tale of an able but insecure and irresolute Queen, advised by ruthless ministers. It is a tale from a hard age of extreme intolerance. That age believed that dissent from the religion of the state was a dire threat to the state. The age did not understand what Campion kept telling it – that he was loyal to the Queen, as secular ruler, but obliged in non-secular affairs to follow his conscience. That is, he was obliged to render unto Caesar the thing's that are Caesar's, but unto God the things that are God's.

How different, how very different, we might complacently think, Elizabethan England is from our own fat, happy, easy-going and prosperous society. We might complacently think that a reversion to Elizabethan standards of poverty could not happen. We might complacently think that the evil of religious persecution could never rise again to Elizabethan levels.

Or could it?

Campion College is approved as a registered Australian Higher Education Institution by the New South Wales Department of Education and Training. Yet it receives no funding or support from any level of government – unlike every other university and school institution in the country. That does appear to be a quite extraordinary state of affairs. Why does the state waste billions – and not just on education – but supply nothing to Campion? The question invites a comparison between Campion and the standard university model in this country, spread over its many universities. How many are there – 30, 40, 50? It does not really matter because by the time one thinks one has finished counting, the number has already risen. But each of those universities is based on a single model. It is stereotyped. It is uniform. It is monolithic. The model of Campion is different. Some questions arise about the differences.

Does Campion, like the standard universities, have the reputation of being run by vast bureaucracies, substantially exceeding the teaching staff in numbers, and in many instances paid salaries reminiscent of sleek bankers – way above their deserts, and way above even the most able and internationally respected of the teaching staff? I think not.

Does Campion, like them, have vast student populations who mill about pointlessly and aimlessly, failing to find an enjoyable and fulfilling communal life? I think not.

Does Campion, like them, have the reputation of perpetrating cruel deceits on people who cannot speak English effectively by inducing them to enter Australia from foreign lands, and undertake degrees which, if anything is to be gained from them, call for an excellent standard of English skill? I think not.

Does Campion, like them, have the reputation of relaxing the standards of assessment to ensure that those foreign students obtain at least a piece of paper, however worthless? I think not.

Does Campion, like them, have the reputation of engaging in these massive frauds on the foreign students, on their non-foreign colleagues, and on the public solely for the purpose of ensuring solvency in university funding and creating supposedly massive 'invisible export earnings'? I think not.

Does Campion, like them, overlook the fact that the expression 'earnings' implies that something of value is supposed to be supplied in exchange for the money received? I think not.

Does Campion, like them, boast of the good will that supposedly contented foreign graduates will feel towards Australia after their exposure to Australian university life? I think not.

Does Campion, like them, have the reputation of ensuring that staff promotion can only be achieved by conducting fake and useless research, by obtaining research grants (whether or not those grants ever lead anywhere, and however much money is wasted on paying administrators to administer them) and by nauseating exercises in self-boosting? I think not.

Does Campion, like some of them, have the reputation of

taking great libraries which cultured and thoughtful academic staff assembled in earlier decades and destroying them by consigning their contents to land fill or worse? I think not.

Does Campion, like them, have the reputation of operating institutions at which there is little liberty to express views diverging from the current orthodoxy because dissent is seen as a moral failing – a mean-spirited and insolent refusal to jump on the virtue bandwagon? I think not.

Does Campion, like them, when a few people exercise even that small degree of liberty, instantly humiliate those few people and howl them down? I think not.

Does Campion, like them, have the reputation of being led by senior officials who persistently deny instances of gross interference with free speech, or if they cannot deny them, discount, downplay or belittle those instances or the people who draw attention to them? I think not.

Campion College was created in the spirit of a great man. He was beatified a few years ago. He was best known by the name under which he achieved universal respect and fame as theologian, writer, novelist, and, like Campion, representative of the human conscience. The name is Cardinal Newman. If Edmund Campion was a great Renaissance all-rounder, John Henry Newman was a great Victorian all-rounder. He had a vision similar to that underlying Campion College. The vision led to the Catholic University of Ireland. It rested on what Newman's biographer, Father Ker, called 'the idea of a liberal education within a confessional religious context' – something resistant both to 'utilitarian attacks' and 'anti-intellectual clericalism'.

But the purpose and function of Campion College rests on even older ideas than that. During a time of collapsing civilisation and cultural despair, monks like Bede, living in their little communities in the Dark Ages, kept alive a tradition of learning and thought in a world poised half way between the rising power of persecuting barbarians and the decaying power of the Roman Empire and its successor kingdoms. Those monks saved a large part of the intellectual capital of the West. They began to build up that capital. As the very long reign of Queen Elizabeth II proceeds, the world we are entering may or may not have emerging similarities with that world of the Dark Ages or the world of Queen Elizabeth I – emerging similarities in material poverty and emerging similarities in moral and intellectual poverty. A career at Campion College may or may not in itself be an asset readily exchangeable into money. But that career will have created a different sort of capital. It will have created a stock of intellectual and moral treasure for those who have experienced it, whether or not they appreciate it fully right now. Those who have experienced Campion College can draw repeatedly and with great advantage on that stock of treasure for the rest of their lives. A small institution like Campion can help ensure the development of a pluralistic tradition, independently of vast and hyper fashionable mega-institutions emanating from and parasitic on the modern state. A small body can develop and preserve qualities which giants may have forgotten, or, if they remember them, may seek to destroy. That is because a small body is independent of the state, nourished by sources of which the state knows nothing.

To you are due congratulations on your achievements here, and an expression of the best of wishes for your future.

Part V
Journeys, Realities & Practicalities

DON'T MENTION THE WAR

Reasons to keep the 'liberal and conservative' band together.

Tony Abbott

The Liberal Party does best when it focuses on creating jobs, making people's lives easier, and fostering pride in our country, not when it debates its own philosophy. It's true, as John Howard recently said, that you can't persuade if you don't believe. But the Liberal Party has never believed in just one big thing. On some issues, Liberals are liberal; on other issues, Liberals are conservative – which is as it should be. At least in English-speaking countries, there's been a warm embrace between liberalism and conservatism because so much of our history is the struggle for freedom; and also because true freedom cannot exist without an orderly society and a framework of law.

A few liberals have taken pains to distinguish themselves from conservatives. Likewise, in this volume, some conservatives take pains to distinguish themselves from liberals (or libertarians, who are not quite the same). But there is, in fact, a very large overlap between people who respect the Western tradition (especially the English-speaking version) and those who cherish freedom as the indispensable feature of a good life.

The poet Tennyson, indeed, had a lovely stanza evoking what's been liberalism and conservatism's mostly happy marriage:

> A land of settled government,
>
> A land of just and old renown,
>
> Where freedom slowly broadens down,
>
> From precedent to precedent

Certainly, the last thing the Liberal Party needs is further polarisation between the instinctive conservatives and the philosophical liberals in its ranks. John Howard's famous description of the Liberal Party as the political custodian, in this country, of both the liberal tradition of John Stuart Mill and the conservative tradition of Edmund Burke still holds true.

Small "l" liberals may dominate a Liberal government from time to time, but they can't hold office without the support of the conservatives in the cabinet and they certainly can't win an election without the votes (or at least the preferences) of conservative middle Australia. The challenge for everyone who wants the Liberal Party to succeed is not to elevate a particular ideological faction into some "winners' circle" but to find ways of keeping small "l" liberals and small "c" conservatives under the same big "L" Liberal tent.

Disagreements and debates within political parties are usually less frequent than those between them; but they can be toxic if not well managed. It was Burke, after all, who defined a political party as a body of men working towards the common interest in accordance with a particular principle on which they all agree. Appealing to a modern democratic electorate, though, usually necessitates compromises within parties as much as it does conflict between them.

Any political party capable of winning elections is inevitably a coalition of people who won't always agree on everything but who have found ways to manage their differences and to unite around particular measures that they can all support. Hence Howard's celebrated metaphor of the Liberal Party as a "broad church".

The differences between conservatives and liberals within the Liberal Party are not dissimilar to those between the pragmatic right and the ideological left inside the Labor Party. Unacknowledged and unmanaged they can become fierce, even crippling. The challenge of leadership is to keep the political focus on those issues where the different strands of internal thinking can more-or-less be reconciled, and to put these at the heart of a coherent political programme, so that it's the differences with other political parties that become the principal contest that voters have to decide.

On those issues where it's necessary to take a position that might be deeply at odds with some inside your own party, the challenge of leadership is to find something bigger where everyone can agree. If this can't be managed, a split – small or large – is almost unavoidable and all splits are damaging, even if they don't threaten the overall unity of the party.

So, what can be taken to characterise a philosophical liberal in Australia today? A liberal typically supports greater freedom, lower taxes, and smaller government. A liberal typically thinks that empowered citizens are much more likely than bigger government to produce a stronger economy and a better society; hence, the principal task of government is to shrink.

A typical conservative would share his or her liberal friends' antipathy to bigger, more intrusive government but would often regard other issues as at least equally pressing: maintaining strong alliances and effective armed forces, for instance; promoting the family and encouraging small business; and respecting values and institutions that have stood the test of time.

Then there are "progressives", sometimes describing themselves as "liberals" but, these days, usually more interested in permissive social policies than in liberal economic ones.

Howard sometimes characterised the Liberal Party as "economically liberal and socially conservative" and that was certainly its centre of gravity in his time. The Howard government was liberal when it reformed the tax system, simplified industrial laws, and reduced government spending. It was conservative when it strengthened the US alliance, increased military spending, introduced work for the dole, increased Family Tax Benefits, freed small business from unfair dismissal laws, and imposed rigorous national testing on schools.

In my time, the Liberal Party was liberal when it cut trade barriers, abolished the carbon tax and the mining tax and cut tax for small business. It was conservative when it stopped the illegal immigrant boats and strengthened national security.

In Howard's time, the most divisive issue was whether Australia should become a republic. The Crown had long been an article of party faith. Sir Robert Menzies had famously said of the young Queen Elizabeth, "I did but see her passing by and yet I love her till I die". When I first joined the party in the 1980s, "we believe...in the constitutional monarchy" was the first item in the "We Believe" statement that all members were expected to subscribe to and that was sometimes recited at the beginning of branch meetings. But when Paul Keating made becoming a republic Labor's policy after the 1993 election, quite a few Liberals decided that it might be time to change after all.

Howard himself was a convinced opponent of anything that might shake the checks and balances in a system of government that he termed a "crowned republic". Yet to manage internal divisions, he dropped support for the monarchy as a formal commitment (even though, to this day, it's still part of the Tasmanian Division's version of "We Believe"). Liberal cabinet ministers were free to support either side of the argument at the 1998 constitutional convention; and to support or to oppose the 1999 referendum on becoming a republic; which, despite the polls and near-universal media support, was soundly defeated.

In my time, the most divisive issue was same sex marriage. More so than with a republic (where there were "liberal" monarchists such as George Brandis), the internal division was largely along instinctual liberal and conservative lines. A "conservative case for same sex marriage" was indeed made – that it could bring more fidelity and stability to same sex couples – but very few self-described conservatives went public in support of changing the time-honoured definition of marriage that had been re-affirmed by the Australian parliament as recently as 2004. Small "l" liberals, on the other hand, largely favoured getting the law out of a legislated definition of marriage that activists had turned into the embodiment of discrimination.

Trying to maintain as binding party policy the Howard-era position that marriage had to be between a man and a woman would have meant an embarrassing defeat on the floor of the parliament as up to a dozen Liberal MPs crossed the floor to support a private members' bill.

As with the monarchy two decades earlier, opposing views were too strongly held by too many MPs for the issue to be resolved by a leader's call or by a party room vote.

Hence the plebiscite: it gave party conservatives and party liberals the chance to make their pitch to the community; and either way it would resolve the issue because no democratic politician can fail to heed an unambiguous national vote.

My colleague Dean Smith, as a "constitutional conservative" although a supporter of same sex marriage, criticised deciding it by a vote of the people in a plebiscite rather than just the parliament in a free vote; but a better conservative position, at least in my view, was that it was best for the whole people to determine something as deeply personal as marriage. After all, the traditional concept of marriage long predated its codification under the Howard government. There was precedent too. The question of conscription – while clearly within the constitutional competence of the Commonwealth parliament – had been put to the people, not once but twice, during the Great War.

It's worth noting that the 50 Liberal Party members who took out an advertisement in favour of same sex marriage, describing themselves as "committed to liberal and conservative values", included many current and former senior cabinet ministers (such as Brandis, Josh Frydenberg, Greg Hunt and Christopher Pyne), but very few who might have described themselves as conservative in any other context.

Until quite recently, except as a term of abuse, "conservative" was not a description that had been widely used in Australia. The first recorded use that I could find was in the Commonwealth parliamentary Hansard of 1901 where then-Prime Minister Edmund Barton denied that he was of "conservative mind".

For someone who spent much time in England, regarded himself as a friend of Winston Churchill, and over a 50 year public life frequently discussed political values, it's remarkable that Menzies had so little to say about conservatism and almost never used the term. Menzies' oft-cited reflection: "We took the name 'Liberal' because we were determined to be a progressive party, willing to make experiments, in no sense reactionary but believing in the individual, his rights, and his enterprise and rejecting the socialist panacea" is sometimes used to make conservatives look like interlopers in the party he formed.

Much less familiar is Menzies' despairing 1974 observation in a letter to his daughter Heather about the party's Victorian state executive: "dominated by what they now call 'Liberals with a small l' – that is to say Liberals who believe in nothing but who still believe in anything if they think it worth a few votes. The whole thing is tragic".

In a 1965 address to the Liberal Party federal council, Menzies said that the key to its success was that it had been "not the party of the past, not the conservative party dying hard on the last barricade, but the party of innovations". And it's true: the Liberal Party has never been "the conservative party" let alone one "dying hard on the last barricade", which no rational party, however conservative, would ever choose. No one has ever claimed that the Liberal Party was merely conservative; and it was Burke himself who pointed out that an entity without the means of change lacked the means of its own conservation.

In a 1974 newspaper article, Menzies declared that:

> When we commenced the Liberal Party we had principles. Principles are apparently nowadays things

that are not to be insisted upon because to insist
upon them is to demonstrate that you are 'reactionary' or 'conservative'. This, of course, is the most
pernicious nonsense. Principles do not change. In
the whole of my political life I have never arrived at
something that I thought to be a matter of principle lightly or casually. They have represented deep
beliefs on my part; and I am old-fashioned enough
to believe that principles, once adopted after much
thought and consideration, do not change.

This sounds like a still-street-smart elder statesman trying to avoid pejorative labels, not someone trying to dis-
sociate himself from political conservativism. In a 1964
speech honouring the life of a Melbourne rabbi, Menzies
spoke of himself as both "orthodox and liberal" which
suggests that, at least in part, he saw himself as a traditionalist.

For most of our first century, Australian politics was about
occupying and utilising a nation-continent, mobilising for
war, grappling with financial crises, and trying to deliver
a "fair go" for the battler. It was less about people's deep
attachments and fundamental values which could usually
be taken for granted. It's hard to credit now, but even in
the 60s and 70s, support for economic development, the
British connection, and some sort of institutional religion
could be taken for granted. The need for national and for
self-improvement was a political creed that united almost
all.

In 19th and 20th century Australia, there were almost
none of the divisions over Crown and Church that, in
earlier times in England, had given rise to the Whigs and
Tories (that ultimately became the British Liberals and
Conservatives). As distinct from Alfred Deakin in the early 1900s, by the time Menzies came to form his version
of the Liberal Party, he was clear that it wasn't to be a

down-under version of the English Liberals who, by that stage, were mostly allies of the Labour Party.

It was really only when cultural issues started to play as big a role as economic ones, and Australians came to identify themselves as "for" or "against" particular social changes, that terms such as "progressive" or "liberal", on the one hand; and "conservative" on the other, came into widespread use.

The first major Liberal to self-apply the term conservative was Malcolm Fraser. In a fine 1980 presentation to the South Australian state council of the Liberal Party, Fraser said that a government concerned to preserve liberal principles and values "must be in some sense conservative".

Dealing with the occasional tension between liberalism and conservatism, Fraser said that:

> Liberalism always emphasises the freedom of the individual and the absence of restraint. In its extreme form it becomes libertarianism and denies the need or efficacy of any constraints on freedom. Conservatism on the other hand stresses the need for a framework of stability, continuity and order, not only as something desirable in itself but as a necessary condition for a free society.

Conservatism, Fraser said, was not a "passing fashion or trend but a considered and serious realisation that central institutions and values are under threat". It was an "accumulated disillusionment" with left wing doctrines that claimed "intellectual and moral superiority" but that when "put to the test either do not work at all or produce unintended consequences which outweigh their supposed benefits". These included "planning which creates confusion and waste", he said; "ill-conceived welfare schemes which create monstrous bureaucracies, high taxes and high inflation"; "nationalised industries that fail to deliver the goods"; "attempts to help minorities which succeed only in creating a new dependency"; and "a concern for the environment which degenerates into ritual and dogma".

As well, Fraser said:

> This resurgence of conservatism expresses a concern to maintain continuity and coherence, to restore human control, in a world which has been subjected to massive and rapid changes...The new conservatism is not opposed to change as such...But it is concerned that the process of change should not proceed in such a headlong and ill-considered fashion that it yields unexpected and undesired consequences...It is concerned to preserve continuity, to ensure that hard-won gains are not carelessly lost, to integrate elements of the old and the new... To the extent that this government is conservative, it is so in these senses and for these reasons, not because it is concerned to protect privilege...

It was really only in opposition during the Hawke-Keating era, that senior Liberals more generally started to examine the conservative elements in their political creed and how these might be in harmony or at odds with philosophical liberalism. Howard led the way, sometimes describing himself as a "Burkean conservative" or once – with equal validity, as Burke was formally a Whig – as a "Burkean liberal".

For my part, I have never felt the need for a qualifying adjective. I regard myself as a conservative but, as such, feel fully at home in a Liberal Party which certainly stands for freedom but which has invariably stood for respect, order and tradition too.

In my 2009 book, *Battlelines,* I said that:

It's no slight on Howard to observe that he was not a systematic philosopher because conservatism is not a systematic philosophy. Unlike liberalism or socialism, conservatism does not start with an idea and construct a huge superstructure based on one insight or preference. Conservatism starts with an appreciation of what is and what has been and tries to discern the good from patterns of conduct. Conservatism prefers facts to theory; practical demonstration to metaphysical abstraction; what works to what's in the mind's eye. To a conservative, intuition is as important as reasoning; instinct as important as intellect. A way of life has far more demonstrative power to a conservative than a brilliant argument. Conservatives are not optimists or pessimists but realists. They have a proper appreciation of the strengths of society as well as its individual and collective capacity for folly. They have an understanding of the need to get things right but also an appreciation of how easily this can go wrong...

For all his personal conservatism, Howard always insisted that a political party that wanted to win government had to have a broad-based political philosophy. To win elections, parties need policies that strike chords with voters, not with theorists. Hence, it's the actual appeal that parties make to voters, not the after-the-event tags applied by academics, that should be taken as best characterising a party's approach...

Perhaps it's enough to say that in some circumstances freedom and in other circumstances a set of rules is the most effective way to encourage people to be their best selves. Howard perhaps came closest to describing what the government was actually trying to do in a speech from 2000. There was, he said, 'a correlation between the principles, the priorities and the aspirations that Australians carry within themselves...and the policy development framework of their national government'. In this speech, he nominated 'self-reliance', 'a fair go', 'pulling together' and 'having a go' as elements of the 'Australian Way'. This was the essence of Howard's approach. He tried to assimilate the values that he thought were at the heart of Australia. His political programme was liberal to the extent that he thought Australians wanted to get on with their own lives, but it was conservative in its emphasis on the source and 'mainstream' content of those values...

My book prompted a response, some months later, from George Brandis in his October 2009 Deakin lecture. In it, he was critical that, "over the past 20 years or so, there had been an attempt to dilute the Liberal Party's commitment to liberalism. This was particularly so during the two periods of John Howard's leadership... (and) recently, Howard's own political legatee... Tony Abbott has taken up the cause of making the Liberal Party more conservative still".

Yet eight years on, Brandis boasted that it was under the "leader of the conservative side of politics" that same sex marriage was on the point of being achieved. Perhaps, by then, he had come to better appreciate the Liberal Party's conservative dimension; or perhaps he'd worked out that political parties rarely prosper by telling a large section of the electorate that "we're not for you".

Of the two big parties, there's no doubt which one most appeals to people who think that freedom is what matters most. But what about people who worry about the social fabric or who are concerned that there's no level playing field on which they can compete? These are far more likely to support a party that's conservative as well as merely liberal. Certainly, the Liberal Party has enjoyed its biggest wins, under Menzies in 1949, Fraser in 1975, Howard in

1996, and me in 2013, when it's been led from the centre-right.

Still the last thing the Liberal Party needs is our own version of identity politics which tags people as "liberals" or "conservatives" and never the twain should meet. Regardless of the emphasis that's placed on the two key strands of Liberal thinking, to some extent we have to be both liberal and conservative. Not only do the two usually go hand in hand but elements of both are needed for electoral success.

A LEGISLATOR'S JOURNEY

From simplistic ideology to nuanced tradition – the instincts of freedom and order in one parliamentarian.

Nick Minchin

The Liberal Party of Australia embraces people and ideas across the Centre-Right political spectrum. Its particular focus from time to time will vary depending on circumstances, the state of the nation, leadership, Party composition and the like.

Most of us attached to the Party also experience being at different points on that spectrum depending on the issue, our stage in life, and our personal circumstances. And many in the Party may relate more readily to John Stuart Mill on one issue, and Edmund Burke on another.

Very few of us exhibit absolute consistency in ideological identification, but most of us have strong tendencies of one kind or another, which are likely to change over time.

I am one of not many who have moved from a libertarian tendency to a conservative tendency over my adult life, involving as it does 32 years of full-time Liberal Party engagement as a Party official and Senator and Minister.

As a teenager I lived in Cleveland, Ohio, USA, for year 12 of high school on an American Field Service scholarship.

Living in the 'land of the free, home of the brave' from 1970-71 was a life-changing experience and a full-frontal exposure to a nation which more than any other takes freedom seriously.

It was a challenging but inspiring year which kindled the fire of libertarianism in my political soul.

My year 12 schooling in the USA was followed by five years at the Australian National University in Canberra, studying Economics and Law. In Economics it was the age of Milton Friedman, the Chicago School and 'rational economics' which I lapped up with delight.

Absorbing the market economics I was being taught consolidated my nascent libertarian tendencies, and when in 1974 John Singleton founded his Workers Party, an avowedly libertarian outfit, I quickly signed on, attended meetings and helped out in the 1974 Federal election.

While forming strong political views at ANU, I was never active politically on campus; I avoided student politics and spent my time studying, working as a barman and waiter, playing sport and surfing. ANU in Canberra in the mid-70s was one heck of a place to be, with my fellow Knox Grammar Old Boy Gough Whitlam trashing the economy and setting up a Constitutional crisis.

I was truly shaken by the incredible damage a Labor Government could wreak in three short years, so after being admitted as a solicitor in 1977, I applied for and was given a job as a research officer at the Federal Secretariat of the

Liberal Party in Canberra at the tender age of 24.

I was committed to doing whatever I could to prevent Labor governing, which by definition meant working full-time for the principal non-Labor Party, the Liberal Party of Australia.

Like so many minor parties, the Workers Party had disappeared, and I was reminded that it was only the Liberals who could truly aspire to govern in place of Labor. But my libertarian tendencies were still fuelled by youthful exuberance.

I spent 14 years as a full-time Liberal Party official, six at the Federal Secretariat, eventually becoming Deputy Federal Director, followed by eight years as the Party's State Director in SA.

They were formative years, during which I acquired a home with a mortgage, got married and had two of our three kids.

As a Party official one hides one's political light under a bushel – but my support for free-market economics and small government remained strong.

What began to change was the development of my social conservatism, no doubt fuelled by the responsibilities of marriage and parenthood, and a return to the embrace of the Christianity of my youth.

Gradually I became the economic liberal and social conservative that John Howard most obviously represents. He became my role model.

When I eventually sought and won Senate preselection in South Australia for the 1993 election, I ran on a clear platform of economic liberalism and social conservatism and carried that predilection with me after becoming a Senator in July 1993.

And increasingly throughout my 18 years as a Liberal Senator for SA, including 10 years as a Minister, I identified as a conservative on the Right of the Liberal Party spectrum.

I never lost my passion for liberty. I fought a one-man war against compulsory voting; I opposed compulsory bicycle helmets; I railed against petty bureaucratic impositions whenever they reared their public head. But increasingly, I understood that individual liberty could not exist in a vacuum; that liberty could easily become licence; and that anarchy was a possible end-point of pure, unadulterated libertarianism.

Increasingly I understood that the preservation of individual liberty required a strong institutional framework that could only be sustained by a conservative disposition.

Liberty is a fragile flower, easily destroyed and hard to reproduce. Without a legal, social, and moral framework conducive to the sustainment of liberty, it will inevitably disappear.

Liberty requires the rule of law, a deeply-embedded democratic culture, a Constitutional system of checks and balances, a social consensus on basic values, social cohesion, economic stability, mutual respect, and law and order.

All those essential underpinnings of liberty are best preserved by a politically conservative culture that respects tradition and well-established institutions; and which is skeptical of radical change for the sake of it.

During my political career I increasingly drew a distinction between the merely behavioural, and the fundamentally moral in my approach to public policy issues.

Liberal Governments should refrain as much as possible from imposing legal obligations or prohibitions on individual behavior that, in the words of Mill, does no harm to others.

So for example while an individual on a bicycle should wear a bicycle helmet, the State should not force that individual to wear a helmet.

Similarly, while qualified electors should vote, the State should not force them to vote.

Citizens in a free country should not be forced to put a fluid like ethanol in the fuel tanks of their cars, simply to satisfy the demands of a particular lobby group.

Smokers should not be forced to pay extortionate levels of tax to consume a product that is legal.

However, there is a set of issues that are on a different level to the merely behavioural. Issues that are of a fundamentally moral character, especially relating to life and death, and that warrant action by the State.

Abortion and euthanasia are two such issues, and illustrate dramatically the gap between a libertarian and a conservative. As a Liberal Senator I exercised my right to a conscience vote to oppose measures relaxing laws relating to euthanasia and abortion.

'Though shalt not kill' is a fundamental injunction that as a social conservative I believe requires action by the State.

One of the most telling Parliamentary debates I was involved in concerned embryonic stem cell research. Even social conservatives divided on that issue. I opposed it, while John Howard supported it.

I joined with socially conservative Labor Senators to vote against allowing the destruction of embryos in the name of medical research, because of my strong view that the State should not permit the wilful termination of innocent life.

Libertarians in the Liberal Party took the opposite view, seeing no reason at all why the destruction of embryos should be prevented.

I understood the harm principle, and presumably so did the libertarians in my party who voted differently on these issues. How is it that they could not recognize the 'harm' in these legislative relaxations?

The hard question that all legislators must ask is: what is the role of the State?

It is incumbent on parliamentarians to really think through their philosophical approach to that question. Just when is state intervention warranted, and when should it be resisted?

Based on my early libertarian inclinations I am deeply skeptical of State intervention to regulate human behaviour where no harm to society or other individuals could result from that behavior.

However, my social conservatism compels me to take a different approach to issues which I categorise as much more profound than merely the behavioural.

The problem is, my conservative disposition means I saw harms which my libertarian colleagues were somehow blind to.

My view that the preservation of liberty requires a strong institutional framework has influenced my approach to issues like same-sex marriage and the republic. I believe the traditional family is one of the fundamental institutions underpinning a free society, and to the extent that SSM threatens that institution, I oppose it.

Similarly, Australia's Federal Constitution, built on the concept of the Crown, is an essential part of our institutional structure underpinning our liberty. Proposals for a republican form of government in Australia are genuinely revolutionary, and do run the risk of doing serious damage to the efficacy of one of the world's most successful Constitutions.

One of the most important lessons I've learned in politics is always to think through the potential consequences of policy proposals or proposed courses of action.

In public life one must consider deeply the possible consequences for individuals, for society, for its institutions and for liberty, of the many propositions for change that swirl around in the political ether. Unintended consequences are the bane of government action, and it was one of my practices as a Minister to ask senior bureaucrats to provide advice on possible unintended consequences of new legislation, to check over their shoulder for the blind spots.

I have come to the view that libertarianism does not provide the necessary philosophical discipline to make the right decisions on the broad sweep of issues that confront a parliamentarian every day. It doesn't perceive the blind spots.

A conservative disposition provides a more cohesive, coherent approach to the basic question of the role of government in a modern society.

My personal journey from ardent libertarian to cautious

conservative has involved constant questioning, and testing of my beliefs and principles, resulting in my firm belief that it is conservatism that is most likely to achieve
the best outcomes for individuals and society as a whole.

FAMILY: THE LIBERTARIAN BLIND SPOT

*Ideology is no match for the most basic guarantee of
formation and freedom – the human family.*

John Anderson

I am always happy to join libertarians in praise of freedom from state interference. Yet in the following pages
I wish to deepen the analysis of freedom by reminding
libertarians that focusing solely on the state is both myopic and dangerous to liberty itself. State expansionism is
provoked by social disharmony, and thus healthy, natural
and civic institutions that promote social harmony best
preserve freedom. I will focus on the family in this chapter, but the analysis could easily extend to other social
capital generators such as churches, charities, sporting
clubs, and voluntary societies. It is right for conservatives
to fight for liberty, but we must be able to appreciate both
the direct pursuit of freedom, and a freedom pursued indirectly by promoting the social institutions whose health
does more than anything else to stave off the expansion of
the state into our private lives.

Abstract and concrete freedom

Another John Anderson, former Professor of Philosophy at Sydney University, said that the life of liberty is 'a perilous and fighting life.'[1] No one would disagree with Anderson, certainly no one who lived through any part of the twentieth century, or who is alive now and paying attention. And yet, despite the obvious fact that freedom's enemies are numerous and powerful, it is remarkably rare for any individual or social movement to openly admit that it is an enemy of liberty, although some, like our so-called 'progressive' warriors, are less adept at keeping their guard up. Strangely, the most oppressive social movements will frequently claim to be liberating their victims.

Thus, Karl Marx assured people in the nineteenth century that 'only in community [with others has each] individual the means of cultivating his gifts in all directions; only in the community, therefore, is personal freedom possible.'[2] In other words, Karl Marx – architect of one of the most oppressive political systems in the history of humankind – sincerely believed that is project was one of freedom. Marx was merely echoing the thought of one of the intellectual harbingers of the French Revolution – the event that inspired so much radical thought of which Marxism was but one expression – who famously said that 'whoever refuses to obey the general will shall be compelled to do so by the whole body. This means nothing less than that he will be forced to be free....'[3] Forcing

---

[1] In fact, Anderson was quoting the Italian philosopher, Benedetto Croce. See *A Perilous and Fighting Life. From Communist to Conservative: The Political Writings of Professor John Anderson*, Mark Weblin (ed.), (North Melbourne: Pluto Press, 2003), p.3.

[2] Karl Marx, *The German Ideology*, C.J. Arthur (ed.), (London: Lawrence and Wishart, 1977), p.83.

[3] Jean Jacques Rousseau, *The Social Contract*, Book I, sec. 8. Available as an ebook.

people to be free was a unique skill of the French Revolutionaries, made possible by the fact that their political programme was essentially constructed around a set of abstract ideals such as *liberty, equality, fraternity*, not to mention *natural rights*.

What lesson are we to learn from this? That ideals are dangerous and should be eschewed for some sort of pure pragmatism? Not at all! The lesson to be learned is not that ideals *per se* are dangerous, but that *abstract* ideals are the real problem. And by an abstract ideal I mean an ideal devoid of any anchoring to something tangible and concrete. Ideals detached from concrete reality are simply vague notions in our minds that trigger feelings rather than genuine cognitive understanding.

One problem with vague and abstract ideals is that if they have no clear meaning, then there is no condition under which we can all agree that they are being realised or not. In other words, when freedom or equality is just a vague concept, its meaning is determined not so much by objective reality, but by feelings, or worse – by those who have the power to declare certain interpretations of an abstract concept the 'correct' one. In other words, the guillotine or the gulag (or, in our age, execution by social media) determines the correct interpretation of 'freedom' or 'equality'.

A better approach to thinking politically is not so much to begin with a set of abstract concepts such as freedom, equality, or solidarity and then build our more specific political beliefs and opinions around them, but to try and appreciate the object that all politics is meant to be about or to serve: human flourishing. The place where we should all begin when thinking about politics and government is to ask what it is to be human. After all, isn't politics supposed to serve the ends of human beings? At least at this point we have something concrete to which our political thinking may be anchored: the human condition.

But even talk of 'the human condition' and 'human nature' can be a little too nebulous. After all, didn't Marx think that his communist utopia was in accord with the human condition? We want to be much more concrete, even less abstract. We want to talk about human beings as observed in various social contexts. In this way we move from political ideology to something more like political experience, or political science.

Responsible political thought anchors itself to some key questions about human beings as observed over time. Even if we grant the fundamental (but unoriginal) premise of liberalism that individuals are unique, we can still ask some key questions: What do human beings seek in their lives (distinguishing between the ends that humans pursue and the infinite variety of means by which they pursue them)? To what extent can we expect the average person to sacrifice her own interests for the interests of others, ranging from close family members to fellow nationals whom they may never have met? In other words, what are human beings capable of in terms of altruism and selfishness? This last question is important for all governments, for all governments fund their programmes through taxation. Thus, to what extent can a government tax its people before its people feel no incentive to work beyond a certain point, knowing that the work involved is hardly worth the reward, thus reducing not only productivity but disincentivising entrepreneurialism, which in time creates a regressive economy? These questions must be approached with a knowledge of psychology, economics, and history.[4] In other words, thinking about politics

---

[4] 'What is the use of discussing a man's abstract right to food or medicine? The question is upon the method of procuring and administering them. In that deliberation I shall always advise to call in the aid of the farmer and

requires us to have an eye firmly on what actually happens in the world, not merely on what we think should happen.

Problems occur when governments get these questions wrong, either through incompetent policy research or ideological blindness. When governments misunderstand what humans live for, or misunderstand the limits of altruism (or selfishness), then governments try to force their citizens' behaviour and lives to fit into a predetermined pattern of what the government thinks they should be. This was one of the great flaws of Marxism in theory and practice. Marx severely underestimated the naturalness of individuals' affections for their own families and friends above everyone else, not to mention people's affections for their religions and nations. Marx mistakenly thought that with the right social conditions people would conceive of themselves not so much as members of a family or religion or nation, but as members of an economic class – as workers. Of course, historically, the greatest disappointment of communists has always been the workers that they seek to liberate, especially when they stubbornly resist setting aside their partiality for their families, religion, and nations for total loyalty to their class as embodied in the communist government.

This gives the lie to the oft repeated dictum that Marxism is a good theory but unworkable in practice. In fact, it is unworkable in practice precisely because it is a *bad* theory. Praising Marxism in theory is like praising the blueprint of a mansion while it collapses in front of you, owing to the architect's obsession with aesthetics over physics. The architect who still insisted that it was a good blueprint, failed only by the realities of physics, would soon find himself deregistered. Lesson? – political theories can

the physician, rather than the professor of metaphysics.'
Edmund Burke, *Reflections on the Revolution in France* (1790).

only be evaluated against their success in the real world, not according to appeals to abstract concepts such as justice, fairness, equality or even liberty itself. The 'nice theory, shame about the history' attitude towards Marxism hardly does justice to the legacy of Marxism in the twentieth century:

- USSR: 20 million deaths;[5]

- China: 65 million deaths;

- Vietnam: 1 million deaths;

- North Korea: 2 million deaths;

- Cambodia: 2 million deaths;

- Eastern Europe: 1 million deaths;

- Latin America: 150,000 deaths;

- Africa: 1.7 million deaths;

- Afghanistan: 1.5 million deaths;

- The international Communist movement and Communist parties not in power: about 10,000 deaths.[6]

Some theory.

But how do we know when a theory is successful? What does it mean for a political theory to be successful? Again, we go back to Politics 101. What is a government supposed to do? Simple, it is supposed to establish or protect the conditions within which individuals, families, and voluntary groups can pursue the goods that make us human in the first place. This approach to politics goes all the

---

[5]   This represents estimation on the conservative side. Some estimates are over 60 million.

[6]   Figures set out in Courtois, Stéphane Courtois (ed.), *The Black Book of Communism: Crimes, Terror, Repression*, (Massachusetts: Harvard University Press, 1999), p.X.

way back to Aristotle in the 4th century BC. When Aristotle called us *political animals* he was not saying that we are naturally Machiavellian or that the greatest activity in which we can be engaged is politics; he was saying that human nature finds its best expression within political societies; that is, societies with governments that protect safety and also allow for a degree of individuality.[7]

For Aristotle, there are certain goods that we all pursue, that we get out of bed to pursue, and they are identifiable by the fact that we desire them for their own sake.[8] For the most part these goods are easy to identify by simply asking, what things do we desire in life that need no justification, or whose appeal only a mad or defective person would question? Health, security, friendship, leisure, knowledge, and creativity are the less controversial among them. The upshot of this approach to human nature is that freedom is not merely freedom from state coercion, but also freedom to pursue the things that make life meaningful. Foundational to all law and public policy is the question of how likely it is to facilitate or hinder people's pursuit of the basic goods that make our lives human. Thus, to the question, what is government supposed to do? – the answer is to set out the conditions within which we can freely pursue the goods that make human life meaningful and joyous.

We can build on this even more by looking at Edmund Burke's famous response to the French Revolution, which anticipated what would become the Reign of Terror (September 1792-July 1794), and also anticipated the gruesome excesses of Marxism in the twentieth century. Against the ideology of the French *philosophes* Burke suggested an approach that he called 'the science of gov-

---

[7] See Aristotle's discussion of the relationship between humankind and the state in *The Politics*, 1.1-3.

[8] Aristotle, *Nichomachean Ethics*, 1.2.

ernment'; and, to be sure, it is no 'short experience that can instruct us in that practical science.'[9] For Burke, a well-running society is immensely complex, constituted by countless 'obscure and almost latent causes, things which appear at first view of little moment, on which a very great part of its prosperity or adversity may most essentially depend.'[10] In other words, for Burke, public policy and legislation must be driven not by abstract theories but by a painstaking understanding of exactly how a society works, not to mention an understanding of the human condition that pays more attention to how we actually are rather than how we ought to be.

Libertarians get something right. In particular, libertarians of the consequentialist school, such as Milton Friedman, rightly stress the appropriateness of small government, not so much because of freedom or rights, but because of the unfortunate tendency of governments to *cause* at least as many problems as they profess to ameliorate. This is a responsible view of government anchored in the practical and observable – Burkean conservatives can agree on it.

Libertarians are also right to stress the agonistic or competitive nature of the relationship between freedom and equality. More equality tends to mean less freedom, and to a significant degree vice versa. Thus, the late Harvard philosopher Robert Nozick's famous example of the hypothetical society whose citizens start off with exactly the same amount of money each, but who choose – entirely voluntarily – to pay money to see Wilt Chamberlain play basketball to their immense entertainment and pleasure. From people's voluntary choices Chamberlain becomes fabulously wealthy. The lesson is that any 'pattern' of fairness or equality imposed on a society will be disrupted

---

[9]   Burke, *Reflections on the Revolution in France.*
[10]   Ibid.

by people's free transactions. The political lesson is of the utmost importance:

> To maintain a pattern one [the state] must either continually interfere to stop people from transferring resources as they wish to, or continually (or periodically) interfere to take from some persons resources that others for some reason chose to transfer to them.[11]

In other words, maximizing equality means maximizing the state's interference in our lives: equality is parasitical on freedom.

Freedom and civil society

The problem with much libertarianism is not so much its conception of liberty as negative, that is, an absence of state interference, but its frequent failure to appreciate the distinction between pursuing liberty directly and indirectly. We pursue liberty directly when we strike down laws that restrict action. We pursue liberty indirectly when we strike down laws or create new laws with the aim of strengthening the natural and social institutions that function as state-limiting forces. With its preoccupation with the state as the single most important institution of oppression, libertarianism frequently overlooks the civic virtue-cultivating institutions that are absolutely necessary for liberty to flourish. What exactly are civic virtues? They are the character traits possessed by individuals required to keep society operating harmoniously; they are the single greatest preservative against state expansion and therefore against the erosion of personal liberty. In this way libertarians should be zealous to identify and protect those natural and social institutions that cultivate civic virtue.

---

[11]   Robert Nozick, *Anarchy, State, and Utopia*, (New York: Basic Books, 2013 [1974]), p.163.

If libertarians want a small state, a state that has no jus-tification to expand more and more into our private lives and pockets, then they need to think seriously about the causes of the social problems that enable, and even drive, the state to expand. There is no space to explore all of the complex social problems that statists use to justify state expansion, but one social trend looms perhaps larger than any in terms of its contribution to social problems: the breakdown of the family and the phenomenon of the ab-sentee father. Sociologists disagree on many things, but on one thing all sociologists agree – the breakdown of the family is the single biggest contributor to poverty and the individual and social maladies that go with poverty: un-dereducation, drug abuse, crime, homelessness, mental illness, and long-term unemployment.

The international sociological evidence for diminished social skills and subsequent hardship and anti-social be-haviour in children from broken homes is indisputable and overwhelming. Girls whose parents divorced are more likely to fall pregnant as teenagers.[12] Similarly, boys whose parents divorce are more likely to father a child with a teenage mother out of wedlock.[13] Teenage pregnancies are almost certain low socio-economic predictors. Chil-dren whose parents divorce will suffer from diminished learning capacity and educational achievement. In other words, they do more poorly at school and don't continue in educational institutions as long as their peers.[14] Divorce

---

[12] Robert J. Quinlan, 'Father Absence, Parental Care, and Female Reproductive Development,' *Evolution and Hu-man Behavior*, 24 (2003): 376–390.

[13] Robert F. Anda, Daniel P. Chapman, Vincent J. Felitti, Valerie Edwards, David F. Williamson, Janet B. Croft, and Wayne H. Giles, 'Adverse Childhood Experiences and Risk of Paternity in Teen Pregnancy,' *Obstetrics and Gynecology*, 100 (2002): 37-45.

[14] E. Milling Kinard and Helen Reinherz, 'Effects of Marital

also contributes to children's 'externalizing behaviors' such as weapon carrying, fighting, substance abuse, and binge drinking.[15] An Australian parliamentary review of the literature of the effects of divorce on children showed that children will feel more hostility and a sense of rejection,[16] which will have subsequent negative psychological and social effects. An exhaustive 2015 report on six OECD countries, including Australia, found that divorce lowered the subsequent earnings of both men and women, with women more likely to experience reduced earning longer than men. Furthermore, in Australia government benefits are 'very important in reducing the effects of divorce on women's equivalised household income.'[17] Research conducted in Australia in 2011 by the Melbourne Institute found that 62% of homeless people identify relationship/family breakdown or conflict as the cause of their initial homelessness.[18] Reflecting back on a lifetime of research-

---

Disruption on Children's School Aptitude and Achievement,' *Journal of Marriage and Family*, 48 (1986): 289-290; Paul R. Amato, 'Children of Divorce in the 1990s: An Update of the Amato and Keith (1991) Meta-Analysis,' *Journal of Family Psychology*, 15 (2001): 355-370; Daniel Potter, 'Psychosocial Well-Being and the Relationship between Divorce and Children's Academic Achievement,' *Journal of Marriage and the Family*, 72/4 (2010), p.941.

[15] Kathleen Boyce Rodgers and Hilary A. Rose, 'Risk and Resiliency Factors among Adolescents Who Experience Marital Transitions,' *Journal of Marriage and Family*, 64 (2002): 1028-1029.

[16] *To Have and To Hold: Strategies to Strengthen Marriage and Relationships*, Parliament of the Commonwealth of Australia, House of Representatives, Standing Committee on Legal and Constitutional Affairs, (Canberra, Australia, Parliament of Australia: 1998), 36.

[17] *The Economic Consequences of Divorce in Six OECD countries*, Australian Institute of Family Studies, Research Report No. 31 – March 2015.

[18] *Journey's Home Research Report No.1*, July 2012 pp.21-22.

ing the relationship between family and society, Co-Director at the National Marriage Project at Rutgers University, David Popenoe, said, 'All the social scientific data that I could unearth, in Sweden, the United States, and other modern nations, pointed strongly to the fact that child outcomes were worse in all family forms apart from married couple families, whether the measure was crime, school completion, teen pregnancies, depression, and almost every other undesirable dimension one could think of.'[19] More pointedly, summarising international peer-reviewed research carried out over three decades, Patrick F. Fagan and Aaron Churchill conclude that:

> Divorce damages society. It consumes social and human capital. It substantially increases cost to the taxpayer, while diminishing the taxpaying portion of society. It diminishes children's future competence in all five of society's major tasks or institutions: family, school, religion, marketplace and government. The reversal of the cultural and social status of divorce would be nothing less than a cultural revolution.[20]

This is not meant so much to be an argument against divorce, but rather a plea to libertarians to consider the relationship between family breakdown and state expansion. Social researchers have also found strong links between fathering and subsequent emotional and social wellbeing of children, boys in particular. For boys, risk of homelessness increases by 10-15% if parents separate.[21]

---

[19] David Popenoe, *War Over the Family*, (Transaction: New Brunswick, NY: 2005), p.xiii.

[20] Patrick F. Fagan and Aaron Churchill, 'The Effects of Divorce on Children,' *Marriage and Religion Research Institute*, January 11, 2012, p.1.

[21] Julie Moschion, Family break-up raises homelessness risk, and critical period is longer for boys, *The Conversation*, June 1 2017.

Fathers are uniquely formative in the lives of both males and females. Long-term peer-reviewed research collated in a Fathering Project report shows that 'high levels of father involvement' have been linked to higher levels of cognitive and social competence, increased social responsibility and capacity for empathy, positive self-control and self-esteem.[22] In several areas, such as social interaction, drug and alcohol abuse, delinquency, and sexual risk-taking, the influence of positive fathering was shown to be more significant than the influence of positive mothering. That is in no way to deny that mothering is less important. Closer to home, a 2011 Australian Institute of Family Studies report summarised research finding that 'Australian fathers play a vital role in their families' and that fathers' parenting is 'sometimes different, but complementary to, the role of mothers.'[23] Furthermore, there are positive associations between measures of fathering and children's socio-emotional and learning outcomes.

As Popenoe, has said:

> A symbiotic relationship exists between the family and civil society. The family in an unfriendly surrounding culture is precarious; the stresses can be overwhelming. And civil societies depend on families to inculcate those civic values – honesty, trust, self-sacrifice, responsibility – by which they can thrive. In this sense, families can be thought of as 'seedbeds of civic virtue.' Such civic values are taught in the home, or they virtually are not taught at all. The school can try to teach these values – as it must – but if they are not taught within the home, early within a child's life, it is usually too late.[24]

---

[22] *How Fathers and Father Figures can Shape Child Health and Wellbeing*, p.2. The Fathering Project.

[23] 'Fathering in Australia among couple families with young children,' Family Matters No. 88 - August 2011, Australian Institute of Family Studies.

[24] Popenoe, *War Over the Family*, p.56.

Healthy families and a robust civil society also preserve liberty. Power's natural inclination is to power, not to impotence, and thus the state's natural inclination is to expand. For those at the helm of the state, every social problem is an opportunity for the state to intervene. This is why it is not sufficient for conservatives to join with libertarians in simply railing against the state. They need to understand and protect the natural and civic institutions – families, churches, friendly societies, and charities – that can address and ameliorate the kinds of social problems by which statists justify their programme of expansionism. In regard to Popenoe's words above, libertarians must be careful not to *unnecessarily* encourage social and economic trends that over time will serve to undermine such institutions, themselves the friends of freedom from the state.

Conclusion

To solve today's problems we cannot be wedded to any conception of freedom in the abstract – as in the French Revolution and the theories of Marx – but rather to what humans *actually* strive towards in life, and the *existing* natural and social institutions that most facilitate their goals.

I count Sir Robert Menzies as an intellectual and political forebear in his appreciation of the importance of the family in this respect. Menzies appreciated the conservation of valuable social institutions in his pursuit of limiting state expansion.[25] Thus, in Menzies' great 1942 'Forgotten People' speech, he spends nearly half of it extolling the importance of the family as the great seedbed of civ-

---

[25] G. Melleuish, 'Can the Liberal Party hold its 'broad church' of liberals and conservatives together?,' *The Conversation*, April 10 2018.

ic virtue.[26] Even before Menzies, the Federation Fathers were deeply informed by an already existing and growing Australian tradition – a conservative instinct which persisted by any other name – as they strove to establish a federal system of government that remained anchored to the institutions and principles of the English Constitution.[27] This Australian tradition does indeed regard liberty as central to flourishing human life. Yet it also recognises the long-standing institutions that have fostered and preserved the civic virtues that keep society harmonious. This is a great inheritance we share as Australians. We must do everything we can to preserve it from intrusive abstractions.

---

[26] R. G. Menzies, 'The Forgotten People' (1942), *The Forgotten People and Other Studies in Democracy*, (Redland Bay, QLD: Jeparit Press-Connor Court, 2017 [1943]), pp.1-10.

[27] S. A. Chavura and G. Melleuish, 'Conservative instinct in Australian political thought: The Federation debates, 1890–1898,' *Australian Journal of Political Science*, 50 (3), 513-528.

Part VI.

Conservative Home.

Conservative World.

THE REVIVALIST

Conservatism is dead. Long live Revivalism.

Oliver JJ Lane

The thing that hath been, it is that which shall
be; and that which is done, is that which shall be
done; and there is no new thing under the sun.

Ecclesiastes 1:9

The reader will not find the claim that there is no point
being a conservative in the 21st century – because there
is nothing left to conserve – particularly original or profound. Indeed, many great men and not least among them
the wonderful Peter Hitchens make a reasonable living
pointing out just that.

In the vernacular of our contemporary meme-laden society, however, this perspective can have the effect of one
great 'black pill'. In other words, it is what we used to call
extremely depressing to find yourself fighting a constant
losing rear-guard action against the avant-garde steam-
roller of modernism.

The fatal temptation is to fall back on the wrong-headed Whiggish idea that 'progress' is inevitable and the only thing left for the isolated conservative is to stand aside and tear his hair out with despair as the chaos unfolds. Observe, once again, the blessed Saint Peter H. who speaks of having given up on all efforts to save Britain from itself but acts now only as an obituarist to our dying society.

Thankfully for the would-be pallbearer, there is a great alternative. We are called upon to set ourselves aside from being either progressives or conservatives – to not be, as Gil Chesterton so famously observed, a person who either makes mistakes or prevents those of others from being corrected.

Instead, we ought to be regressive, and proudly so. To imitate those wonderful Victorians who mitigated the industrial chaos of their own age so successfully by looking back to Medieval England.

I call the wonderful people rediscovering this tradition of constructive backwards-looking by the title of 'Revivalists'.

The Revivalist symbol: St Pancras station

The astonishingly beautiful St. Pancras railway station hotel, completed 1876 in the polychromatic, High Gothic Revival style, is the most powerful and enduring symbol of Revivalism one could hope for. The age of steam, powered by industry and mechanisms by necessity engineered down to the very last thousandth of an inch could very well have been one characterised by 'clean' lines, and 'efficient' design.

But, thank God and to the great benefit of us all, it was not. The Victorians rooted themselves during a time of then-unprecedented pace of change and development, first in the reassuring leitmotif first of Classical civilisation, and then in European Medieval history. Establishing a sense of place, purpose, and permanence and not allowing a people to become lost in a rapidly developing world is essential, and how better to do so than by the most public art form, architecture.

The Victorian master builder or engineer understood instinctively what the great American poet Longfellow wrote in *The Builders*, that:

> In the elder days of Art,
> Builders wrought with greatest care
> Each minute and unseen part;
> For the Gods see everywhere.

How impossibly idealistic this dead standard seems betwixt the dull grey concrete tower and the sheet-glass needle. Some would walk, shivering beneath these crimes and shrug them off as 'just the way the world is now – you can't turn the clock back!' But the Revivalist *knows* such heights are obtainable by man and didn't come as a mere unrepeatable fluke.

This ideal was powerfully expressed through the Victorians' own revivalism in buildings like the Crossness Pumping station ('a cathedral of ironwork', which only survives today because the metalwork is so massive it was too expensive for 20th century philistines to demolish), a sewage treatment plant that never meant to be seen by the public in ordinary operation and yet was built as a temple to sanitation. It is thankfully now in the process of restoration.

The genesis of St Pancras itself has been the subject of great writings by greater minds, but its journey from a proud expression of a confident people reacting to progress in a natural and healthy way to a brush with obliteration by the modernist wreckers is deeply instructive. The building itself is a colossal brick memento mori, a painful reminder of how much we have lost to modernism and how close we came to losing more.

It is hard to believe now, seeing the refurbished and vibrantly alive St Pancras today, that the British state which came to own it through the nationalisation of the railways in 1948 once was desperate to demolish it. Having been prevented from doing so, it instead pursued a policy of deliberate neglect for decades. Old railwaymen who had occasion to visit the hotel after its 'conversion' to offices by its resentful guardian recall the incongruous and crude hanging of rectangular strip lights from the grand ceiling mouldings, holes knocked through walls to allow wiring to pass, with the cabling runs nailed directly into decorative plaster.

A 2005 account in *Building* magazine by a visitor before its Revival recalls the vandalism visited upon the station by a government denied demolition. But a determined group of campaigners and enthusiasts swam against the tide of modernism to preserve the then deeply unfashionable Gothic style, and the visitor contrasted an image of the building in its heyday to the present, writing:

> There's a sepia photograph of stiff Victorian guests waited on by a battalion of staff in the same lofty, curving coffee lounge. The Victorian version is adorned with textured wallpaper, marble columns and a ceiling crusted with mouldings, whereas today's is hidden under white plaster, but where patches have been peeled away, the glowing colours underneath are tantalisingly revealed. The past seems almost within touching distance – just waiting for someone to bring it back to life.

Saving this building was not mere conservatism. The astonishing 16 million bricks fired to match the originals, 18,000 new panes of glass for the roof, and 300,000 roof slates to revive this building back to its original purpose can be, if we let it, a guide to the broader Revival our society needs.

The late Gavin Stamp, a leading light of the Young Georgians, another of the crucial Revivalist movement, modernism-refusenik groups to whom Revivalism owes so much (his richly illustrated book *Gothic for the Steam Age* has the power to cure even the foulest moods), pointed out this grounding to ease change also took form in the 1920s and 30s, during the interwar house building boom.

Stamp convincingly argued that the reaction to the coming of the motor-car age was fundamentally a revival of Tudor taste in the creative arts, just as Gothic had been to steam. The defining feature of early 20th-century house building was Tudor, a style as loathed by architectural establishment snobs today as it was then.

This style, as Stamp notes, was also leapt upon by brewers building huge numbers of new inns to serve expanding suburban communities and the A-road network. To them, the Olde English style spoke of pleasant, warm beer and roast beef, rather than the hard spirits and debauchery of the inner cities. In a decade where prohibition of alcohol had taken hold in the United States and was a spectre haunting Europe, this grounding in the pastoral innocence of the Yeoman's England rather than Hogarth's London was crucial – a Revivalism in service of commerce.

The Revivalist Creed, a.k.a:

Who are these strange people who want to make the world a more beautiful place anyway?

Setting out life along Revivalist principles is not only desirable, I have discovered through some years of amusing and enlightening experiment, it is also practical and rewarding. As an antidote to the existential dread of the plastic ready-meal and the 88% Acrylic, 7% Polypropylene, 5% Polyester pullover, I have found nothing better.

If you have thought it worth your while to read this far you will, it is quite certain, already know a great many proto and even realised Revivalists. Whether they know they are brothers in arms quite yet or not, there are certain qualities by which ye shall know them.

Think always of the ordinary sort of fellow, who upon looking upon the latest glass & steel monstrosity to disfigure our city skylines, or the crumbling cast concrete civic monstrosity gifted to us by the great disaster that was the 20th century, has his private doubts. The man that looks and who asks himself – under his breath lest he be overheard and tutted at by some passing snob – 'why can't cities be beautiful any more?'

Know that in his heart lies the glimmer of hope that we may yet be saved. In terms of the radicalisation process, it is only a few short steps from despairing at whatever unworthy filth has been crowned as 'art' by the impossibly elite, incestuous, and diseased cultural establishment to actually doing something about it. We are called upon, surely, not to be idle observers but passionate actors, doing the good thing wherever the opportunity presents itself.

Revivalists, as I know them, by their very nature, are counter-culturalists and reactionaries. They are a varied and fascinating group of curmudgeonly individualists committed, perhaps not a little ironically, to saving a homogenous and harmonious society.

And to some extent, they have to be. It takes a certain degree of bloody-mindedness to look at the new world being created for us and to not only consciously realise it is wrong – the position of the conservative – but to understand instinctively that much that is precious has been already lost and to merely attempt to hold the tide is pointless.

Revivalism is an idea whose time has come, again. You are not by any means the only disillusioned conservative confronted with the sudden mainstream culture horror at plastic ocean pollution to look at his wax-paper wrapped sandwich and realise that we've been the inadvertent environmentalists all along.

The Revivalist, although reluctant to give offence, will derive much pleasure from his bona fide, if inadvertent, eco-credentials outranking those of the abrasive, loud-mouth, plastic-shod vegan. That old tweed coat hanging on the peg offers much to the worker-consumer suddenly starkly aware of the dreadful implications of shallow, fast fashion. It is organic and sustainable – we shall have sheep and plants to dye those fabulous colourways long after the petrochemical industry that sustains our polyester world has finally vanished.

The Revivalist Home

Urban living for thinking, critically minded people has been the norm for the past century, after the country house set grindingly rolled towards endangered species classification and were replaced by – at least within commuting distance – stockbroker types.

Yet the first-rank Western city as a home to the Revivialist is under persistent and pernicious assault from two sides – quite apart from the degrading onslaught of modernist architecture and crass 'public art'.

On one hand, massive excess demand – often driven by open borders policies and migrants that gravitate towards urban centres – is driving purchase prices to totally unobtainable levels. This is a serious matter for the nascent family that understands a sense of place, investment in the future, and full expression of the wonderful domestic bond between man and woman requires property ownership.

On the other, is the rising tide of violence. The lives of young, nicely brought up children destroyed by drug addiction. And that is not, of course, to mention the apparently unending scandal of migrant community child rape gangs blighting towns and cities – a phenomenon that, we hope, will remain confined to northern towns and cities of the United Kingdom and not blight other Western nations.

This leaves one reaching the inevitable conclusion that to bring up children solely in the 21st century city is, even with the best parenting imaginable, a roll of the dice with their bodies and minds.

Retreat, albeit temporary, from our once great cities is therefore inevitable and necessary for all but the wealthiest Revivalists, who in any case have the means to insulate themselves from the existential dread of the soul-crushing commute and violent city.

Some would paint this course of action as pure cowardice. Better, perhaps, to remain in the immoral, multicultural swamp and reform it from the inside. But even with the stiffest resistance and mental fortitude, the reek of the city corrupts. See this impact writ large in Westminster or Washington – the moral swamp.

The importance of removing yourself from this influence

as an important step towards contributing to the coming revival has been made recently in a most enlightening interview with *The Federalist* by traditionalist sculptor Alexander Stoddart. Speaking of the art he creates and the innate ability of the great majority of people to notice and call out without embarrassment the modernist nonsense pushed on us by the artistic establishment, Stoddart observes:

> So as far as the resurgence or revival of Occidental values is concerned, you can't look to New York or London, but you can look to other places. And your ordinary John Doe from the provinces has got a strong olfactory sense for a fraud, just because he hasn't been living in a place where the miasma is constant. He's too far out there, he's not a part of the Mandarin coterie.

So this is why being a provincial is a very important thing, because you can actually maintain clear breathing, your nose stays close to nature, and you can smell the fraud when you come into a room.

To Stoddart, being a 'provincial' isn't something to apologise for – it is virtuous and essential. Crucially, he links those key ideas, 'the resurgence or revival of Occidental [Western] values', to anti-urban living.

It is not enough to merely exist in the countryside, of course, to be an individual in splendid isolation. The provincial joy is real community, so absent from anonymous city streets, and ample space to build depth and character to resist the modern, and revive the good.

With that in mind, I bandy the words of Alasdair MacIntyre's *After Virtue*, a work certainly familiar to metaphorically besieged Christians seeking to survive the 21st century. Looking back to the against-all-odds survival of the faith in monastic communities through the dark ages, he concluded:

> What matters at this stage is the construction of local forms of community within which civility and the intellectual and moral life can be sustained through the new dark ages which are already upon us. And if the tradition of the virtues was able to survive the horrors of the last dark ages, we are not entirely without grounds for hope. This time however the barbarians are not waiting beyond the frontiers; they have already been governing us for quite some time.

In other words – we've a generation or three ahead of us before any form of surviving traditional culture not cryogenically frozen and carefully shepherded away from the roaming eye of the barbarian will totally cease to meaningfully exist. Dark days are coming, and perhaps the time is now to start burying treasures and building walls.

This above all else, I believe, is what we are called to do at this very moment – to make our families and immediate communities seed banks of tradition, ready to spread and germinate when society is ready again.

Indeed, perhaps I would go further. So much has been lost already and the sooner the worthwhile is revived, the better off we shall be in the long term. This is especially true of those things that existed in living memory. Better to act now, surely, than trying to rediscover in centuries' time through social archaeology what customs and ways long ago turned to metaphorical dust.

With this need to act in mind, and having mercifully escaped the once-great metropolis of London, I have been putting these principles into action in England's rural south-west. This has been a very literal act of Revival, taking a previously uninhabited 16th-century cottage, the meadows and fields that once surrounded it grown tall with young trees and dense undergrowth and making it a working house again.

Restoring the cottage itself has proven to be the greatest asset in building a friendship network of fellow Revivalists – people who upon hearing that someone somewhere is making something beautiful again, just can't resist coming to have a look. Or lending that one traditional, specialist tool, or offering a weekend's labour in the particular area of expertise they've developed in their own Revival project.

I have found it quite remarkable how tolerant of the old way those considering the leap can be, when drawn to a rural beacon of anti-Urban life. The ancient cottage totally devoid of city amenities like mains water, drainage, or gas – water being drawn from a well in the garden and heat coming from a single iron stove – is a tonic.

There wasn't even hot water piped to the bathroom or a single flushing loo upon our arrival, but these issues – along with a total rethatch and reclamation of swampland around it into useful growing acreage – have now been overcome.

The hard work of this – and of keeping animals, growing vegetables – is enormously important to developing a strong, self-reliant, and stoic state of mind. What a refreshing change from the damaging and disturbing notion pushed on us by the mainstream media that men must talk about their emotions or else run the risk of killing themselves.

I've observed this improvement clearly in myself, and also in the developing personalities of the small core group of friend-volunteers who have travelled from across the country to help us build a rugged and sustainable outpost of civilisation for the long term.

As if this were not challenge enough, we are now also restoring a substantial Victorian-era property to become our permanent family home as well. Rooms enough, we hope for our growing family and spares for visiting like-minded Revivalists – a place to learn craft, share experience, and enjoy the fruits of our labour.

I say restoring, but I must be brutally honest – we are essentially undoing the evil of the 20th century. Undoing the damage done to the carpenter's work, lovingly re-laying the hand-fired polychromatic tiles, uncovering the old passageways and nooks carelessly boarded up by modernising morons in decades past.

This stewardship of place, the desire to pass on something in a better condition than it was received, was until comparatively recently a normal and healthy part of human existence in Western civilisation. While the progressive has worked to weaken this impulse with punitive death taxes, it remains. To the Revivalist, the family is everything.

And isn't family, after all, what it's all about? While the socialist will subject man to the imagined greater good and the party-loyal conservative will parrot lazy lines about the supremacy of the individual, you must surely know that society is made up of families.

And more than that, I dare say – society is a transient plaything moulded and abused by politicians and think-tankers – *civilisation* relies on a decent bedrock of families.

It cannot be said enough, and especially in this era of appalling identity politics, that by far the most important thing for us to work for is the family. Children of happy marriages must conserve it and pass on that inheritance to their own, and those from broken homes must be Revivalists and rediscover something good our great-grand-parents knew, but the 20th century worked to destroy forever.

It is all well and good, of course, admiring the antique silk umbrella you so gallantly keep in service with minute repairs, or the heritage wallpaper carefully picked out to restore the old drawing room, and indeed the zero-food miles vegetables you grow in your garden. But good grief, it is all for nothing if there isn't a civilised man on earth to admire your hard work in a century's time.

But starting a family – especially for the university educated young in the 21st century West – can appear to be difficult, if not an unattainable goal. Alas, it is easy and seductive to fall into this trap of thinking, that yes, of course! I wish to start a family, but first I just need one more postgraduate degree. Just one more pay rise. No children until we've had our astonishingly expensive dream wedding and at least bought a house. My partner just isn't quite settled in her career yet...

Your whole life will dance merrily past your eyes while you wait for that perfect moment to get on with it. The simple fact is the average age of the first time mother in Europe is now 30, and simple biology following on from how very late we now leave starting a family is forcing small family sizes of just one or two children on us.

For the vast majority of us whose ancestors were not Dukes or Scions of Industry, our forebears successfully reproduced in conditions that would be considered unacceptably squalid today. Each and every one of us is the beneficiary of an unbroken chain of hundreds of generations of human beings who, whatever else they achieved in life, were at least able to have sex successfully. How dreadful it would be for you to be the first ever in your direct family line to not even manage that.

We must, as Karl Marx almost certainly didn't say, seize the means of reproduction. Having a big family of your own is the most direct and rewarding thing any reader of this book can do, I hope, to make this world a better place.

As widely loathed by over-educated city dwellers as they are, with this in mind you absolutely have to note the clearly Revivalist policies being put in place in former communist countries in central Europe as we speak. Hungary is now giving decent cash loans to new families and writing them off once the mother has had her third child. For those with four children, the government will exempt the mother from income tax for life. Bold steps indeed, even if the free market conservative will find the blatant use of taxpayer's money crude and distasteful. Poland is making similar moves, but in the realms of Revivalist dreamland politics one particular policy sticks out as an incredible example of bold leadership on a matter that money-men will find utterly incomprehensible, but the mother or grandmother might weep in gratitude for.

Starting in 2018 and slowly easing the change through increasing the number of weekends affected every year, Poland is mandating that shops close on Sundays – to give employees and consumers at least one day a week off. And this is time meant specifically to spend with family.

God bless Poland.

A Call to Action

The small, superficially inconsequential changes we can make to our daily lives to improve ourselves and those around us, lead in time to greater things. The left understands this, using the power of small nudges in the other direction to demean and dilute a society ready for demolition and replacement in bright, shining concrete.

This is why the barbarians in office inflict on us so many tiny and seemingly inconsequential depredations. The debasement of our built environment, art, our language, the abolition of chivalry.

I am just five years in, barely scratching the surface of what is possible. But I have found the water warm and encourage you to follow.

A conservative politician may promise when seeking election to roll back the frontiers of the state but we know this is simply not enough. We must roll back the frontiers of the 20th century, the social conventions and lazy expectations that still dominate our civilisation but which can be defeated with good grace and stoicism. It is time to live in the mode of the *status quo ante bellum* – for the good of us all.

> People hate anything well made, you know: it gives them a guilty conscience.
>
> *John Betjeman*

DEMOCRACY, POPULISM, AND LIBERALISM

*Populism and nationalism may presage a revival of
conservatism, traditionally and properly understood.*

Roger Kimball

Whatever else it is, The Declaration of Independence is
a paean to nationalism and populism, properly understood. Remember, mankind is endowed by its creator
with certain 'unalienable' rights. To secure those rights,
people institute governments, whose legitimacy is under-
written by 'the consent of the governed.' Should a government cease to secure the happiness and prosperity of
the governed, 'it is the Right of the People to alter or to
abolish it, and to institute new Government, laying its
foundation on such principles and organizing its powers
in such form, as to them shall seem most likely to effect
their Safety and Happiness.'

The ideas of nationalism and populism emerged tarnished
from the twentieth century, partly because of their association with totalitarian movements that deployed nationalist and populist rhetoric to pursue the destruction of
nations and the liberty of their people, partly (and this is a
side of the issue that is often neglected) because of various
world-government schemes that regarded nations as an

impediment to the achievement of supra-national utopia.

In 2005, the political philosopher Jeremy Rabkin published a fine book called *Law Without Nations? Why Constitutional Government Requires Sovereign States*. Rabkin ably fleshes out the promise of his subtitle, but it would be folly to think this labor will not have to be repeated. As the apparently aborted promise of Brexit demonstrates, the temptation to exchange hard-won democratic freedom for the swaddling comfort of one or another central planning body is as inextinguishable as it is dangerous. As the English philosopher Roger Scruton has argued, 'Democracies owe their existence to national loyalties—the loyalties that are supposedly shared by government and opposition.' Many utopians argue that such loyalties are a threat to peace. After all, wasn't it national loyalty that sparked two world wars? No, it was that perverted offspring, totalitarianism, which wrapped itself in the banner of nationalism to achieve transnational ends. Scruton quotes Chesterton on this point: to condemn patriotism because people go to war for patriotic reasons, he said, is like condemning love because some loves lead to murder.

It is one of the great mysteries—or perhaps I should say it is one of the reliable reminders of human imperfection—that higher education often fosters a particular form of political stupidity. Scruton anatomizes that stupidity, noting 'the educated derision that has been directed at our national loyalty by those whose freedom to criticize would have been extinguished years ago, had the English not been prepared to die for their country.' This peculiar mental deformation, Scruton observes, involves 'the repudiation of inheritance and home.' It is a stage, he writes,

> through which the adolescent mind normally passes. But it is a stage in which intellectuals tend to become arrested. As George Orwell pointed out, intellectuals on the Left are especially prone to it,

and this has often made them willing agents of foreign powers. The Cambridge spies [Guy Burgess,
Kim Philby, et al.] offer a telling illustration of what
[this tendency] has meant for our country.

It is also telling that this *déformation professionelle* of intellectuals encourages them to repudiate patriotism as an
atavistic passion and favor transnational institutions over
national governments, rule by committee or the courts
over democratic rule. Rabkin reminds us of the naïveté—
what others have called 'idealism'—that this preference
requires. In order to believe that international bodies will
protect human rights, for example, you would have to believe

> that governments readily cooperate with other
> governments on common projects, even when
> such cooperation promises no direct exchange of
> benefits to each side. In the end, you must believe
> that human beings cooperate easily and naturally
> without much constraint—without much actual en-
> forcement, hence without much need for force. To
> believe this you must believe that almost all human
> beings are well-meaning, even to strangers. And
> you must believe that human beings have no very
> serious disagreements on fundamental matters.

The persistence of such beliefs is no guide to their cogen-
cy or truth. What that other Jeremy, Jeremy Bentham,
long ago called 'nonsense on stilts' presents a spectacle
that is perhaps unsteady but nonetheless mesmerizing.
And when it comes to the erosion of the nation state and
its gradual replacement by unaccountable, transnational
entities such as the EU, the UN, or the so-called 'World
Court,' the results are ominous. As Andrew C. McCarthy
has noted,

> [w]ith the potent combination of a seismic shift
> in public attitudes away from democratic self-de-

termination and toward oligarchic juristocracy (or rule by courts), as well as a sweeping infrastructure of so-called 'international human rights law,' this movement is now poised to realize much of its goal: A world in which the nation state, the organizing geopolitical paradigm and engine of human progress since the Treaty of Westphalia, substantially gives way to a post-sovereign order of global governance led by supra-national tribunals (or tribunals that, though nominally 'national,' pledge fealty to the higher calling of 'humanity'). Like other utopian projects, the end of this one is tyranny.

Today, the nation state, that territorially based network of filiation bound together through shared history, custom, law, and language, is under greater siege than at any time since the dissolution of the Roman Empire. The external threat of radical Islam—pardon the pleonasm—may be the greatest threat to Western civilization since 1571 when the Battle of Lepanto checked the incursion of what we used to call the paynim foe into Europe.

But in the end, perhaps the greatest threat to the West lies not in its external enemies, no matter how hostile or numerous, but in its inner uncertainty—an uncertainty that is all-too-often celebrated as an especially enlightened form of subtlety and sophistication—about who we are. The nation state is a bedrock of Western identity—a foundation we can abandon, whether through the embrace of judicial or bureaucratic fiat or the slow-drip method of unchaperoned immigration, only at our peril.

The attack on the nation state—a less orotund formulation might say our unwitting self-demolition—proceeds apace on several fronts. So does the attack on the reservoir of political sentiment—what is usually derided as 'populism'—that underwrites the nation state.

It is curious how certain words accumulate a nimbus of positive associations while others, semantically just as innocuous, wind up shouldering a portfolio of bad feelings. Consider the different careers of the terms 'democracy' and 'populism.' Do you know any responsible person who would admit to being opposed to democracy? No one who does not enjoy a large private income would risk it. But lots of people are willing to declare themselves anti-populist. The discrepancy is curious for several reasons.

For one thing, it is a testament to the almost Darwinian hardiness of the word 'democracy.' In the fierce struggle among ideas for survival, 'democracy' has not only survived but thrived. This is despite the fact that political thinkers from Plato and Aristotle through Cicero and down to modern times have been deeply suspicious of democracy. Aristotle thought democracy the worst form of government, all but inevitably leading to ochlocracy or mob rule, which is no rule.

In Federalist 10, James Madison famously warned that history had shown that democratic regimes have 'in general been as short in their lives as they have been violent in their deaths.' 'Theoretic politicians,' he wrote—and it would be hard to find a more contemptuous deployment of the word 'theoretic'—such politicians may have advocated democracy, but that is only because of their dangerous and utopian ignorance of human nature. It was not at all clear, Madison thought, that democracy was a reliable custodian of liberty.

Nevertheless, nearly everyone wants to associate himself with the word 'democracy.' Totalitarian regimes like to describe themselves as the 'Democratic Republic' of wherever. Conservatives champion the advantages of 'democratic capitalism.' Central planners of all stripes eagerly deploy programs advertised as enhancing or extending 'democracy.' Even James Madison came down on the side of a subspecies of democracy, one filtered through the modulating influence of a large, diverse population and an elaborate scheme of representation that attenuated (Madison said 'excluded') the influence of 'the people in their collective capacity.'

'Democracy,' in short, is a eulogistic word, what the practical philosopher Stephen Potter in another context apostrophized as an 'OK word.' And it is worth noting, as Potter would have been quick to remind us, that the people pronouncing those eulogies delight in advertising themselves as, and are generally accepted as, 'OK people.' Indeed, the class element and the element of moral approbation—of what some genius has summarized as 'virtue signaling'—are key.

It is quite otherwise with 'populism.' At first blush, this seems odd because the word 'populism' occupies a semantic space closely adjacent to 'democracy.' 'Democracy' means 'rule by the demos,' the people. 'Populism,' according to The American Heritage Dictionary, describes 'A political philosophy directed to the needs of the common people and advancing a more equitable distribution of wealth and power'—that is, just the sorts of things that the people, were they to rule, would seek.

But the fact is that 'populism' is ambivalent at best. Sometimes, it is true, a charismatic figure can survive and even illuminate the label 'populist' like a personal halo. Bernie Sanders managed this trick among the eco-conscious, racially sensitive, non-gender-stereotyping, anti-capitalist beneficiaries of capitalism who made up his core constituency.

But it was always my impression that in this case the term 'populist' was fielded less by Sanders or his followers than by his rivals and the media in an effort to fix him in the public's mind as one of the many lamentable examples of not-Hillary, who herself was presumed to be popular though not populist.

There are at least two sides to the negative association under which the term 'populist' struggles. On the one hand, there is the issue of demagoguery. Some commentators tell us that 'populist' and 'demagogue' are essentially synonyms (though they rarely point out that *demagogos* simply meant 'a popular leader,' e.g., Pericles). The association of demagoguery and populism describes what we might call the command-and-control aspect of populism. The populist leader is said to forsake reason and moderation in order to stir the dark, chthonic passions of a semi-literate and spiritually unelevated populace.

Populism, in short, seems incapable of escaping the association with demagoguery and moral darkness. Like the foul-smelling wounds of Philoctetes, the stench is apparently incurable. Granted, there are plenty of historical reasons for the association between demagoguery and populism, as such names as the brothers Tiberius and Gaius Gracchus, Father Coughlin, Huey Long, not to mention a certain Bavarian corporal named Adolf, remind us.

Still, I suspect that in the present context the apparently unbreakable association between populism and demagoguery has less to do with any natural affinity than with cunning rhetorical weaponization. 'Populism,' that is to say, is wielded less as a descriptive than as a delegitimizing term. Successfully charge someone with populist sympathies and you get, free and for nothing, both the imputation of demagoguery and what was famously derided as a 'deplorable' and 'irredeemable' cohort. The element of existential depreciation is almost palpable.

So is the element of condescension. Inseparable from the diagnosis of populism is the implication not just of incompetence but also of a crudity that is part aesthetic and part moral. Hence the curiously visceral distaste expressed by elite opinion for signs of populist sympathy. When Hillary Clinton charged that half of Donald Trump's supporters were an 'irredeemable' 'basket of deplorables,' when Barack Obama castigated small-town Republican voters as 'bitter' folk who 'cling to guns or religion or antipathy to people who aren't like them or anti-immigrant sentiment or anti-trade sentiment,' what they expressed was not disagreement but condescending revulsion.

I think I first became aware that the charge of populist sympathies could have a powerful political, moral, and class delegitimizing effect when I was in London last June to cover the Brexit vote. Nearly everyone I met, from Tory ministers to taxi drivers, from tourists to tradesmen, was a Remainer. The higher up the income and class scale you went, the more likely it was that your interlocutor would be in favor of Britain's remaining in the European Union. And the more pointed would be his disparagement of those arguing in favor of Brexit. The Brexiteers were said to be 'angry,' yes, but also ignorant, fearful, xenophobic, and racist.

Except that they weren't, not the ones I met, anyway. For them, Brexit turned on a simple question: 'Who rules?' Is the ultimate source of British sovereignty Parliament, as had been the case for centuries? Or is it Brussels, seat of the European Union?

The question of sovereignty, I believe, takes us to the heart of what in recent years has been touted and tarred as the populist project.

Consider Britain. Parliament answers to the British voters.

The European Union answers to—well, to itself. Indeed, it is worth pausing to remind ourselves how profoundly undemocratic is the European Union. Its commissioners are appointed, not elected. They meet in secret. They cannot be turned out of office by voters. If the public votes contrary to the wishes of the E.U.'s commissars in a referendum, they are simply presented with another referendum until they vote the 'right' way. The E.U.'s financial books have never been subject to a public audit. The corruption is just too widespread. Yet the E.U.'s agents wield extraordinary power over the everyday lives of their charges. A commissioner in Brussels can tell a property owner in Wales what sort of potatoes he may plant on his farm, how he must calculate the weight of the products he sells, and whom he must allow into his country. He can outlaw 'racism' and 'xenophobia'—defined as harboring 'an aversion' to people based on 'race, colour, descent, religion or belief, national or ethnic origin' and specify a penalty of 'at least' two years' imprisonment for infractions. He can 'lawfully suppress,' as the London Telegraph reported, 'political criticism of its institutions and of leading figures,' thus rendering the commissars of the E.U. not only beyond the vote but also beyond criticism.

It's a little different in the United States. I'll come to that below. At the moment, it is worth noting to what extent the metabolism of this political dispensation was anticipated by Alexis de Tocqueville in his famous passages about 'democratic despotism' in *Democracy in America*. Unlike despotism of yore, Tocqueville noted, this modern allotrope does not tyrannize over man—it infantilizes him. And it does this by promulgating ever more cumbersome rules and regulations that reach into the interstices of everyday life to hamper initiative, stymie independence, stifle originality, homogenize individuality. This power, said Tocqueville, 'extends its arms over society as a whole.'

> It does not break wills, but it softens them, bends them, and directs them; it rarely forces one to act, but it constantly opposes itself to one's acting; it does not destroy, it prevents things from being born; it does not tyrannize, it hinders, compromises, enervates, extinguishes, dazes, and finally reduces each nation to being nothing more than a herd of timid and industrious animals of which the government is the shepherd.

Tocqueville's analysis has led many observers to conclude that the villain in this drama is the state. But the political philosopher James Burnham, writing in the early 1940s in *The Managerial Revolution*, saw that the real villain was not the state as such but the bureaucracy that maintained and managed it. It is easy to mock the apparatchiks who populate the machinery of government. Thus James H. Boren writes wickedly that 'the noblest of all of man's struggles are those in which dedicated bureaucrats, armed with the spirit of dynamic inaction, have fought to protect the ramparts of creative non-responsiveness from the onslaughts of mere citizens who have demanded action on their behalf.' But the comic potential of the morass should not blind us to the minatory nature of the phenomenon. Indeed, it presents a specimen case of the general truth that the preposterous and the malevolent often co-mingle. The shepherd of which Tocqueville wrote was really a flock of shepherds, a coterie of managers who, in the guise of doing the state's business, prosecuted their own advantage and gradually became a self-perpetuating elite that arrogated to itself power over the levers of society.

Sovereignty, Burnham saw, was shifting from Parliaments to what he called 'administrative bureaus,' which increasingly are the seats of real power and, as such, 'proclaim the rules, make the laws, issue the decrees.' As far back as the early 1940s, Burnham could write that '"Laws" today in the United States . . . are not being made any longer by

Congress, but by the NLRB, SEC, ICC, AAA, TVA, FTC, FCC, the Office of Production Management (what a revealing title!), and the other leading 'executive agencies.' And note that Burnham wrote decades before the advent of the EPA, HUD, CFPB, FSOC, the Department of Education, and the rest of the administrative alphabet soup that governs us in the United States today.

I am convinced that the issue of sovereignty, of what we might call the location of sovereignty, has played a large role in the rise of the phenomenon we describe as 'populism' in the United States as well as Europe. For one thing, the question of sovereignty, of who governs, stands behind the rebellion against the political correctness and moral meddlesomeness that are such conspicuous and disfiguring features of our increasingly bureaucratic society. The smothering, Tocquevillian blanket of regulatory excess has had a wide range of practical and economic effects, stifling entrepreneurship and making any sort of productive innovation difficult.

The question of sovereignty also stands behind the debate over immigration: indeed, is any issue more central to the question 'Who governs?' than who gets to decide a nation's borders and how a country defines its first person plural: the 'We' that makes us who we are as a people?

Throughout his 2016 Presidential campaign, Donald Trump promised to enforce America's immigration laws, to end so-called 'sanctuary cities,' which advertise themselves as safe havens for illegal aliens (though of course they do not call them 'illegal aliens'), and to sharpen vetting procedures for people wishing to immigrate to America from countries known as sponsors of terrorism.

The President sometimes overstated and not infrequently misstated his case. Semantic precision is not a Trumpian speciality. But political effectiveness may be. Behind the Sturm und Drang that greeted Trump's rhetoric on immigration, we can glimpse two very different concepts of the nation state and world order. One view sees the world as a collection of independent sovereign countries that, although interacting with one another, regard the care, safety, and prosperity of their own citizens as their first obligation.

This is the traditional view of the nation state. It is also Donald Trump's view. It is what licenses his talk of putting 'America First,' a concept that, pace the anti-Trump media, has nothing to do with Charles Lindbergh's isolationist movement of the late 1930s and everything to do with fostering a healthy sense of national identity and purpose.

The alternative view regards the nation state with suspicion as an atavistic form of political and social organization. The nation state might still be a practical necessity, but, the argument goes, it is a regrettable necessity inasmuch as it retards mankind's emancipation from the parochial bonds of place and local allegiance. Ideally, according to this view, we are citizens of the world, not particular countries, and our fundamental obligation is to all mankind.

This is the progressive view. It has many progenitors and antecedents. But none is more influential than 'Perpetual Peace: A Philosophical Sketch,' a brief essay that Immanuel Kant published in 1795 when he was seventy-one. The burden of the essay is to ask how perpetual peace might be obtained among states. The natural condition of mankind, Kant acknowledges, is war. But with the advent of 'enlightened concepts of statecraft,' mankind, he suggests, may be able to transcend that unfortunate habit of making war and live in perpetual (*ewigen*) comity.

Kant lists various conditions for the initial establishment of peace—the eventual abolition of standing armies, for example—and a few conditions for its perpetuation: the extension of 'universal hospitality' by nations was something that caught my eye. Ditto 'world citizenship.' 'The idea of . . . world citizenship,' he says at the end of the essay, 'is no high-flown or exaggerated notion. It is a supplement to the unwritten code of the civil and international law, indispensable for the maintenance of the public human rights and hence also of perpetual peace.'

Kant makes many observations along the way that will be balm to progressive hearts. He is against 'the accumulation of treasure,' for example, because wealth is 'a hindrance to perpetual peace.' By the same token, he believes that forbidding the system of international credit that the British empire employed 'must be a preliminary article of perpetual peace.' Credit can be deployed to increase wealth, ergo it is suspect. Kant says that all states must be 'republican' in organization. By that he means not that they must be democracies but only that the executive and legislative functions of the state be distinguished. (Indeed, he says that democracy, 'properly speaking,' is 'necessarily a despotism' because in it the executive and legislative functions of governments are both vested in one entity, 'the people.') He looks forward to the establishment of a 'league of nations' (*Völkerbund*), all of which would freely embrace a republican form of government.

It would be hard to overstate the influence of Kant's essay. It stands behind such progressive exfoliations as Woodrow Wilson's 'Fourteen Points,' not least the final point that looked forward to the establishment of a League of Nations. You can feel its pulse beating in the singing phrases of the 1928 Kellogg-Briand Pact, which outlawed war. It is worth noting that among the initial fifteen signatories of that noble-sounding pact, along with the United

States, France, and England, were Germany, Italy, and Japan. What does that tell us about the folly of trusting paper proclamations not backed up by the authority of physical force? It is one thing to declare war illegal; it is quite another to enforce that edict.

Kant's essay also directly inspired the architects of the United Nations and, in our own day, the architects of the European Union and the battalions of transnational progressives who jettison democracy for the sake of a more-or-less nebulous (but not therefore un-coercive) ideal of world citizenship.

I would not care to wager on how many of the hysterics who congregated at airports across the country to protest Donald Trump's effort to make the citizens of this country safer were students of Kant. Doubtless very few. But all were his unwitting heirs. 'Universal hospitality': how the protestors would have liked that! (Though to be fair to Kant, he did note that such hospitality 'is not the right to be a permanent visitor.') I have no doubt that the motivation of the protestors had many sources. But to the extent that it was based on a political ideal (and not just partisan posturing or a grubby bid for notoriety and power), the spirit of Kant was hovering there in the background.

Kant was not without a sense of humor. He begins his essay by noting that he took his title from a sign outside a Dutch pub. 'Pax Perpetua' read the sign, and below the lettering was the image of a graveyard. Perhaps the universal perpetuity of death is the only peace that mankind may really look forward to. Kant clearly wouldn't agree, but it was charming of him to acknowledge that the idea of a genuine perpetual peace for mankind might be regarded by many as nothing more than a 'sweet dream' of philosophers.

What has been called the populist spirit aims to rouse us from that 'sweet dream'—what James Madison might have called the 'theoretic' reverie of the meddling class whose designs for our salvation always seem to involve the extension of their own power and prerogative. In this sense, the issue of sovereignty also stands behind the debates over the relative advantages and moral weather of 'globalism' vs. 'nationalism'—a pair of terms almost as fraught as 'democracy' and 'populism'—as well as the correlative economic issues of underemployment and wage stagnation. 'Theoretic' politicians may advocate 'globalism' as a necessary condition for free trade. But the spirit of local control tempers the cosmopolitan project of a borderless world with a recognition that the nation state has been the best guarantor not only of sovereignty but also of broadly shared prosperity. What we might call the ideology of free trade— the globalist aspiration to transcend the impediments of national identity and control—is an abstraction that principally benefits its architects.

In the end, what James Burnham described as the 'managerial revolution' is part of a larger progressive project. The aim of this project is partly to emancipate mankind from such traditional sources of self-definition as national identity, religious affiliation, and specific cultural rootedness, partly to perpetuate and aggrandize the apparatus that oversees the resulting dissolution. Burnham castigates this hypertrophied form of liberalism (what we might call 'illiberal liberalism') as 'an ideology of suicide' that has insinuated itself into the center of Western culture. He acknowledges that the proposition may sound hyperbolic. 'Suicide,' he notes, may seem 'too emotive a term, too negative and 'bad.' 'But it is part of the pathology that Burnham describes that such objections are 'most often made most hotly by Westerners who hate their own civilization, readily excuse or even praise blows struck against it, and themselves lend a willing hand, frequently enough, to pulling it down.' The issue, Burnham saw, is that modern liberalism has equipped us with an ethic too abstract and empty to inspire real commitment.

A TRADITIONALIST FOREIGN POLICY

The two principles that should inform properly conservative foreign policy, and how extreme liberalism has failed the world.

Daniel McCarthy

The hunt for a foreign-policy tradition that can rightly be called conservative plausibly begins with Edmund Burke. *Reflections on the Revolution in France* supplies an outlook that is translated directly into policy in Burke's subsequent writings on the revolution, notably 'Thoughts on French Affairs' and the *Letters on a Regicide Peace*. Revolutionary France was not just a military threat in itself, it was the exporter of an ideology that threatened to destroy all order within as well as between the states of Europe. Every land would be divided between supporters and opponents of the revolution's principles, with the result that an entire civilization would be plunged into civil war. Burke likened the situation to the revolutions and wars of religions that had followed the French Revolution, or the *stasis* to which city after city in the Hellenic world succumbed during the Peloponnesian Wars. He urged Britain to war, and to make no peace with the France until the last revolutionary embers were doused.

Opposing revolution in splendid isolation

The first precept of a traditional conservative foreign policy, then, is that revolutionary ideologies must be prevented from spreading, especially when they are backed by a great military power. Yet there is a second precept, supported by no less an historical authority, that may seem to conflict with the first. This second precept is to cherish 'splendid isolation,' a term not coined by the third Marquess of Salisbury but often applied anyway to his foreign policy, and to that of the Conservative Party in general during the 19th century. The Conservatives were the party of empire, but the empire was enough: Britannia did not need to be involved constantly in the intrigues of the European continent or anywhere else outside of her dominion. In idealized terms, the grand strategy was not one of 'isolationism,' as that term is used pejoratively by interventionist liberals, but of what is now called 'offshore balancing.' The Royal Navy would be supreme upon the seas and act when necessary to vindicate British interests or maintain balance among the great powers. But what John Quincy Adams said of U.S. foreign policy on July 4, 1821 could be said with almost equal justice of Britain as well: 'she goes not abroad in search of monsters to destroy.'

Adams, who was U.S. secretary of state at the time, made his remark in reply to an essay in the *Edinburgh Review* that had accused Americans of failing to adopt a foreign policy to support the dissemination of liberalism. The essay proposed that Britain and America work together against the reactionary forces ascendent in post-Napoleonic Europe. Adams took the occasion of his speech on the 45th anniversary of the Declaration of Independence to draw an implicit distinction between the French and American Revolutions: the American one was for export only by example. America, said Adams, is the well-wisher to the freedom and independence of all. She is the champion and vindicator only of her own. ... She well knows that by once enlisting under other banners than her own, were they even the banners of foreign independence, she would involve herself, beyond the power of extrication, in all the wars of interest and intrigue, of individual avarice, envy, and ambition, which assume the colors and usurp the standard of freedom. The fundamental maxims of her policy would insensibly change from liberty to force. ... She might become the dictatress of the world: she would be no longer the ruler of her own spirit.

Burke had acted as a parliamentary agent for the colony of New York before the American Revolution, and he had counseled Parliament and George III to make the concessions necessary to avert war with the colonies. He did not welcome the Americans' separation from Britain, but he believed it would be both counterproductive and wrong to force them to remain. For Burke, as for John Quincy Adams, the American Revolution was fundamentally unlike the French Revolution, and however republican the Americans might be, their understanding of freedom did not entail the overthrow of the European order, as the Jacobins' ideology did. Adams, in rejecting the attempt of liberal journalists at the *Edinburgh Review* to shame America into an activist foreign policy, proved Burke right. In foreign policy, from the first, the United States was Burkean rather than liberal or Jacobin.

Adams was the author of the Monroe Doctrine, a foreign-policy principle promulgated two years after his July 4 speech that said the United States would act to prevent the establishment of new European colonies in the Americas or the re-establishment of colonies where subjects had declared their independence and had been recognized by the U.S. The spirit that informed the doctrine was much the same as the one behind 'splendid isolation' in the British case: it involved a minimal commitment and did not seek to foment revolution or determine other nations' forms of government, even within the Western hemisphere. Rather, the U.S. signaled that it would not allow the Americas to be drawn, or drawn back, into the imperial politics of Europe.

Even in Europe, ravaged as it had been by the French Revolution and Napoleon, a conservative foreign policy was upheld by statesman such as Clemens von Metternich, the foreign minister and later chancellor of the Austrian Empire in the first half of the 19th century. Metternich pursued a Burkean program of suppressing revolutionaries, though for Austria there was no question of balancing Europe's powers by remaining 'offshore.' Continental conservatives were in tragic circumstances: they could not fully restore the prestige and solidity of the *ancien regime* no matter how vigorously, or leniently, they went after revolutionaries. The damage was done, and harsh measures often provoked new resistance. Yet peace endured among the powers of the Continent, if not within them, for a half-century or so after the Congress of Vienna and only broke down completely with the beginning of the First World War, ninety-nine years after Napoleon's exile to St. Helena.

The foreign policy of the 19th-century British Conservative Party can hardly be reduced to splendid isolation, and U.S. foreign policy had drifted far from the course set by John Quincy Adams and earlier statesmen by the time the Spanish-American War erupted in 1898. The scramble for new empires at the end of the century and the rise of Germany and Japan to great-power status were developments for which the conservative precepts of a hundred years before were inadequate. Had Burke or Adams been alive, they perhaps would have cautioned against colonial adventures, but the world's shifting balance of power posed a greater difficulty, one that had nothing to do with revolutionary ideology. Was a united, industrially ascendent Germany a force that had to be checked? British leaders thought so. Americans were more skeptical, yet Woodrow Wilson's promises to keep out of World War I proved to be no barrier to his taking the country into the conflict after his re-election as president.

The outcome of the war, however, vindicated traditional conservative concerns in foreign-policy. A new revolutionary ideology, Bolshevism, had seized power in Russia during the war and was spreading in Germany. The wars of the French Revolution and Napoleon had ended with the reimposition of a conservative order upon Europe at the Congress of Vienna. World War I ended with the creation of a liberal order, including a German republic under a heavy penalty of reparations and a variety of weak new states in the lands that were formerly the Austro-Hungarian empire. Revolutionary ideologies, first of the left, then of the right in the form of fascism and Nazism, flourished in a Europe where no traditional conservative authorities could crush them.

The United States found acquiring formerly Spanish imperial possessions in the 1890s and fighting in the trenches of Europe two decades later to be a bitter experience. Americans did not wish to be involved too deeply in the feeble postwar order, and when war came again twenty years later, the U.S. public remained reluctant to mobilize. Britain had emerged a victor in World War I, but a victor whose weaknesses and limitations had been exposed. The country was ill-equipped for another war with Germany. In short, there was no one willing to and capable of applying conservative precepts effectively in the interwar environment. And so there was soon another war.

After the Second World War, the United States changed its strategic posture. The U.S. was never going to create traditional conservative regimes, in the 19th-century sense, in the lands it occupied, and there was no going back to such traditional regimes in any case. But the new regimes the U.S. would foster in Japan, Germany, and elsewhere would be anti-revolutionary, not the breeding grounds for revolution that the states which emerged from World War I had been. The U.S. would guarantee the basic character and disposition of the new regimes by maintaining forces within them, or by incorporating them within alliance structures. This was not exactly liberal nation-building, nor was it the punitive peace that had followed World War I. American reconstruction efforts were facilitated not by the innate appeal of American values, but by the obvious alternative that awaited World War II's losers if they rejected the U.S. model: reconstruction along Soviet lines instead.

The two principles of traditional conservative foreign policy were often at odds during the Cold War. The United States treated Soviet Communism as a threat comparable to what Burke had seen in Jacobinism. Americans of the political right, like Burke before them, wished to brook no compromise with this force that would overturn Western civilization. Yet the other conservative impulse in foreign policy, toward restraint and balance, accepted 'Containment' as an adequate strategy in Europe and engaged in creative Realpolitik, including Richard Nixon's eventual embrace of Communist China. This was not 'splendid isolation,' but it was perhaps the closest thing that might be achieved in a bipolar and ideologically riven world order. At times, the tension between conservative Realpolitik and the right's counterrevolutionary anti-Communism worked to good effect, maintaining a strong moral and ideological front against the USSR while achieving in practice everything that could be achieved through diplomacy and measures short of war. The peaceful conclusion of the Cold War through the combination of both conservative impulses ranks as a supreme accomplishment in the foreign policy of the last century.

The results of extreme liberalism in international affairs

Yet after the Cold War, the United States abandoned conservatism in foreign policy, with even Republican presidents pressing for liberal and democratic revolutions across the globe. The liberalism that had been a revolutionary ideology in the 19th century made an alliance, if at times an awkward one, with conservatism during the Cold War, as both liberalism and conservatism were opposed to Communism. With the end of the Cold War, ideological liberalism began to return to its original, revolutionary character, this time with the unilateral, hegemonic power of the United States behind it. The liberal conditions that American power created abroad under the two Republican Bushes and Democratic Presidents Clinton and Obama, however, were typically as weak and prone to extremism as the liberal regimes that had been created after World War I, if not more so. Since 2003, the result has been civil war and the growth of Iranian influence in Iraq, continual U.S. occupation of Afghanistan without any hope of a stable native democratic regime taking root, and warlordism and slavery unleashed in Libya. Revolutionary Islamist ideology infects all three countries, and many other parts of the Middle East, Asia, and Africa as well. Americans have lost thousands of sons and daughters, and trillions of dollars, in these wars and misadventures, and the cost in U.S. morale has been incalculable.

The extreme liberalism pursued by America's leaders since 1989 extends to economics as well, and has resulted in the rapid, continuous expansion of China's military as well as market advantage. In Western Europe, meanwhile, the liberal democracies whose liberalism was kept in check after World War II by the threat of Soviet Communism have embraced a now self-destructive ideological liberalism, with the result that parties of the broadly liberal center face grave challenges from nationalists and populists. Europe after World War II seemed to have escaped the tragic circumstances of its politics since the French Revolution. Now those circumstances have returned, albeit in what remains for now a sub-critical condition.

Liberalism in international affairs has failed the world, from the U.S. to Western Europe to the Islamic world and the Far East. A traditional conservative foreign policy—modified to suit the conditions of the 21st century—is needed now as much as in the aftermath of the French Revolution or during the Cold War. Western Europe is in need of conservative, anti-revolutionary government that can reverse liberal excesses without going to right-wing extremes. The United States would do well to conserve its power, including its morale, by eschewing wars to promote liberalism and democracy and instead fostering a global balance, drawing traditional allies such as Western Europe and Japan closer through the logic of national interest and counterrevolutionary commitments rather than liberal idealism and institutions. In much of the rest of the world, liberalism means not freedom but weakness and susceptibility to revolution. The growth of good order in developing states, the post-Communist bloc, and the Islamic world will be slow, and the West should view these places through realistic and conservative rather than liberal and hopeful eyes.

Burke, Lord Salisbury, and John Quincy Adams are far from infallible guides to foreign policy, even when properly appreciated for the spirit of their views rather than the direct applications they had in mind for their own times.

Yet in the wisdom of conservative statesmen such as these we find the beginnings of an antidote to the excesses of liberalism in the post-Cold War world. Revolutionary ideology remains a deadly threat to civilization, though at present it is not joined to a great power state like 1890s France or the Soviet Union. The ethos of splendid isolation, in the form of strong yet modest measures such as offshore balancing and the Monroe Doctrine, is still the best guide to using military strength wisely. Neither of these precepts provides a solution to all the difficulties posed by the rise of China, to mention only the largest of the 21st century's challenges, but the example of World War I shows that conservative traditions in foreign policy have their limits. Even here, however, the answer may lie in a combination of the creative Realpolitik that served conservatives so well during the Cold War with an adjustment of our economic and cultural priorities at home. A stronger, more self-sufficient West is a more secure West, one that maintains a balance within its own civilization, regardless of what happens elsewhere.

AFTERWORD

Catherine Priestley

I can best trace the origins of this project to the Spring of 2015. In a 24-hour Sydney café called Hernandez. Hernandez is just the right place for late-night conversation. The coffee is constant, oil paintings adorn the walls, and its clientele are suitably eccentric.

For a certain, small group of students, Hernandez became the place to analyse and lament, when Malcolm Turnbull seized the leadership from Tony Abbott in September. We debated the issue into the early hours. On the one hand, the parliamentary Liberal Party had done the very deed which had destroyed the former Labor government; on the other, one or two among the young fogeys were quite taken with Turnbull's orange ties.

Even in the early days, there was a sense that the fallout would be drawn-out and damaging; this was not a clean wound. When viewed through the lens of this collection, it seems apparent that the Abbott-Turnbull spill signalled the coming apart of the conservative and liberal alliance in Australian politics.

The essays hope to bring these two strains of thought into sharper focus.

It should be clear now that conservatism is a tradition, not an ideology. It is based on instincts, not artificial 'golden rules' written in the 19th century. Indeed, the eminent philosopher Sir Roger Scruton says it is this reliance on instincts which makes conservatism so difficult to define.[1]

---

[1]   Scruton, Roger, and Murray, Douglas, 7 May 2019. "Douglas Murray and Roger Scruton on the future of

The difficulty in defining and understanding the conservative has made him easy prey for the hegemonic ideology of our time: liberalism. In her 1975 introduction to John Stuart Mill's *On Liberty,* Gertrude Himmelfarb said that, for good or for bad, a certain idea of *liberty* is now the only moral principle to command general assent.[2] Liberalism's simple axiom that people should be free to do what they like, so long as it doesn't harm anyone else, determines the outcome of most debates.

This collection should also have made clear the tension between the conservative cast of mind and liberal ideology. On multiple social and economic issues, we see the two approaches arriving at drastically different outcomes. It is unsurprising, then, that factionalism breeds in parties that insist on the fusion of traditional conservatism and ideological liberalism.

This collection, however, hopes to be constructive, rather than destructive, for such parties. It may provide pointers for an agenda for prospective and current party supporters. It sheds light on the history and meaning of the two world-views fighting it out, clarifying the lay of the land in centre-right parties. It will hopefully assist the conservative to understand and articulate what she believes, so she is not caught unawares, knee-deep in a factionalism the basis of which is not clear.

Towards the completion of this project, some years after our Hernandez soirees, two of us were at a university college cocktail party, talking until the early hours. The party included university students and young professionals, who had all, it seemed, been through some recent evolu-

conservatism." Podcast audio. *Spectator LIVE*. Spectator Radio. 7 May 2019. Accessed 7 July 2019.
[2] Gertrude Himmelfarb, introduction to *On Liberty* by John Stuart Mill (Penguin Books Ltd, 1974), 1.

tions in thought. Initially captured by a libertarian preoccupation with free speech and markets, they are now fascinated by history, philosophy and tradition; they want to explore the great minds and literary geniuses of Edmund Burke, G.K. Chesterton, Blessed John Henry Newman, T.S. Eliot, Les Murray, St John the Evangelist and St Paul – to name a few.

Ensuring personal freedom is one thing, but freedom for what? Those who ask this question are seeking the true meaning of their life. Surely there is nothing more thrilling than discovering the history of man's attempt to understand himself and his purpose. It is the unending conversation, as perfectly captured by Kenneth Burke's famous analogy:

> Imagine that you enter a parlor. You come late. When you arrive, others have long preceded you, and they are engaged in a heated discussion, a discussion too heated for them to pause and tell you exactly what it is about. In fact, the discussion had already begun long before any of them got there so that no one present is qualified to retrace for you all the steps that had gone before. You listen for a while until you decide that you have caught the tenor of the argument; then you put in your oar. Someone answers; you answer him; another comes to your defense; another aligns himself against you, to either the embarrassment or gratification of your opponent, depending upon the quality of your ally's assistance. However, the discussion is interminable. The hour grows late, you must depart. And you do depart, with the discussion still vigorously in progress.

This collection was inspired by conversation; a conversation that we hope continues.